The Captive Press

The Captive Press

Foreign Policy Crises and the First Amendment

Ted Galen Carpenter

CATO
INSTITUTE
Washington D.C.

Library of Congress Cataloging-in-Publication Data

Carpenter, Ted Galen.
    The captive press : foreign policy crises and the First Amendment / Ted
Galen Carpenter.
        p.   cm.
    Includes bibliographical references and index.
    ISBN 1-882577-22-1 (cloth). — ISBN 1-882577-23-X (paper)
    1. Government and the press—United States.   2. War in the press—
United States.   3. Freedom of the press—United States.   4. GOus.   I. Title.
PN4738.C27   1995   95-18582
071'.3—dc20   CIP

Cover Design by Randy White.

Printed in the United States of America.

CATO INSTITUTE
1000 Massachusetts Ave., N.W.
Washington, D.C. 20001

To Barbara, for being there in good times and bad, always providing the needed support and encouragement.

Contents

Preface

The relationship between government and the news media is crucial in a constitutional republic. Generations of Americans have recognized the importance, indeed the indispensability, of a free press to our system of limited government and individual liberty. The commitment to the freedom of the press enshrined in the First Amendment is tested most severely whenever America appears to be under siege by foreign enemies—a problem that has arisen with increasing frequency in the 20th century. Political leaders have shown a tendency to view media criticism of the nation's foreign policy during such periods as a manifestation of disloyalty and an insidious threat to national security. Their assumption appears to be that press freedoms, like politics, should stop at the water's edge.

There are a number of excellent studies of the relationship between government and the press during specific international conflicts, such as the Vietnam War. There are also some excellent books on more specialized issues, such as the role of battlefield correspondents. What has been lacking is an examination of patterns in the relationship between government and the media during foreign policy crises and of the significance of those patterns. This book is a modest attempt to help fill that void.

The Captive Press explores the conflict between the demands of national security and the requirements of a vigorous, free press. It reviews the press-government relationship during foreign policy crises throughout the nation's history, focusing especially on the period since World War II. The thesis is fairly straightforward: as the United States has pursued a global interventionist foreign policy in the last half century, the tensions between the national security bureaucracy and a free press have grown more acute. Officials have enticed or pressured journalists to abandon their role as monitors of policy and become members of the nation's foreign policy team, a ploy that has often proved successful. Whenever attempts at seduction have been insufficient, the government has resorted to a variety of measures to intimidate or circumvent the media. The implications of that two-pronged strategy of co-option and coercion for the long-term vitality of the First Amendment are, at the very least, troubling.

It should be emphasized that the author has never been a journalist or a member of the national security bureaucracy. Although the validity of judgments made by an admitted "outsider" can be questioned, an "external audit" of the roles played by the journalistic and policymaking communities has some unique strengths. It is less likely than are analyses by policymakers or journalists to become the hostage of implicit institutional biases and the tunnel vision they tend to produce. In addition, because I am not a member of the media or policymaking communities, there is less pressure to pull punches because of fear of offending friends and colleagues.

I owe a debt of gratitude to many people who helped make this book possible. Edward Crane, William Niskanen, David Boaz, and the other members of the Cato Institute staff have been unstinting in their moral and tangible support. Crane, Jonathan Kwitny, Leon T. Hadar, Stephen S. Rosenfeld, and Stanley Kober offered helpful comments and suggestions on an earlier draft. Lisa Palluconi spent many hours tracking down elusive sources and did so with unflagging good humor. My editor, Elizabeth W. Kaplan, deserves great credit for doing her usual thorough and uncompromising job of improving the quality of the manuscript. Any remaining errors of fact or interpretation are, of course, entirely my own.

Introduction: The Erosion of Press Freedoms

A people who mean to be their own governors must arm themselves with the power that knowledge gives. A popular government without popular information or the means of acquiring it is but a prologue to a farce or a tragedy or perhaps both.

—James Madison

Madison's observation is as true today as it was in 1822.[1] There is always an inherent tension between the requirements of national security as perceived by public officials and the freedoms of speech and press guaranteed by the First Amendment. That tension has been most pronounced during wars or other foreign policy crises. Justice Oliver Wendell Holmes, speaking for a unanimous U.S. Supreme Court in the landmark 1919 case of *Schenck v. United States*, expressed the view of those who believe that First Amendment freedoms may have to give way to the exigencies of national security. "When a nation is at war," Holmes argued, "many things that might be said in times of peace are such a hindrance to its effort that their utterance will not be endured so long as men fight, and no Court could regard them as protected by any constitutional right."[2]

The tension between press freedoms and national security claims has existed since the earliest years of the Republic. It is no accident that the first serious postrevolutionary attempt to limit the freedom of speech and of the press, the Alien and Sedition Acts of 1798, was a response to criticism of John Adams's administration's conduct of foreign affairs during a period of extreme tension between the United States and France that culminated in an undeclared naval war. The Alien and Sedition Acts set the pattern for subsequent relations between the press and government. Especially in times of crisis, the federal government has sought to enlist journalists and other opinion shapers as allies in telling the administration's version of events or, failing that, to suppress those who insist on leveling criticisms.

1

Such attitudes have become especially virulent and pervasive during the 20th century, as the United States has adopted an increasingly interventionist role in world affairs. In the name of a multitude of national security justifications, genuine or bogus, serious and perhaps permanent damage is being done to the vitality of a free press.

Interventionism and the Problem of a Free Press

The logic expressed by Justice Holmes—subordinating freedom of expression to the requirements of national security—was unsettling enough when confined to periods of declared war. As long as the American Republic remained at peace most of the time, wartime restrictions on First Amendment freedoms could be regarded as regrettable aberrations. The emergence of the Cold War, which caused America to spend more than four decades in a twilight zone between war and peace, eliminated that comforting rationalization. As the United States undertook an array of global political and military commitments and remained constantly prepared for the onset of combat, "abnormal" wartime restrictions and practices increasingly threatened to become the norm.

The danger that national security demands will have a corrosive effect on freedom of expression has not abated with the end of the Cold War, for U.S. officials show a determination to continue pursuing a global interventionist policy in the post–Cold War period. President Bill Clinton's pledge in his inaugural address that the United States would respond with military force, if necessary, not only when America's vital interests are challenged but when the "will and conscience of the international community is defied" offers little hope of a more limited role. Clinton's stress on the need for "continuity" in U.S. foreign policy and his refusal to eliminate any of the formal or informal security guarantees to allies and clients that the United States accumulated during the Cold War also indicate that Washington's appetite for intervention has diminished little. Consequently, the tension between expansive national security objectives and First Amendment freedoms remains a serious concern.

The requirements of a global interventionist foreign policy run directly counter to the goals of an unrestricted press and vigorous public debate. Advocates of interventionism typically regard criticism of foreign policy initiatives as, at best, a nuisance or, at worst,

2

undermining the government's global strategic and political objectives. Many of them see a hostile, or even a merely inquisitive, press as a threat to national security.

From the perspective of a regime committed to interventionism, a critical press is inconvenient, even dangerous, for several reasons. First, investigative journalism exposes many of the cover stories, official rationales, half truths, and outright lies that surround various foreign policy decisions. The public's awareness or ignorance of such information can greatly influence its support for an initiative.

Critical coverage also may cast doubt on the wisdom or effectiveness of existing policies, leading to an erosion of public confidence and support. National security practitioners certainly believed that was the case during the final years of the Vietnam War when a barrage of negative stories brought home to the American people that officialdom's predictions of imminent victory were clearly not being fulfilled.

Another problem for proponents of interventionism is that the glare of publicity makes it difficult or even impossible to maintain the secrecy needed for covert operations—an essential weapon in a superpower's arsenal of tactics. In the days before intense press scrutiny, the Central Intelligence Agency pursued a variety of covert missions, most notably the successful coups in Iran (1953), Guatemala (1954), and the Congo (1960) and the unsuccessful attempt to oust Indonesian leader Achmed Sukarno in the late 1950s. Since the revelations of CIA misconduct during the Watergate scandal, and the public's subsequent revulsion, it has been much more difficult for the agency to conduct effective covert (especially paramilitary) operations.

During the 1980s the press routinely reported on "covert" U.S. assistance to the Afghan *mujaheddin* and Angola's UNITA insurgents. News stories about the CIA-directed mining of Nicaragua's harbors and the agency's other actions in support of the Contras' campaign to oust the leftist Sandinista regime in Nicaragua made the entire operation a matter of public record. The most surprising feature of the Iran-Contra affair was that the Reagan administration was able to maintain the secrecy of its initiative for as long as it did, given the intensity of the media's scrutiny. Writing in 1987, political scientist Gregory Treverton noted, "Of the forty or so covert operations underway in the mid-1980s, at least half were the subject of

3

some press account."[3] The United States now engages in the most overt "covert" activities of any great power in history, and advocates of an interventionist foreign policy are not at all reconciled to having every U.S. move reported to the American people and the world.

Finally, interventionists are wary of an unfettered press because they believe that criticism of the government's foreign policy creates the impression of domestic disunity. That perception supposedly erodes the confidence of allies and adversaries alike in the constancy and reliability of U.S. global commitments. Such uncertainty may impel clients to distance themselves from America's cause or, even worse, embolden a potential aggressor. The bitter controversy over the Vietnam War and the resulting policy paralysis in the United States, interventionists contend, led directly to Soviet geopolitical gains in Southeast Asia, southern Africa, and Afghanistan during the next decade.

A Love-Hate Relationship

Although government officials may acknowledge for the record that an independent press is an integral part of a democratic political system, they tend to regard the fourth estate as a necessary evil and seek to either seduce or restrict it. Not surprisingly, officials charged with responsibility for foreign policy prefer to formulate and execute decisions away from the prying eyes of journalists. However, they also recognize that the press can be an effective conduit for disseminating government propaganda and thereby manipulating public opinion.

Members of the news media exhibit a similar love-hate attitude toward policymakers. As Americans, reporters are not immune to nationalistic and jingoistic sentiments, and on more than a few occasions they have been receptive to appeals to patriotism—to be Americans first and journalists second. Correspondents, editors, pundits, and publishers who work for major media outlets also tend to see themselves as members of an opinion-making elite. They consider themselves on an intellectual and social par with high-level policymakers, an attitude that increases the prospect of their being co-opted by ambitious and determined policymakers.

The perception of membership in the political and policy elite is one factor explaining why relatively little prescient, "cutting-edge" criticism of U.S. foreign policy initiatives has come from the main-stream media. Under normal circumstances, that portion of the press and high-echelon political leaders tend to view world events and U.S. options through similar intellectual prisms. With rare exceptions, it is only when a split occurs in the political community that one sees a large number of negative comments about the existing policy from mainstream journalists. That was clearest during the Vietnam conflict. The crescendo of media criticism of Washington's course followed, or at least accompanied rather than preceded, the break-down in the political consensus. A similar pattern could be seen in connection with the U.S. military intervention in Somalia in 1992–93. The mainstream media echoed the political establishment's over-whelming support of the enterprise during the initial months, and the news stories coming out of Somalia were almost uniformly upbeat. Once U.S. forces began to sustain casualties and there appeared to be substantial sentiment in Congress for terminating the mission, however, critical articles and broadcasts appeared with far greater frequency.

In addition to the elitist factor, there is an important institutional incentive that biases many media figures toward an activist U.S. foreign policy. As the late investigative journalist Warren Brookes pointed out, journalists—especially those based in Washington—exist to report on the activities of government. If government were smaller and less intrusive, or regarded as less central to American life, their own careers would also tend to be less prominent. Because the competition for column space or air time is fierce, there is an inherent incentive to hype the importance of one's subject. In addi-tion, a reporter is more likely to get newsworthy information from important sources (usually government officials) if those sources are pleased with previous stories.[4]

Although such factors are present on every press beat, they are especially relevant to media coverage of defense and foreign policy. Because of the shroud of secrecy surrounding the formulation and execution of foreign policy, journalists in that field are unusually dependent on inside sources. Officials are unlikely to feed "exclu-sives" to reporters or columnists who have a habit of criticizing their actions, and there may be no alternative access to the needed information. An anti-interventionist perspective, therefore, is a quick route to obscurity for journalists who want to advance their careers.

Perhaps even more important, a generally noninterventionist U.S. role in world affairs would mean less work for journalists who cover those issues. Indeed, because the American people tend to be uninterested in foreign affairs generally—except when there is a crisis directly involving the United States—those beats, which have been so prestigious since World War II, would become occupational backwaters.

Despite such powerful incentives for members of the media to "go along to get along," journalists have at times viewed the government's stewardship of foreign and defense policy with skepticism, if not hostility. That tendency has been most apparent when military enterprises have clearly gone awry, as in the cases of the U.S. interventions in Vietnam, Lebanon, and—most recently—Somalia. Even when an overwhelming majority of the press has been generally sympathetic to an administration's objectives, there have always been iconoclasts. Moreover, even mainstream journalists have voiced criticism, constructive or otherwise, of specific aspects of the nation's overall international strategy. However well meant, their criticism has rarely been welcomed by political leaders.

Just as some incentives encourage cooperation between government and the media, others foster tension. Despite important overlapping interests, the two institutions do have different missions and purposes. Journalists by training or temperament are dedicated to filing interesting stories ahead of the competition. They are not necessarily deterred if that goal sometimes requires obtaining and publishing information that government leaders would prefer remain outside the public domain. The traditions of the journalistic profession also emphasize the duty of the press—sometimes referred to as a "First Amendment obligation"—to monitor and criticize the activities of government, and at least some journalists take that mission seriously. Although career incentives as well as appeals to patriotism and the need to protect the nation's security often dampen the inclination to scrutinize and criticize the government's foreign policy initiatives, they seldom eliminate it.

Conversely, the national security bureaucracy conceives of its duty as implementing policies to further goals that serve the best interests of the nation. Most policymakers are probably sincere in that view, although there is obviously an enormous potential for confusing the welfare of a particular administration, department, or group of vested interests with the welfare of the American people. Indeed, the institutional and career incentives that Nobel laureate James Buchanan and other "public-choice" economists have shown to determine the behavior of government agencies apply as readily to the national security bureaucracy as to any other sector of the federal government. In addition, policymakers take great pride in their expertise and do not welcome outside scrutiny, much less criticism. They typically regard nongovernmental critics as dangerous (even if well-intentioned) amateurs or malicious adversaries. Although that attitude exists in any policymaking institution, nowhere is it more prevalent than in the national security bureaucracy. There, the myth of expertise reigns supreme. Because members of the press are the most visible monitors and critics of the nation's foreign and defense policies, officials are especially concerned about journalists' activities.

Former secretary of state Henry Kissinger offers a candid view of the complex "symbiotic" relationship between journalists and government officials from the perspective of the latter.

> Much as the journalist may resent it, he performs a partly government function. . . . Officials seek him out to bring their pet projects to general attention, to settle scores, or to reverse a decision that went against them. Whatever the official's motive, it cannot be disinterested. At a minimum he seeks to put himself in his best light. . . .
>
> The journalist has comparably interested motives in his contacts with the official. He must woo and flatter the official because without his goodwill he will be deprived of information. But he cannot let himself be seduced—the secret dream of most officials—or he will lose his objectivity. A love-hate relationship is almost inevitable.[5]

Seduction or Repression

Given the problems that can be caused for an interventionist foreign policy by a vigorous, inquisitive press, it is not surprising that officials have used a variety of methods to control the media. During the two world wars and the first two decades of the Cold War, the preferred technique was to co-opt journalists. As well as appealing to reporters' patriotism, policymakers fed "friendly" members of the media important news stories while freezing out their competitors.

There were other aspects of the policy of inclusion: convincing journalists that they and officials must cooperate to protect the nation from mortal adversaries and appeals to snobbery—implying that officials and journalists were both part of a knowledgeable elite that sometimes had to keep "sensitive" information from a public that was incapable of evaluating it responsibly. Such seduction strategies were quite successful as long as most members of the media accepted the notions that America was engaged in a life-or-death struggle with dangerous foreign enemies and that policymakers were managing the country's security strategy competently. Both assumptions were shaken by the Vietnam debacle, and throughout the 1970s and 1980s the relationship between the press and the national security bureaucracy became more confrontational. The performance of the media as government cheerleader during the Persian Gulf War, however, may signal a return to the earlier pattern.

When its efforts to induce members of the press to be part of the foreign policy team rather than detached observers are not effective, the government treats recalcitrant reporters, columnists, and analysts as enemies to be neutralized. Officials have used a variety of techniques to thwart critics. The most common measure is to invoke the need for secrecy in matters of national security to conceal any information that might contradict official positions or otherwise undermine the case for existing foreign policy initiatives. That ploy has led to a vast overclassification of materials on defense and foreign policy issues. When that stratagem proves insufficient, government leaders are not above resorting to intimidation.

Officials use smear tactics, such as impugning the patriotism of individuals who produce accounts critical of U.S. foreign policy, to discredit them in the eyes of the popular audience. That tactic was especially virulent during the McCarthy era in the early 1950s, but it has an unsavory pedigree dating back to the passage of the Alien and Sedition Acts and has been prominent on many other occasions, most recently during the Persian Gulf War. When news stories quote or otherwise rely on classified information, officials also threaten to prosecute both the "leakers" of information and the journalists who print that information under the Espionage Act of 1917.

Lurking in the shadows is even more potent full-blown censorship. Press censorship was a prominent feature of U.S. mobilization efforts in World War I and World War II, and during the Cold War era there was a detailed stand-by plan for a censorship code to be used in case of national emergency. In addition, several administrations have attempted to impose another form of censorship by obtaining—through either legislation or court precedents—an American version of the British Official Secrets Act, which prohibits publication of any material the government determines to be a state secret.

Officials have also discovered an especially effective way of stifling potential criticism of military interventions: restricting media access to the theater of operations. The Reagan administration used that tactic quite successfully during the invasion of Grenada in October 1983. Reporters were prevented from covering the assault for the first 48 hours, and military escorts were required thereafter. When the Bush administration sent forces into Panama in December 1989, reporters were similarly excluded from covering the action and were confined to a U.S. military base during the most crucial hours of the fighting.

After the Grenada operation, the government-imposed limits on media access to combat zones became institutionalized. Reacting to criticism of the wholesale exclusion of the press from Grenada, the Pentagon proposed the creation of media pools—small groups of designated reporters who would provide coverage of events for all of their colleagues. In theory the pool system guarantees at least some media coverage of military operations, but in reality it facilitates the government's control of the flow of information. Even worse, the arrangement is an acknowledgment that reporting on military enterprises is not a First Amendment right but a privilege bestowed by the government—a privilege that can be modified or withdrawn at the discretion of political authorities.

The effectiveness of the isolation strategy became all too apparent during the Persian Gulf War. Pentagon officials used a variety of measures—press pools, requiring reporters to be accompanied by military escorts on all interviews, and mandatory prefiling reviews (i.e., censorship) of stories—to prevent negative coverage. At the same time, the Pentagon obligingly provided generous amounts of "information" through carefully managed briefings. The result was that the American people heard, saw, and read primarily what the government wanted them to about Operations Desert Shield and Desert Storm. Television screens were filled with government-supplied video images of precision-guided munitions striking their targets, military aircraft leaving on or returning from missions, and upbeat soldiers training for the assault to liberate Kuwait. Newspapers and magazines were also filled with accounts supplied by the Pentagon. The combination of restricted independent media access and the Defense Department's concerted propaganda blitz produced the precise result desired by the government. Never has a military enterprise been so thoroughly covered while so little meaningful information was conveyed to the American people.

Both the effort to co-opt or manage the press and the attempt to exclude or intimidate it have been government staples throughout the interventionist era. Only the mix of those tactics has shifted with time. Moreover, during the gulf war, the two tactics dovetailed almost perfectly. Through astute manipulation and sophisticated propaganda techniques combined with erecting an array of obstacles that prevented the media from conducting independent forays to gather information, the government effectively neutralized opposition to its policy. In that war the press was *both* co-opted and intimidated.

After the Persian Gulf War many prominent journalists vowed that they would never again allow the government to so manipulate the news media. Press coverage of the crises in Somalia and Yugoslavia, however, has exhibited many of the unhealthy tendencies that were evident in the gulf episode. Too many news stories about those countries read as though they were written by the most stridently interventionist officials in the State Department. As there was in the months leading up to Operation Desert Storm, there has been an insufficient willingness to question the government's interpretation of events and issues or to place developments in a meaningful political, social, or historical context. Once again, the press seems content to be a lapdog rather than a watchdog.

Restoring the Sentinel of Liberty

Government efforts to inhibit scrutiny of its foreign policy initiatives should greatly concern the American people. An unfettered press is a prerequisite for meaningful debate on public policy issues, and there is no issue more important than that of war and peace. A press that the government has either intimidated or domesticated has abdicated its role as the sentinel of liberty. If the government co-opts, censors, intimidates, or otherwise silences the news media, it can virtually preclude meaningful debate on its policies, thereby postponing or even stifling the expression of opposing points of view. Dictatorial regimes have always understood the utility of controlling the press (witness the pervasiveness of their censorship measures), but democratic governments are not immune to the temptation to limit or preclude debate.

Knowledge is, indeed, power, and control of information frequently determines the locus of power in a political system. Americans who value liberty and democracy would do well to remember that fact and resist calls to sacrifice First Amendment freedoms on the altar of national security.

1. Press and Government in Wartime: The History of an Ambivalent Relationship

The tendency of First Amendment freedoms to wither during foreign policy crises became evident even during the early years of the Republic when Americans found their domestic politics caught up in the struggle between revolutionary France and the conservative European monarchies led by Great Britain. George Washington's concern, expressed so eloquently in his farewell address, that foreign entanglements might diminish the commitment to domestic liberty, proved to be prophetic as the administration of President John Adams moved to quash opposition to its foreign policy. As the United States drifted into undeclared naval warfare with its onetime ally, France, conservative elements in the governing Federalist party increasingly viewed their pro-French opponents as unpatriotic, even treasonous. The Federalists' response to mounting criticism of the Adams administration's foreign policy was the passage of four statutes in the summer of 1798, collectively known as the Alien and Sedition Acts.

Three of those measures—the Naturalization, Alien, and Alien Enemies Acts—were directed at a group of anti-Federalist editors and pamphleteers of French or English extraction who had not yet become U.S. citizens. As devices for intimidation, those acts were well crafted. The most pernicious statute, the Alien Act, gave the president the authority "to order all such aliens as he shall judge dangerous to the peace and safety of the United States, or shall have reasonable grounds to suspect are concerned in any treasonable secret machinations against the government thereof, to depart out of the territory of the United States, within such time as shall be expressed in such order."[1] In other words, the president had unrestricted power to expel any alien critic from the country.

The Sedition Act was more directly designed to silence all foreign policy critics, whether aliens or U.S. citizens. That measure prohibited the publication of any "false, scandalous and malicious writing" directed against any branch of the Ù.S. government, with intent to "defame" or bring it "into disrepute" or to excite against it "the hatred of the good people of the United States," for the purpose of "opposing or resisting any law" or any lawful presidential act, or to "aid, encourage or abet any hostile designs of any foreign nation against the United States, their people or government."[2] A partisan Federalist newspaper, the *Gazette of the United States*, offered a candid interpretation of the legislation. "It is patriotism to write in favor of our government—it is sedition to write against it."[3] The possible penalty for violating the act was a fine of $2,000 and a two-year prison term.

Three things are especially notable about the Alien and Sedition Acts. First, they were enacted in the midst of a foreign policy crisis when it appeared that the United States might soon be at war with France. Despite the acrimonious nature of the debate that had gone on for several years, it is unlikely that a majority in Congress would have passed such restrictive legislation without the impetus of a war scare. As historian Dumas Malone noted, the acts could not have passed "except under conditions of fear and patriotic hysteria."[4] The onset of a foreign policy crisis was enough to cause otherwise sensible political leaders to undermine the press freedoms guaranteed in the Constitution—a document that had been ratified less than a decade before.

Second, the Alien and Sedition Acts represented such broad grants of power that they enabled governmental officials to silence foreign policy critics for virtually any reason. The architects of existing policy were empowered to judge whether their adversaries should be allowed to present opposing arguments. Finally, the underlying assumption was that critics of the incumbent government's foreign policy were not honorable opponents who simply held different views but disloyal elements that ought to be suppressed.

All three features would recur in later efforts to restrict First Amendment rights in the name of protecting the nation from external enemies. The Alien and Sedition Acts were in some respects less odious than subsequent measures, including legislation passed during both world wars and the Cold War. For all of their menacing potential, the three Alien Acts were never enforced, and only 25 people were arrested for violating the Sedition Act. Moreover, the Alien Act had a provision for automatic expiration two years from the date of passage, and the Sedition Act similarly expired automatically in March 1801. That limitation contrasts favorably with the open-ended restrictive statutes enacted during the 20th century. The Sedition Act also explicitly allowed truth as a defense, a protection that was absent, for example, in the Sedition Act of 1918.[5]

The American people reacted angrily to those initial attempts to infringe on their constitutional rights. Anger at the Alien and Sedition Acts was reflected in approval of the defiant Kentucky and Virginia resolutions in 1799 and became an important factor, possibly even the single most important factor, in the Federalist party's defeat at the hands of Thomas Jefferson's Republicans in the election of 1800.[6] That feisty animosity toward the federal government's attempt to curtail debate was in stark contrast to the passivity that Americans have displayed in the 20th century toward similar depredations in the name of national security.

The reaction against the Alien and Sedition Acts also had the salutary effect of strengthening respect for freedom of expression. It is notable that the federal government did not seriously entertain notions of censoring the press during the War of 1812. The only significant exception was Gen. Andrew Jackson's effort to place restrictions on journalists who were covering the battle of New Orleans. Always the high-handed autocrat, Jackson even briefly jailed one writer who protested the censorship and then ousted the judge who ordered the writer freed on a writ of habeas corpus.[7] But it was clear that Jackson was operating without authorization from Washington.

Official tolerance of dissent was even more evident during the Mexican War. The absence of efforts to curtail debate was especially heartening since both conflicts were extremely unpopular among portions of the public. (New England bitterly resisted going to war against Britain in 1812 and contemplated secession from the Union, and anti-slavery groups in northern and eastern states considered the Mexican War little more than an imperial land grab to expand the geographic dominion of slavery.) There were only intermittent and ineffectual efforts to censor battlefield reports and no serious effort at all to stem the flood of anti-war news stories and editorials.

Civil War Press Restrictions

The relationship between press and government was quite different during the Civil War, however, as the intolerance of dissent

15

symbolized by the Alien and Sedition Acts reemerged. Almost from the outset, both the Union and the Confederate governments sought to impose battlefield censorship. Their actions were in part a response to an important advance in technology that had far-reaching implications for the transmission of information, the telegraph. The proliferation of telegraph lines in the 1850s dramatically changed the speed with which the press could report on battles and troop movements. Journalists suddenly had the ability to describe military engagements as they were taking place—a development that blurred the line between press reports and military intelligence.[8] In theory at least, indiscreet news stories filed by journalists could provide invaluable intelligence to the enemy. Not surprisingly, neither Union nor Confederate generals (or their political superiors) relished that prospect.

Gen. William Tecumseh Sherman probably held the most hostile view. "War correspondents are a nuisance and a danger at headquarters and in the field," he wrote on one occasion. They "should be treated as spies" because "their publications reach the enemy, [and] give them direct and minute information of the composition of our forces." Expressing the attitude not only of some of his contemporaries but of many later military leaders, Sherman concluded, "Napoleon himself would have been defeated with a free press."[9]

Censorship by both sides in the Civil War, however, went far beyond insisting on delaying the transmission of battlefield dispatches. Although the restrictions on press freedoms imposed by Confederate authorities were more rigid and comprehensive than those imposed by their Union counterparts, the defeat and dissolution of the Confederacy meant that those precedents had little lasting importance. The same could not be said of the measures that the Lincoln administration and its military command adopted. Indeed, the actions of the Union government set the pattern for wartime censorship in the 20th century.

At the beginning of the war, Union authorities called on newspapers to exercise voluntary censorship but failed to provide any meaningful guidelines about what was permissible and what was not. That approach was inherently unworkable; even publications that strongly supported the Northern cause found themselves running afoul of implicit restrictions desired by military and political leaders. Equally significant, opponents of the administration had no intention of abiding by requests to modify their coverage of the war effort.

16

As would be the case in future wars and foreign policy crises, when the government failed to get its way by urging the press to be cooperative and "patriotic," it resorted to coercion. Union authorities adopted a compulsory censorship system and proceeded to prosecute violators. There were two notable features of the Lincoln administration's censorship regime that would reappear during the 20th century. First, although the ostensible reason for imposing restrictions on the press was to prevent the disclosure of information that could undermine military operations, the guidelines were disturbingly vague. Moreover, the way the censorship system was applied demonstrated that the authorities wanted to curb far more than reports that might provide valuable intelligence to the enemy; they wanted to suppress any criticism of their war policies, and that motive struck a direct blow at the First Amendment. Newspapers were prosecuted for publishing "false reports" that were deemed harmful to the Northern cause, a standard so vague and subjective that it could mean anything officials wanted it to mean.

How dangerously arbitrary the Union censorship system had become was apparent when military authorities temporarily shut down the *Chicago Times* for the "crime" of incessantly criticizing the Lincoln administration.[10] Phillip Knightley notes that Secretary of War Edwin Stanton exhibited a fondness for repressive measures. "Stanton took to suspending newspapers that had broken his censorship rules, arresting editors, threatening proprietors with court-martial, and banning correspondents from the front." At one point he even issued orders to shoot a correspondent for the *New York Herald Tribune* who had refused to hand over a dispatch he had written for his paper (an order that fortunately was not carried out).[11]

The second precedent-setting feature of the government's treatment of the press during the Civil War was enforcement techniques. Union leaders employed a variety of tactics. In February 1862 the War Department issued an order taking military control of all telegraph lines, and one section of that order contained a none-too-subtle threat to uncooperative papers. "All newspapers publishing military news, however obtained, not authorized by official authority, will be excluded thereafter from receiving information by telegraph, or from transmitting their papers by railroad."[12] The military backed up that threat by monitoring all telegraph transmissions.

Authorities also resorted to more direct punitive measures. The Post Office denied use of the mails to several papers it deemed disloyal. An overzealous U.S. marshal seized copies of the *New York Daily News* when they arrived by train. The Lincoln administration launched criminal prosecutions of offending editors and publishers. On a few occasions, the military even went beyond postpublication prosecution and suspended the publication of newspapers for printing "false" reports. In addition to the action taken against the *Chicago Times*, in 1864 military leaders imposed a three-day suspension on both the *New York World* and the *New York Journal American*. Not only were the papers temporarily banned, but the editors were jailed.[13] Such actions were blatant cases of prior restraint, one of the most odious censorship tactics that the First Amendment was designed to prevent. Prior restraint during the Civil War was all the more offensive because it was enforced by military leaders acting on their own authority, without reference to any law. Victims could not rely on the democratic process or the safeguard of judicial review for protection.

Although speech and press freedoms suffered during the Civil War (as did other constitutional rights), it was the onset of a foreign policy crisis, World War I, that did lasting damage to those liberties. The oppressive measures used in the Civil War did not last long beyond the end of the fighting. There were some efforts at censorship (especially of the battlefield variety) during the Spanish-American War, but the brevity of that conflict prevented a serious and sustained confrontation between press and government.[14] Moreover, the vigorous debate on the policy level that had existed during the months leading up to the U.S. intervention—including efforts by the Hearst and Pulitzer chains to goad the United States into declaring war—continued during and after the fighting and focused primarily on whether the acquisition of colonies would corrupt the American Republic.

The First Amendment as a World War I Casualty

Another vigorous debate occurred before America's entry into World War I, as pro- and anti-interventionist newspapers and magazines covered a wide range of issues related to the European conflict. That freedom of expression came to an abrupt halt, however, when the United States entered the war in April 1917. A stifling conformity, orchestrated by the administration of President Woodrow Wilson, descended on the nation and remained not only for the duration of the conflict but far beyond. The Wilson administration's repressive actions during World War I placed First Amendment freedoms in greater danger than they had been in at any time since the Alien and Sedition Acts of more than a century before, and significant precedents were set for controlling the press in the name of national security. Administration officials co-opted most elements of the press as part of a massive propaganda campaign to "sell" the war effort to the American public, and critics who would not be co-opted were intimidated or suppressed. For the first time in American history, the government claimed a legal and moral right to exercise monopoly power over information on international affairs.

Battlefield censorship equaled or exceeded anything practiced during the Civil War. The rules for accrediting war correspondents to the American Expeditionary Force suggested a pervasive government demand for ideological conformity. They required the reporter to swear that he would "convey the truth to the people of the United States" but refrain from disclosing facts that might aid the enemy. (It would soon become obvious that officials thought that any account that placed the war effort in a less than positive light was aiding the enemy.) In addition, the correspondent or the sponsoring newspaper had to post a $1,000 bond to cover the cost of his maintenance and equipment and a $10,000 bond to ensure that he would conduct himself "as a gentleman of the press." If the military concluded that the correspondent violated any of the censorship rules, the latter bond was automatically forfeited.[15]

As would occur so often in the future, responsibility for censoring press dispatches was assigned to a prominent journalist—much as prison officials use inmate trustees to keep other inmates in line. In this case, the job was given to former *New York Herald* reporter and Associated Press correspondent Frederick Palmer. It was not coincidental that Palmer had been the only American correspondent accredited to the British army and had produced gushingly pro-British dispatches throughout the war. He was certain to be an enthusiastic booster of the Wilson administration's war effort. To further ensure discipline, Palmer was commissioned a major in the U.S. Army and assigned to public relations. He quickly found himself in an untenable position, accused by his onetime colleagues of being too stingy with information. According to Phillip Knightley, "Palmer became more and more the army officer, dispensing only the sparsest information in releases and then usually confining them to laudatory reports on American operations. Since the correspondents were determined to give their reading public the facts about what was happening to their sons, husbands, and brothers in France, trouble was inevitable."[16]

Military censorship sometimes reached ludicrous levels. When correspondents tried to send a story about the French presenting American forces with cases of wine as a goodwill gesture, for example, censors banned it because it suggested "bibulous indulgence by American soldiers which might offend temperance forces in the United States."[17] On another occasion, reporters discovered that Palmer and his associates had taken to reviewing and censoring even the expense reports that the reporters sent back to their newspapers.

More serious than such petty restrictions was the military's attempt to conceal logistical snafus and general mismanagement that sometimes needlessly placed the health and even the lives of American soldiers in jeopardy. Although the disclosure of such information could arguably have "given aid to the enemy," the motives of political and military leaders were suspect. For example, when three enterprising reporters discovered serious and pervasive supply shortages, Gen. John Pershing drafted a cable to the War Department suggesting that the correspondents be allowed to write an account, under Palmer's control, of the supply problems. Pershing's reasoning was that some "moderate criticism" by reasonably friendly sources would be preferable to risking a massive loss of public confidence if more hostile press elements back home broke the story. Secretary of War Newton D. Baker turned down Pershing's request on the grounds that such critical stories, no matter how moderate their tone, would shake public confidence in Pershing and the war effort.

Both Pershing and Baker seemed concerned about their reputations at least as much as they were worried that such information might aid the enemy. They disagreed primarily about the best strategy of information control. Pershing preferred a damage-limitation strategy to risking an uncontrolled breach, while Baker opted for outright suppression. The outcome of either strategy was to deny the American public accurate information about the war effort.

Restrictions on coverage were severe throughout the war, and several journalists had their credentials revoked for violating the ground rules. With rare exceptions, the public back home learned only what military authorities wanted them to learn about the ebb and flow of the combat in France.

As stifling as the battlefield information policy was, the status of freedom of information on the home front was even worse. An ubiquitous government propaganda apparatus was directed by the Committee on Public Information, an agency that Wilson created by executive order only seven days after Congress approved the declaration of war against Germany. George Creel, the Denver journalist appointed to head the agency, immediately promulgated a "voluntary" censorship code for the press and then enlisted nearly 150,000 journalists, writers, scholars, and other communicators in the propaganda campaign.[18] Creel and other members of the administration were convinced that a domestic propaganda offensive was essential to mobilize public opinion behind the war effort.

Although a majority of Americans probably supported U.S. entry into the European conflict when Wilson sent his war message to Congress, most did so reluctantly, and sizable pockets of anti-war sentiment remained. Only 73,000 men enlisted in the military during the initial six weeks of the war, which impelled a desperate Wilson administration to raise a conscript army. The Creel committee's job was to make the American people more "war conscious" and generate public enthusiasm for U.S. involvement. Frank Cobb, editor of the *New York World*, later described how the mission of the Committee on Public Information complemented the overall war effort.

> Government conscripted public opinion as they conscripted men and money and materials. Having conscripted it, they dealt with it as they dealt with other raw materials. They mobilized it. They put it in the charge of drill sergeants. They goose-stepped it. They taught it to stand at attention and salute.[19]

Creel's propaganda strategy stressed two themes. One was glorification of the U.S. war effort as an idealistic crusade to advance the cause of freedom and democracy throughout the world, and the other was the caricature of a loathsome German menace led by the "Beast of Berlin," Kaiser Wilhelm II. The German people became the "Hun" who was despoiling Europe and seeking to extend his dominion over the whole Western Hemisphere.

It might be tempting to snicker at the crudity of such propaganda, but it succeeded admirably in heightening the war consciousness

21

and enthusiasm of most Americans. Indeed, it generated an unprecedented wave of hysteria about dissenters and people who were unfortunate enough to have German ancestry. At times, the campaign against all things German reached ludicrous proportions. Several states prohibited the teaching of German or the conduct of church services in that language. Statues of prominent Germans, including Revolutionary War hero Friedrich von Steuben, were removed from public parks, and the city fathers of Cincinnati even banned pretzels from free-lunch counters in saloons.

Far worse than such petty idiocies was the treatment of German Americans as well as pacifists, socialists, and other opponents of the war. Rumors of espionage and sabotage swept the country, and "patriotic" groups, such as the National Security League and the National Protective Association, actively encouraged by the Wilson administration, were organized to deal with the imaginary menace. Those vigilantes demanded a display of "100 percent Americanism" from all members of their communities. Suspect individuals were threatened, forced to publicly kiss the American flag, and subjected to beatings or literally tarred and feathered.[20]

Vigilante groups were encouraged in their intolerance by the government's own attempts to quash dissent. Wilson's initial answer to opponents of the war was the Espionage Act of 1917. Although Congress passed that legislation in the heat of wartime, the Wilson administration had contemplated imposing censorship even before the United States entered the war. As early as August 1916, Secretary of War Baker had recommended to Congress the enactment of a censorship statute. Some two months before the declaration of war, Rep. Edwin Yates Webb (D-N.C.), chairman of the House Judiciary Committee and one of the administration's closest political allies, introduced such legislation. Webb's measure would have authorized life imprisonment for anyone who circulated or published military information, false statements, or reports "likely or intended to cause disaffection in, or to interfere with the success of, the military or naval forces of the United States."[21]

Although the life imprisonment provision was softened and there were some modest differences in language, the Espionage Act bore a striking resemblance to the earlier Webb bill. Such premeditation suggests that the Espionage Act was not merely an overreaction in time of war. In any case, the legislation was the most serious attempt to constrain First Amendment freedoms since the expiration of the Alien and Sedition Acts. In addition to specifying criminal penalties for attempts to obstruct the draft, the Espionage Act provided for imprisonment of anyone making "false reports" to help the enemy— the same vague standard used by military authorities during the Civil War to harass dissenters. It soon became evident that federal prosecutors considered the mere circulation of anti-war literature a violation of the Espionage Act.

That statute harbored another offensive censorship clause. It empowered the postmaster general to deny use of the mails to any publication that, in his opinion, advocated insurrection, treason, or resistance to the laws of the United States. Postmaster General Albert Burleson promptly used his new powers to exclude a variety of pacifist, socialist, and isolationist newspapers, magazines, and pamphlets. Even if a paper avoided publishing an "illegal idea," it could still be excluded from the mails for betraying, as one postal censor put it, "an audible undertone of disloyalty" in ostensibly legal comments.[22] For those victimized by such capricious censorship, the only recourse was a lengthy and invariably futile trek through the federal court system.

The government's assault on First Amendment freedoms accelerated as the war progressed. The Trading with the Enemy Act, passed in October 1917, authorized the president to censor all international communications and gave the postmaster general sweeping censorship authority over the foreign-language press in the United States. Yet the administration still claimed that it had inadequate means of checking disloyalty and asked Congress for still broader powers.

Those powers were granted in the May 1918 amendments to the Espionage Act, changes that were popularly termed the Sedition Act. The Espionage Act, at least theoretically, required the government to prove that injurious consequences would result directly from prohibited utterances. The Sedition Act dispensed entirely with that obstacle and extended the power of the federal government over verbal and printed opinion regardless of consequences. And the substantive provisions were so vague as to seem calculated to exert the maximum chilling effect on freedom of expression. The act forbade disloyal, profane, scurrilous, or abusive remarks about the form of government, flag, or military uniform of the United States. The statute also prohibited any language designed to obstruct the war effort in any way. Again, the postmaster general was given carte blanche to deny use of the mails to any persons who, in his opinion, were circulating seditious material.[23]

The Sedition Act was the culmination of governmental measures that sacrificed First Amendment rights to the perceived exigencies of foreign policy. There was more freedom of expression in France, even though the front lines of the invading German army were sometimes less than 50 miles from Paris, than there was in the United States, more than 3,000 miles from the carnage. But France had few vocal opponents of the war; the United States harbored many. It is revealing that on several occasions Creel "asked" editors not to print stories that had already been widely published in Britain, France, or other allied countries.[24] Those requests strongly suggest that officials had motives other than concern about protecting the security of military operations. The Wilson administration's actions indicated a determination to forge a national unity behind the war effort no matter what the cost to constitutional liberties. Dissenters could not be tolerated in America because they might convince the normally noninterventionist public that the Wilsonian crusade to "make the world safe for democracy" was a bloody fraud. Journalist Walter Karp indicted Wilson for fostering such an atmosphere of intolerance and argued that the president's conduct betrayed a deep character flaw.

> Cherisher of the "unified will" in peacetime, Wilson proved himself implacable in war. Despising in peacetime all those who disturbed "the unity of our national counsel," Wilson in wartime wreaked vengeance on them all. Exalted by his global mission, [he] esteemed himself above all men and their puling cavils. He could no longer tolerate, he determined to silence, every impertinent voice of criticism, however small and however harmless. Nothing was to be said or read in America that Wilson himself might find disagreeable. Nothing was to be said or read in America that cast doubt on the nobility of Wilson's goals, the sublimity of his motives, or the efficacy of his statecraft. Wilson's self-elating catch phrases were to be on every man's lips or those lips would be sealed by a prison term.[25]

That was no exaggeration. Consider the picture painted by two historians who were relatively sympathetic toward the Wilson

administration and the mission of the Committee on Public Information. Using a hypothetical midwestern farm family as an example,
James R. Mock and Cedric Larson observed,

> Every item of war news they saw—in the country weekly,
> in magazines, or in the city daily picked up occasionally
> in the general store—was not merely officially approved
> information but precisely the same kind that millions of their
> fellow citizens were getting at the same moment. Every war
> story had been censored somewhere along the line—at the
> source, in transit, or in the newspaper office in accordance
> with "voluntary" rules established by the CPI. The same
> mimeograph machines furnished most of the Washington
> news, and the same cable censorship had passed all items
> from abroad.[26]

Such homogenization and regimentation of information were not
exactly what the authors of the First Amendment had had in mind.
Indeed, the restrictive measures bore an ominous resemblance to
the informational systems that would soon become the hallmark of
totalitarian systems.

The same totalitarian ethos was evident in the proposal sent to
Wilson by long-time Democratic party activist Breckinridge Long
to establish a newspaper board to better coordinate press treatment
of the war effort. Long lamented that, to the categories of industry
that had been integrated into the federal apparatus to prosecute the
war, "there is one notable exception—the press." The operation of
the existing censorship program, he concluded, "leaves much to be
desired," and a press board made up of leading journalists and
publishers was needed to make censorship more systematic and
effective. Long conceded that experience and professional competence would be important qualifications for the board members.
"Above all, however, they must have demonstrated their absolute
loyalty to the administration and the prosecution of all its plans."[27]

Long's enthusiasm for conformity did not stop there. In words
that foreshadowed the concept of organic nationalism and the führer
principle that would animate the European fascist movements of
the interwar years, he stressed,

> Responsibility would be single; power would be great; obli-
> gation would be, through the administration, to the country.
> The daily press would automatically become a part of the

25

> administration. They would feel that they were a part of it.
> Their patriotism and sense of obligation would cause them
> to respond to the help of the body to which they would be
> attached, of which they would feel themselves a part. The
> advantage to the country would be great. Public opinion
> would respond to proper treatment. Impressions most con-
> ducive to the accomplishment of the national purpose would
> be scattered throughout the land. Conjecture would cease.
> Misunderstanding would be minimized.[28]

Although Wilson and Creel ultimately dismissed Long's proposal as impractical, they did not disagree with his logic or objectives. Wilson replied to Long that "[I] need hardly say that I sympathize with the object you have in mind of organizing the newspaper men in some serviceable way to put the news service upon a higher plane of intelligence and public duty." The president's belief that the censorship system already in place was insufficient and his frustration with the decentralized nature of the American press, which made more systematic control difficult, were both quite evident: "There are too many irregular, irresponsible and unmanage-able forces amongst us, and while the members of a particular group would no doubt be honor bound by their engagements, they could bind nobody else and control nobody else."[29] In a similar vein, Creel lamented, "The press is the only profession in the world without an organization of any kind. There is no one body to speak for it, to make bargains for it, or to enforce discipline of any kind."[30] The desire for total regimentation was there, only the means were elusive.

The short-term results of the Espionage and Sedition Acts and other restrictive measures were severely damaging to First Amend-ment rights. More than 2,000 people were prosecuted and 1,055 convicted under those laws—the overwhelming majority for merely criticizing the government. It is testimony to the real motive for the legislation that not a single enemy spy was ever convicted of violat-ing the Espionage Act. Some of the prosecutions seemed especially partisan and vindictive. Socialist party leader Eugene V. Debs, for example, received a 10-year prison term for daring to express his distaste for the war in a speech in Canton, Ohio. Other prosecutions bordered on the bizarre and would have been humorous had it not been for the consequences borne by the victims. Movie producer Robert Goldstein was sentenced to prison for 10 years for distributing a film about the American Revolution. The reason? His film depicted British atrocities and therefore "incited hostility" against an ally of the United States in the current war! Moreover, according to the Court of Appeals for the Ninth Circuit, the "truth or falsity" of the incidents depicted on the film was "not the essence of the inquiry." Indeed, the court conceded that the picture "might be a truthful representation of an historical fact" yet still run afoul of the Espionage Act.[31]

There was virtually no limit to the government's attempts to stifle dissent. As constitutional scholar Zachariah Chafee Jr. noted,

> It became criminal . . . to state that conscription was unconstitutional though the Supreme Court had not yet held it valid . . . to urge that a referendum should have preceded our declaration of war, to say that war was contrary to the teachings of Christ. Men have been punished for criticizing the Red Cross and the Y.M.C.A.[32]

As bad as they were, the prosecutions under the wartime statutes barely begin to measure the destructive impact on freedom of expression. Although the chilling effect is inherently difficult to gauge, there is little doubt that many opponents of the war were intimidated into silence if not a bogus endorsement of Wilson's crusade by the draconian penalties meted out to their more outspoken compatriots. Those prosecutions established a legacy of governmental intolerance toward foreign policy dissenters that has periodically plagued the Republic—particularly during times of crisis—ever since. Walter Karp captures the atmosphere of intimidation.

> Fear and repression worked its way into every nook and cranny of ordinary life. Free speech was at hazard everywhere. Americans were arrested for remarks made at a boarding house table, in a hotel lobby, on a train, in a private club, during private conversations overheard by the government's spies. Almost every branch of Wilson's government sprouted its own "intelligence bureau" to snoop and threaten and arrest. By 1920 the Federal Bureau of Investigation, a swaddling fattened on war, had files on two million people and organizations deemed dangerously disloyal.[33]

The wartime repression of speech and press freedoms also left a more tangible legal legacy. When the Supreme Court finally reviewed sedition cases—after the war ended—it upheld the government's actions. Speaking for a unanimous Court in the landmark case of *Schenck v. United States*, Justice Oliver Wendell Holmes upheld the constitutionality of the Espionage Act.[34] Holmes conceded that Schenck's conduct (circulating pamphlets advocating resistance to the draft) would have been legal in normal times. But in wartime, he said, the government had the legitimate authority to proscribe utterances that might undermine the nation's defense effort. Although Holmes attempted to limit constraints on freedom of expression by formulating the "clear and present danger" test, his deference to restrictive legislation in times of crisis gave the government extraordinary latitude to silence critics. Consequently, the *Schenck* decision, far from contributing to the growth of First Amendment freedoms, as some constitutional historians have claimed, actually legitimized constriction of those rights.

The tangible legacy of the wartime censorship statutes was evident in legislation as well. Although Congress repealed the Sedition Act in 1921, the Espionage Act and the Trading with the Enemy Act remained on the books. Furthermore, during both the conflict and the years following, more than two dozen state legislatures enacted criminal syndicalist laws patterned after the Sedition Act of 1918. Advocacy of radical causes remained a risky undertaking in many locales well into the 1920s.[35] Restraints originally designed for a wartime emergency thus became part of the nation's legal framework even during a period of unquestioned international peace.

The worst legacy of the U.S. experience in World War I was not restrictive legislation or even the public hysteria that made patriotism synonymous with intolerance. It was the willingness of both government officials and the public to abandon the commitment to long-standing fundamental liberties for the pursuit of foreign policy objectives. The wisdom of American entry into the war remains a matter of debate among historians, but even if one accepts the proposition that it was a necessary step, the security of the United States was hardly so menaced that wholesale regimentation and repression were required. It is difficult to justify infringements on domestic liberties exceeding those of the Civil War period to meet a "threat" that was largely confined to a battlefield more than 3,000 miles away from the American homeland. Even the argument that the suppression of dissent was necessary to protect the lives of U.S.

troops does not hold up well. The United States had waged other conflicts without such massive repression, and there is no credible evidence that the public disputes about war policy increased the number of casualties.

Not only did the Wilson administration exhibit a cavalier attitude toward constitutional rights, those Americans who dared to resist the incursions of the executive branch and Congress found no protection or even retrospective vindication in the courts. In virtually every instance, the courts upheld the legality of the extraordinary powers exercised by the government during the war.

The atmosphere of intolerance and hysteria fostered by the Wilson administration did not dissipate with the end of the fighting. Since Germany had been defeated, the infamous Hun could no longer serve as a target of American patriotic wrath, but a new satanic threat emerged after the Bolshevik revolution in Russia. Despite the acute weakness of the political left in the United States in the immediate postwar period—the once powerful Socialist party had been badly damaged by its stubborn opposition to the war—jittery Americans feared that the Republic was on the verge of a communist revolution. A proliferation of labor troubles (especially the Seattle general strike in February 1919), and the discovery of bomb plots against some prominent public officials in April 1919, inaugurated a new round of public hysteria that became known as the Red Scare. Socialist legislators were expelled from several state legislatures simply because of their political affiliation, radical activists were assaulted in various communities, and the editorial offices of left-wing publications were vandalized. The treatment meted out to dissenters during the war thus resurfaced in the postwar era.

As it had during the war, the Wilson administration abetted rather than quelled attacks on civil liberties. On several occasions during his September 1919 tour to generate public support for U.S. membership in the League of Nations, the president even charged that opponents of the league (mainly conservative Republicans) were dupes of the Bolsheviks.[36] The worst offender in the administration was Attorney General A. Mitchell Palmer, who launched a concerted campaign to crush the illusory communist threat. Palmer instructed the Federal Bureau of Investigation to concentrate its efforts on infiltrating and disrupting communist organizations, and he lobbied incessantly for congressional passage of a peacetime sedition act—

a legislative proposal that Wilson officially endorsed in his annual message to Congress. Some 70 sedition bills were introduced in Congress during the fall of 1919 and the winter of 1920. The version that Palmer embraced (the Graham-Sterling bill) would not only have made permanent the wartime restrictions of the Sedition Act of 1918 but would have prohibited "incitement" to sedition—an offense so vague that it could mean virtually anything that federal prosecutors wanted it to mean.

Although Congress resisted the administration's latest effort to obliterate the First Amendment, Palmer was able to wage his own war against the Red Menace. The culmination of his effort came on the night of January 2, 1920, with the so-called Palmer raids, when thousands of federal agents and local police executed a simultaneous assault on the headquarters of alleged communist organizations throughout the country.

Eventually, the victims of the Palmer raids received hearings and the other elements of due process, but the fact that the raids occurred at all indicated how the wartime habits of repression had damaged the commitment to civil liberties. Robert K. Murray, the foremost historian of the Red Scare, concludes that in 1919 and 1920 "America's soul was in danger." The nation was "deserting its most honored principles of freedom—principles which had made it great and given it birth." And Murray has little doubt about the primary culprit: "The war was largely to blame. During the conflict the demand for absolute loyalty had permeated every nook and cranny of the social structure." In spite of a pervasive desire for a return to peacetime normality, "the American public of 1919 was still thinking with the mind of a people at war."[37]

It was not until the Harding administration, which began in 1921, that the wartime repression and hysteria truly abated. Harding soon released Debs and others who still languished in prison for violating the Espionage and Sedition Acts, and Americans increasingly turned their attention to other matters. But even with the return of normalcy, a residue of intolerance and constricted liberties remained. Some 35 states had criminal syndicalist laws, and the demand for "100 percent Americanism" persisted well into the decade. It is difficult to escape the conclusion that the Wilsonian crusade to make the world safe for democracy came perilously close to destroying the First Amendment and other vital components of democracy at home.

Government Mastery of the Press in World War II

The prevailing view of historians is that the government's record on First Amendment rights in World War II was markedly superior to its performance in World War I. That conclusion is debatable at best. It is true that the atmosphere of hysteria seemed less pervasive, and certainly the suppression of dissent was less blatant; there was no repetition of the hundreds of sedition prosecutions, for example. But that was largely due to the dearth of opposition to the war after Pearl Harbor—in significant contrast to the persistence of a sizable anti-war faction in 1917–18. The general absence of heavy-handed government suppression was not necessarily evidence of greater tolerance.

As it had been in World War I, the authority to censor and otherwise control the press was established early and decisively. Indeed, the administration of Franklin D. Roosevelt attempted to impose restrictions almost a full year before the United States entered the war. On December 30, 1940, Secretary of the Navy Frank Knox asked the news media to refrain from publishing information about a variety of topics, including the construction of new ships and the strength of various naval units. Although that step took the form of a "request," Knox and other administration officials hinted that restraints might become mandatory if cooperation was not forthcoming. In addition, Army and Navy officials developed comprehensive censorship plans that would take effect in the event of a national emergency.

When the Japanese attacked Pearl Harbor, the U.S. government responded immediately with censorship measures. The Federal Bureau of Investigation temporarily assumed control over both news reports and telecommunications into and out of the United States. On December 15, 1941, Roosevelt relieved the FBI of those responsibilities and appointed Byron Price, an editor for the Associated Press, to head the new Office of Censorship. Congress confirmed Roosevelt's actions three days later with the passage of the First War Powers Act, authorizing the censorship of all communications between the United States and any foreign country.[38] In addition to monitoring communications between the United States and other countries, Price's agency issued the Code of Wartime Practices to which publishers and broadcasters were "requested" to adhere. Some of the guidelines bordered on the bizarre. For example, man-on-the-street interviews were banned because they might be used to convey coded messages to Nazi or Japanese agents. Even weather forecasts were severely restricted lest the ubiquitous German intelligence apparatus gather information about weather patterns that would facilitate an invasion of North America, even though the nearest German army was some 3,000 miles away from U.S. shores.

The Code of Wartime Practices was supplemented from time to time by the Office of Censorship as well as by the military commanders in the various combat theaters. Battlefield restrictions varied widely from place to place and were seemingly more closely related to the personalities and whims of specific military commanders than to any coherent security rationale. Censorship was especially severe in the Pacific theater where both Gen. Douglas MacArthur and Adm. Ernest King severely restricted the press. MacArthur, ever the consummate egotist, constantly pressured reporters to file stories that placed the troops—and their commander—in the best possible light.[39] King's strategy also seemed motivated primarily by a desire to protect his and the Navy's reputation. At his direction, the Navy repeatedly withheld information on military setbacks, and even when such negative information was released, it was typically paired with stories of battlefield successes.

The Navy's disingenuous practices began immediately after the attack on Pearl Harbor. So thorough was the suppression of independent press accounts out of Honolulu that nothing but official communiqués emerged for four days. Those official accounts claimed that only one "old" battleship had been sunk and a few other ships damaged, while "heavy casualties" had been inflicted on the Japanese. Although the Navy eventually retreated from such absurdly optimistic descriptions, subsequent reports were only marginally more accurate, and the full scope of the damage was not disclosed until the final months of the war. Phillip Knightley justifiably questions the motives for the cover-up.

> It cannot be argued that these lies were necessary to conceal from the Japanese the extent of the disaster they had inflicted on the U.S. Pacific Fleet. The Japanese knew exactly how much damage they had done, and reports in Tokyo newspapers accurately stating the American losses meant that the Americans knew that the Japanese knew. The American censorship was to prevent the American public from learning the gravity of the blow.[40]

That U.S. officials would attempt to keep the American people in the dark on such matters is hardly surprising, given the attitude of censors in the Pacific theater and their superiors in Washington. According to Price's deputy, Theodore F. Koop, "War touches every individual, and no one can remain aloof as a more-or-less interested spectator. Newspapers . . . and broadcasting stations must be as actively behind the war effort as merchants or manufacturers."[41] That comment accurately summarized the attitude of military leaders and civilian policymakers in the Roosevelt administration toward the proper role of the press.

Although the censorship system was less heavy-handed in the North African and European theaters, it was not necessarily less restrictive. One of the favorite tactics of the censors was to delay the filing of unflattering news stories for days and sometimes even for weeks, while a "security review" was conducted. Meanwhile, the military's official version of events went forward speedily and had a chance to shape public opinion before it could be challenged by contradictory information.

Another disturbing aspect of the battlefield censorship system was its misuse to censor political or policy news in the name of military security requirements. Probably the most blatant example was the blocking of reports in April 1945 that Gen. Dwight D. Eisenhower had ordered U.S. forces advancing toward Berlin to halt, thereby enabling Soviet forces to capture the city. Given the virtual collapse of German military units by that stage of the war, security justifications for withholding such information from the public were feeble at best. Such stories might, however, have raised questions about the reasons for the willingness of U.S. leaders to let the Soviet Union achieve a dramatic symbolic and psychological triumph in the heart of Europe. Conservative Americans, some of whom had never fully trusted the USSR despite the rhetoric about the Grand Alliance against Hitler, would almost certainly have voiced objections. The motive for that act of censorship seemed to have had more to do with protecting the flanks of the U.S. political and military leadership than with genuine security concerns.

An even more worrisome example was General MacArthur's continuing censorship of news dispatches after fighting ceased in the Pacific theater. He did not lift such restrictions until October 6, 1945, some two months after Japan's surrender, and then only when the

Truman administration—responding to intense pressure from news organizations—directed him to do so. In the intervening weeks, "correspondents chafed under a censorship that they said grew tighter and tighter in regard to criticism of occupation policies."[42] In other words, a censorship system that existed ostensibly to protect the security of military operations in wartime was kept in place to stifle dissenting views on U.S. political policies in Japan during peacetime.

Most rigorous battlefield censorship in World War II was probably superfluous. Virtually all reporters were enthusiastic supporters of the war and willingly responded to requests to sanitize or withhold unpleasant information. Stories of allied atrocities were notably absent—even though such incidents did occur—and accounts of dubious policies or even outright military blunders seldom appeared.[43] Indeed, the entire image of the conflict was one of a heroic, victorious crusade by noble democracies against odious totalitarian aggressors—an image that, although true in some respects, ignored the troublesome detail that one important totalitarian power was part of the "democratic" coalition.

As would be the case in the Persian Gulf conflict nearly a half century later, press accounts dwelt on the wonders and accomplishments of sophisticated U.S. weaponry while downplaying, if not ignoring, the filth, brutality, and suffering that accompany any war.[44] U.S. censorship authorities actively encouraged that antiseptic portrayal of the war. One directive, for example, admonished radio stations "to steer clear of dramatic programs which attempt to portray the horrors of combat."[45] Most reporters embraced that objective on their own, although Ernie Pyle and a few others made a credible effort to accurately describe the day-to-day lives of combat personnel.

Despite some battlefield abuses and some questionable censorship practices on the home front, the restrictions on information were less brazen than they had been during World War I. As a guiding principle, Price and his subordinates endeavored to draw a distinction between a legitimate right to criticize the government and freedom to be "criminally careless with military information." Although that standard was sufficiently vague to invite abuse, little occurred. The overwhelming majority of the press willingly collaborated in the administration's propaganda campaign. That was true not only of battlefield correspondents but of writers, editors, and broadcasters back home as well.

In contrast to the situation that prevailed in World War I when the Committee on Public Information exercised both censorship and propaganda functions, the Roosevelt administration divided them between the Office of Censorship and the Office of War Information (OWI). The latter agency was established by executive order in June 1942 to serve as liaison between the communications media and Washington, to "explain" government policies to the public, and to ensure a free flow of information about the war—consistent, of course, with national security requirements.

The Roosevelt administration understood the important role of propaganda to an even greater extent than had the Wilson administration. Indeed, the president took steps to establish several embryonic propaganda agencies before the United States entered the fighting. The most significant was the Foreign Information Service (FIS), nominally headed by Col. William G. "Wild Bill" Donovan, but in fact directed by playwright and presidential speech writer Robert Sherwood, one of Roosevelt's confidants. Sherwood gathered around him an assortment of journalists, broadcasters, and writers— virtually all of them staunch advocates of U.S. intervention in the war. Among their earliest and most significant projects was the creation of a radio service—the Voice of America—to disseminate the views of the U.S. government (or more precisely, the Roosevelt administration) on the world crisis. The "information" provided by the FIS was often flagrant pro-war propaganda—paid for by U.S. tax dollars. The objectivity of the FIS both before and during the war can be gauged by Sherwood's statement that "all U.S. information to the world should be considered as though it were a continuous speech by the President."[46] Yet several dozen members of the journalistic community lent their talents to the effort, willingly acting as conduits of propaganda for the government.

The function of the FIS was to present the Roosevelt administration's foreign policy to foreign audiences in the most favorable terms. The OWI served a similar function for domestic readers and listeners. To head the OWI, Roosevelt appointed Elmer Davis, who had served as reporter and editorial writer for the *New York Times* before moving on to become a broadcaster for CBS. *Time* described him as one of the best newsmen in the business, an assessment that was widely held in the profession.

Any hopes that Davis and his OWI colleagues might have entertained of protecting the flow of information and avoiding the experiences of World War I quickly dimmed. The executive order establishing the agency was hopelessly vague, recognizing the right of the public "to be truthfully informed about the common war effort" but failing to say anything about how questions of national security would affect the release of information. As noted, the Navy frequently withheld (or at least delayed) negative reports until they could be paired with stories of combat successes, and the Army was not much better. Even Davis was frustrated by such practices, especially Admiral King's obstructionism. Davis later commented that he "always suspected that Admiral King's idea of war information was that there should be just *one* communiqué. Some morning we would announce that the war was over and that we won it."[47]

The political organs of government were only slightly more indulgent of the OWI. Civilian leaders wanted not only to run the war without outside monitoring or interference but to develop postwar policies in the same manner. If they saw a significant role for the OWI at all, it was simply as a convenient channel for propaganda. As the war progressed, that attitude frustrated even some journalists who were enthusiastic supporters of the crusade against fascism. Historian Allan M. Winkler concludes, "Newsmen who felt their primary allegiance was to the people at large were increasingly ill-disposed . . . to cooperate with what some viewed as the president's publicity bureau—an agency that seemed either unnecessary or unhelpful or both."[48] The administration's efforts to "guide" press coverage caused columnist Raymond Clapper to complain that FDR was taking "the whole technique of a controlled press beyond anything we have experienced in this country."[49] Since Clapper was familiar with the Wilson administration's conduct in World War I, that was an extraordinarily harsh criticism.

Although the frustration of journalists who took the First Amendment seriously was understandable, they should scarcely have been surprised at the Roosevelt administration's actions. U.S. leaders wanted an institutional cheerleader to proclaim the wisdom of demanding unconditional surrender from the Axis powers, the enduring nature of the Grand Alliance with Britain and the Soviet Union, and the feasibility of a postwar world free from violence and aggression—a world built on FDR's four freedoms. And while some journalists complained about the sterility of the debate and the government's self-serving restrictions on information, many more were willing to look the other way, and some were eager accomplices in disseminating the government's propaganda.

The OWI diligently tried to fulfill its mission of encouraging newspapers, magazines, radio, and the movie industry to produce favorable accounts of the war effort and America's allies. For example, the OWI attempted to neutralize possible public criticism of Washington's de facto alliance with the Stalinist USSR. The administration's concern on that score was well-founded. Several public opinion surveys taken in late 1942 and early 1943 showed widespread public skepticism about the trustworthiness of the USSR and lower, but still disturbingly high, levels of skepticism about Britain, China, and other allies. Other surveys taken at the same time also showed that a third of the people were willing to accept a separate peace with Germany or to agree to something less than Germany's unconditional surrender. Both positions ran directly counter to administration policy.[50]

OWI officials worked to bring public opinion into closer accord with FDR's wartime and postwar objectives. Cooperative filmmakers and journalists responded with alacrity, producing an endless stream of news stories and feature films that painted the Axis enemies in terms even more dire than the reality. Portrayals of the Japanese were especially odious, featuring blatantly racist stereotypes that are a national embarrassment in retrospect. In account after account, the Japanese were depicted not merely as congenital aggressors but as scarcely human and certainly not deserving of the slightest mercy. Typical of that approach was a radio program, *A Lesson in Japanese,* narrated by actor Frederic March, that contained the following passage.

> Have you ever watched a well-trained monkey at a zoo? Have you seen how carefully he imitates his trainer? The monkey goes through so many human movements so well that he actually seems to be human. But under the fur, he's still a savage little beast. Now, consider the imitative little Japanese who for seventy-five years has built himself up into something so closely resembling a civilized human being that he actually believes he is just that.[51]

Opinion elites similarly cooperated with the OWI in blunting public concern about Washington's alliance with Stalin. Hollywood produced such gushing films as *North Star*, *Song of Russia*, and *Mission to Moscow* that bore utterly no resemblance to real life in the USSR. Members of the print medium also portrayed America's ally in glowing terms. *Life* informed its readers that the Russians were "one hell of a people" who "think like Americans." The authors of another *Life* article described the NKVD (predecessor of the KGB) as "a national police force similar to the FBI."[52] By painting unrealistic pictures of the USSR, the government's propaganda network almost certainly contributed to the public disillusionment that set in during the immediate postwar period and contributed to the uncompromising attitudes toward Moscow that characterized the Cold War. Even worse, those portrayals led to later witch-hunts for the "communist traitors" who had misled the American people.

The OWI not only orchestrated the whitewashing of the USSR's record, it openly sought to increase public receptivity to statist policies at home. Probably the most egregious example was "Battle Stations for All," a 123-page pamphlet published in 1943 that extolled the virtues of rationing, increased taxation, price controls, rent controls, and other measures aimed at "taking the profit out of war."[53] That pamphlet offended even some staunch supporters of the war— particularly moderate and conservative Republicans who suspected that the public was being conditioned to accept a highly activist and intrusive government as a normal part of American life.

Although the Roosevelt administration preferred the velvet glove of co-option in its dealings with the press, there were reminders that the iron fist of coercion would be used if necessary. Publicly, Roosevelt extolled the virtues of the First Amendment, even in wartime. Addressing the Society of Newspaper Editors shortly before the attack on Pearl Harbor, the president stated,

> Suppression of opinion and censorship of news are among the mortal weapons that dictatorships direct against their own people and against the world. As far as I am concerned, there will be no government control of news unless it is of vital military information. . . . It would be a shameful abuse of patriotism to suggest that opinion should be stifled in its service.[54]

Once the United States officially entered the war, however, FDR's attitude was quite different. Certainly the president's private comments—as well as those of other government leaders and key administration supporters—suggested that opposition to the war effort would not be tolerated. Roosevelt believed that articles in the *Chicago Tribune*, the *New York Daily News*, and other conservative publications critical of Britain and the Soviet Union might warrant prosecution under the Espionage Act of 1917. "The tie-in between the attitude of these papers and the Rome-Berlin broadcasts is something far greater than mere coincidence," FDR fumed on one occasion.[55] Liberal supporters urged the administration to take substantive action against such critics. Freda Kirchwey, editor of the *Nation*, asserted that the "treason press" in the United States constituted "an integral part of the fascist offensive." Disloyal publications "should be exterminated exactly as if they were enemy machine guns in the Bataan jungle."[56]

Interventionist liberals had exhibited marked intolerance for opponents of their foreign policy views even before Pearl Harbor. Roosevelt ordered the FBI to investigate leading anti-war individuals and organizations during 1940–41 in an effort to link them to fascist governments. Administration officials and interventionist partisans repeatedly attempted to smear Sen. Robert Taft (R-Ohio), Rep. Hamilton Fish (R-N.Y.), journalist John T. Flynn, aviation hero Charles Lindbergh, and other anti-war leaders as pro-fascist.[57] When the United States entered the war, those tactics intensified with the publication of such books as *Illustrious Dunderheads, Sabotage! The Secret War against America,* and *Under Cover* that included numerous allegations or innuendoes that isolationists were in league with a fascist fifth column to undermine the war effort.[58] As Kirchwey had done, they also included demands that domestic fascist propaganda—by which they meant virtually anything that questioned the policies of the Roosevelt administration—be banned.[59] In short, members of the noninterventionist community were victims of a liberal interventionist version of "McCarthyism" a decade before that term came into vogue.

Roosevelt seemed inclined to take the advice of his more zealous followers and adopt draconian restrictions on press critics. His conception of First Amendment freedoms was alarmingly narrow when it came to matters of national defense. In marked contrast to his 1941 speech to the Society of Newspaper Editors, he privately asserted that freedom of the press was "freedom to print correct news" and freedom to criticize government policies "on the basis of factual truth." He saw "a big distinction between this and freedom to print untrue news."[60]

FDR conveniently ignored the thorny problem of who was to define "correct" news or determine whether a criticism was factual or just. At least in wartime, the implication was that the government should have the power to pass judgment on the worthiness of its critics. In essence, FDR subscribed to the view of First Amendment rights embodied in the Alien and Sedition Acts more than a century before. The danger inherent in that approach is self-evident even if the policy is implemented by extraordinarily tolerant chief executives, and presidents rarely fit that description when they are busy pursuing interventionist initiatives that they believe are in the national interest. Wilson, Roosevelt, and most of their successors tended to view "correct news" and "factual truth" as synonymous with an endorsement of the incumbent administration's foreign policy.

His usual sensitivity to political realities restrained FDR from launching a frontal assault on powerful mainstream critics such as the *Chicago Tribune*. But the administration did employ criminal sanctions against highly unpopular fascist and quasi-fascist opponents of the war. That the government even bothered to prosecute a handful of pro-fascist propagandists for sedition was disquieting. None of the defendants had the slightest ability to foment serious opposition to the war. In the first place, the overwhelming majority of Americans—including those who had been staunch noninterventionists—supported the war effort after the Japanese attacked Pearl Harbor. Moreover, the defendants' fascist associations or pretensions hopelessly tainted them, rendering their influence nil.

Such prosecutions may have been an overreaction to an insignificant threat, but an alternative explanation is more probable. In a subtle but effective way, the Justice Department's action warned more mainstream critics that a similar fate might await them unless they kept their dissent under rigorous control.[61] For journalists who recalled the numerous sedition prosecutions of World War I, a subtle reminder was probably sufficient. Even the staunchly pro-FDR biographer James MacGregor Burns conceded, "The trial did serve to muzzle 'seditious' propaganda, but it also revealed Roosevelt as a better Jeffersonian in principle than in practice."[62]

In some respects, the government's policies on freedom of expression in World War II were as corrosive as its conduct a generation earlier. The government fostered an illusion of greater tolerance of dissenting views, but the mechanisms of control and intimidation were merely more insidious. The unhealthy legal precedents established during the first global conflict were reiterated and strengthened during the second. Moreover, manipulation and control occurred with far less provocation. In World War I a sizable anti-war minority did exist, and vigorous criticism of U.S. involvement in the fighting might well have undermined the war effort. Faced with that problem, the Wilson administration chose to abridge freedom of expression. During World War II no significant anti-war faction existed. Yet the Roosevelt administration demonstrated that it had little patience with outright opponents, however ineffectual, or mainstream critics, however mild their criticisms. That legacy of World War II did not bode well for the treatment of individuals who dared to criticize the direction of U.S. foreign policy as the Cold War struggle with the Soviet Union began.

The mindset created in World War I and consolidated in World War II—that the press was either a tool to be used for the dissemination of government propaganda or an adversary to be silenced—continued into the Cold War era and beyond. The government's attitude toward the news media became increasingly arrogant. One example of that attitude during the waning months of World War II was the virtual exclusion of the press from the Yalta and Potsdam Conferences, where the "Big Three" allied governments decided the geopolitical architecture of postwar Europe. At Yalta FDR's press secretary, Stephen Early, admitted to inquiring journalists that Roosevelt and Churchill had agreed with Stalin that no reporters of any nationality would be allowed to attend the conference.[63]

The willingness of an American president to acquiesce to the wishes of a totalitarian regime about press coverage of a conference with historic policy implications was disquieting. At least Churchill and his advisers leaked some, albeit sketchy, information to British journalists. That action was hardly an adequate substitute for independent press coverage, but it was superior to the conduct of the U.S. delegation, which seemed not only willing but eager to cooperate with the Soviet-requested news blackout. The veil of secrecy only marginally dampened press speculation about the deliberations at the time, but it subsequently contributed to a variety of myths about the Yalta Conference, including allegations that a sick or treasonous FDR approved a Soviet scheme to subjugate Eastern Europe.

Historian Louis Liebovich notes, "It was probably a mistake on Roosevelt's part not to have worked harder to provide more and better information to U.S. newsmen during the eight days of meetings. The secrecy combined with the health issue ensured that Yalta would always be subject to second guessing."[64] What Liebovich fails to appreciate is that FDR's conduct was entirely consistent with his assumption that he had a constitutional writ to conduct the nation's foreign policy free from scrutiny.

Unfortunately, FDR's successor, Harry S Truman, exhibited many of the same traits. That became evident when the Big Three leaders sought to impose a news blackout of the July 1945 Potsdam Conference—although at least this time some U.S. reporters were able to be in the city. Again, a U.S. president sided with Stalin against Churchill, agreeing that brief, nondescript press releases of the deliberations would be the only information given to the news media. The administration's attitude provoked some criticism by political opponents. In a speech on the floor of the Senate, Alexander Wiley (R-Wis.) excoriated the administration's insistence on secrecy. "It is high time that [press] delegates to the Potsdam Conference were stopped being treated like indiscreet maidens who talk too much. This is censorship and a ghastly example of dictatorial behavior. Correspondents are being spoonfed a dish of trivial mush."[65]

Perhaps the most corrosive effect of the wartime experience with censorship was on the journalistic community itself. Knightley describes the willingness of battlefield correspondents to accept government controls.

> War correspondents went along with the official scheme for reporting the war because they were convinced that it was in the national interest to do so. They saw no sharp line of demarcation between the role of the press in wartime and that of the government, and they became so accustomed to censorship that when it finally ended, in 1945, one correspondent was heard to say in some bewilderment, "But where will we go now to get our stories cleared?"[66]

What was true of war correspondents was also true of the news media generally. As Theodore F. Koop conceded, "So firmly had the idea of checking with a government authority been implanted in the minds of radio and newspapermen that it was difficult for them to reconvert to peacetime freedom."[67]

Koop was correct. Although journalists echoed Senator Wiley's demand for more openness about the Potsdam Conference, it is revealing that virtually none of the editorials and articles discussing the issue vigorously sought the right to cover the actual deliberations. Instead, they respectfully requested that the press corps receive adequate news briefings so they might better analyze the progress of the meetings.[68] That supplicant mentality was hardly consistent with a healthy exercise of First Amendment rights.

World War II marked the beginning of another chapter in governmental co-option of the news media on defense and foreign policy issues. Whereas co-option of the media had been temporary in 1917–18, this time it would persist long after the guns fell silent. One of the most prominent casualties of the two global conflagrations of the 20th century was the concept of independent, unfettered, and skeptical press coverage of foreign policy.

2. The Velvet Glove: Seducing the Press

Precedents for controlling the press in the name of national security were firmly established during both world wars; the federal government used the dual tactic of co-opting friendly elements and intimidating or suppressing would-be critics. Any expectation that America would return to its tradition of vigorous debate on all subjects, including foreign affairs, after World War II proved unfounded. As the United States entered that state of perpetual crisis known as the Cold War, the patterns established during the two world wars exerted considerable influence, albeit usually in more subtle forms.

Even during the embryonic stages of the Cold War, government efforts to manipulate the mainstream media and silence unorthodox critics were evident. Members of the Truman administration, especially Secretary of State Dean Acheson, routinely used the press to float trial balloons and promote misleading policy rationales. The "selective leak," while certainly not unknown before the late 1940s, became a prominent feature of the administration's campaign to sell its interventionist foreign policy to the public. That technique was double-edged. Reporters who were "cooperative" became privy to valuable information for exclusive stories; uncooperative types were frozen out.

There was also more subtle pressure exerted on the press to do nothing that might undermine national security during a period of ongoing confrontation with the USSR. As Theodore F. Koop had mused in 1946, "The success of the [voluntary] wartime censorship in keeping military information out of circulation can set a dangerous precedent for men who in peacetime want to keep ideas out of circulation."[1] The parallels were unsettling. As they had during wartime, government leaders viewed the press as part of the nation's foreign policy team, not as an external monitor. Secretary of Defense James Forrestal clearly was operating on that premise when, during a meeting with media representatives in March 1948, he expressed

45

the need for "an assumption by the information media of their responsibility in voluntarily refraining from publishing information detrimental to our national security."[2]

Forrestal's apparent desire to extend wartime "voluntary censorship" practices to a period in which the United States was not engaged in an armed conflict was disquieting, since no one could know how long the Cold War might last. Even more disquieting was the vague standard of "information detrimental to our national security." That concept implied more than the wartime restrictions on information that might prove militarily useful to the enemy. Among other things, it raised the question: detrimental according to whom? Almost any account that uncovered malfeasance, incompetence, or deceit on the part of U.S. policymakers could be construed as detrimental to national security by officials who had a vested interest in advancing a particular policy agenda or protecting their professional reputations. Forrestal's implicit assumption was that the objectives of the media and the national security bureaucracy were—or at least ought to be—the same. Indeed, on another occasion, he expressed that assumption explicitly. "The American press," he wrote to Gen. George C. Marshall, "should be an instrument of our foreign policy."[3]

Forrestal's attitude toward the media was still evident nearly two decades later. In 1965 Assistant Secretary of Defense for Public Affairs Arthur Sylvester bluntly told journalists that in time of war (by which he meant the undeclared Vietnam War) the news media had the obligation to become the "handmaiden" of government.[4] On another occasion, before the onset of the massive U.S. involvement in Vietnam, Sylvester described the government's overall information policy on national security issues as an attempt to "wed the pen and the sword."[5]

During the first two decades of the Cold War, much of the press viewed its role in the same way. An increasing number of journalists failed to heed the warning of Walter Lippmann that there "were certain rules of hygiene" in the relationship between journalists and government officials "which one has to observe." Members of the press, he admonished, "cannot become the cronies" of officials if they are to do their jobs. At least "an air space," if not a wall of separation, was essential.[6] James Russell Wiggins later observed that Lippmann "was only voicing sentiments thoroughly understood by the press in the nineteenth century but which seem to be less and less understood in the twentieth century."[7] "Air space" was noticeably lacking from the late 1940s to the late 1960s, and the consequences of the government's successful co-option of the press were insidious and pervasive.

Most members of the press echoed the Truman administration's rationale for such initiatives as the Truman Doctrine, the Marshall Plan, and the North Atlantic Treaty Organization. Few questioned the assumptions that those measures were necessary in the struggle to defend the democratic West from the onslaught of communist expansionism and that no alternative policies were available. Yet we now know that much of the anti-communist rhetoric was a calculated tactic by the Truman administration to garner public support for what might otherwise have been controversial initiatives.[8] Administration leaders concluded that it was essential to minimize the aspects of realpolitik inherent in programs to contain Soviet power and instead to stress the moral and crusading themes of anti-communism. Without those rationales, they feared, the American people would resist expensive and burdensome obligations, perhaps even relapse into a policy of "isolationism."

Alarmism was used as a tactic early in the Cold War. In retrospect, it is apparent that the aid package for Greece and Turkey—the occasion for promulgating the Truman Doctrine pledging the United States to "support free peoples who are resisting attempted subjugation by armed minorities or by outside pressures"—was designed to deal with the power vacuum in the Eastern Mediterranean caused by the abrupt withdrawal of Britain's long-standing military presence. But the proposed doctrine was not presented to Congress or the public as a limited geopolitical measure. Instead, the administration took the advice of Sen. Arthur Vandenberg (R-Mich.) that it would be necessary to "scare hell" out of the American people to win support.[9]

The resulting propaganda campaign was an exercise in oversimplification. Administration spokesmen portrayed the authoritarian Greek and Turkish governments as bona fide members of the "free world." Long-standing Russian desires to gain greater access to the Mediterranean through the Bosporous and the Dardanelles—an objective that predated the reign of Tsar Peter the Great in the late 17th century—were cited as definitive evidence of a plot by Stalin and his henchmen to subvert and conquer Turkey. Although administration officials understandably used whatever arguments they thought would advance their goals, despite the violence that might be done to historical accuracy and even rudimentary logic, the press had a moral obligation to at least raise questions about such inaccuracies. Yet very few media accounts disputed the administration's apocalyptic justifications for the proposed aid. Even fewer questioned the broader, long-term policy implications of the Truman Doctrine—even though congressional critics warned (correctly, as it turned out) that such a commitment would make the United States the military patron of any regime, however odious, that professed to be anti-Soviet.

There was even less critical scrutiny of the Marshall Plan that the administration promulgated the following year. Yet scholars have since made strong cases that the extensive program of economic assistance was motivated at least as much by a perceived need to redress the growing trade imbalance between Western Europe and the United States as by any conviction that the plan would stave off communist takeovers.[10] Even NATO, which seemed explicitly designed to thwart Soviet expansionism, was more a device to make it difficult to decouple U.S. and West European security interests; most leaders on both sides of the Atlantic privately acknowledged that the danger of a Soviet invasion was remote—although Soviet attempts at subversion and intimidation were a credible threat.[11] A considerable amount of the evidence that would have cast doubt on the administration's version of events was available in the public domain at the time—if journalists had bothered to look for it.

The Truman administration was remarkably effective in using the mainstream press to implement its propaganda offensive.[12] With the significant exceptions of the *Chicago Tribune* and its sister East Coast publication, the *Washington Times-Herald*, major newspapers and magazines rarely questioned the administration's official rationale for its Cold War measures. What criticism did emerge generally faulted Truman and his cohorts for being insufficiently rigorous in combating the communist menace.

The absence of media skepticism about U.S. foreign policy continued with few exceptions throughout the Eisenhower and Kennedy years.[13] What is so striking in retrospect is the lack of inclination to challenge the official version of events even when government explanations were manifestly dubious.

One finds very few stories, for example, about the repression practiced by South Korean dictator Syngman Rhee, although ample evidence existed. Instead, most of the press parroted Washington's assertion that American troops were fighting and dying in Korea to protect freedom and democracy.[14] Granted, there was no question that the South Korean government was less vicious and repressive than its North Korean adversary, and the evidence is overwhelming that North Korea started the conflict that plunged the peninsula into a bloody war. Nevertheless, the Rhee government was far from democratic, and the media's failure to point out that fact created a misleading impression.

It was also significant that most of the stories that did deal with South Korean corruption, brutality, or military incompetence were filed by European, Australian, and other non-American correspondents.[15] The absence of critical accounts is unsurprising since not one major U.S. newspaper consistently opposed the war. (Even the *Chicago Tribune* turned against the effort only after the Chinese intervention made it a much bloodier and more costly undertaking.) The same was true of American news magazines; even among liberal and left-wing journals, the ultraleft *National Guardian* was virtually alone in denouncing the U.S. intervention.

So tame was the mainstream press that reporters reacted with mystified dismay when the government began to show signs that the voluntary censorship regime instituted during the early stages of the fighting might not be so voluntary. Correspondents had made the error of filing stories indicating that the U.S. troops that had been hastily dispatched to Korea from Japan to meet the onslaught of North Korean forces were ill equipped and ill trained and were, therefore, not faring well in combat. Gen. Douglas MacArthur later contended that as gloomy and doubtful as the situation was during the initial weeks of the war, "the news reports painted it much worse than it actually was."[16] Army officials promptly extended the "voluntary" censorship code to rule out any criticism of the conduct of allied soldiers on the battlefield or (probably more relevant) the decisions made by United Nations commanders in the field. MacArthur fondly recalled receiving a letter from the managing editor of the *Chicago Sun-Times* stressing that paper's willingness to cooperate and noting that it had already imposed self-censorship to ensure that stories detrimental to the war effort would not appear. According to

MacArthur, once again "a free press exhibited its fullest commitment to the burdens of a free society."[17]

The notion that responsible journalism was defined as support for the war was not confined to the editors of the *Sun-Times*. Marguerite Higgins of the *New York Herald Tribune* implored the government to realize that reporters were fully behind the war effort and were only trying to be helpful to the Truman administration's cause. "So long as our government requires the backing of an aroused and informed public opinion," she wrote, "it is necessary to tell the hard bruising truth. It is best to tell graphically the moments of desperation and horror endured by an unprepared army, so that the American people will demand that it does not happen again."[18] Although Higgins believed that candor was compatible with patriotism, other correspondents sought to demonstrate their loyalty by urging the government to institute mandatory censorship so they would have better guidance about what they could and could not report. The influential trade journal *Broadcasting* reported that many journalists hailed the imposition of formal censorship in December 1950 as "long-awaited and much needed."[19] That attitude was not exactly the hallmark of a vigorous, independent press.

Military officials did not always appreciate the media's subservience, however. Even well-intentioned accounts could contain information that might reflect badly on the war effort and the military as an institution, thereby damaging careers and reputations. Not only the severity but the breadth of censorship varied markedly with the fortunes of war. When the U.S. cause was faring well, censorship eased; whenever there were setbacks, the military censors became markedly less tolerant; indeed, they were sometimes downright surly. That pattern had been seen during both world wars and would be again in future conflicts.

Journalists had most freedom during the weeks following MacArthur's spectacularly successful amphibious flanking maneuver at Inchon in September 1950 and the resulting rout of North Korean forces that soon enabled UN units to liberate Seoul and then to advance to the Yalu River border with China. They had much less freedom during the weeks following North Korea's invasion of South Korea—when U.S. and South Korean forces were pushed back into a small area around the southern port city of Pusan—and the months following the intervention of Chinese troops in November 1950.

During the latter period, allied forces were repulsed from the Yalu and had to withdraw south of the 38th parallel, sustaining heavy casualties, and South Korea's capital, Seoul, was again surrendered.

Less than a month after the first encounter with Chinese units, MacArthur's headquarters terminated the "voluntary" censorship arrangements and imposed rigorous restrictions on newspaper accounts, broadcasts, magazine articles, and photographs from Korea. The new requirements included the usual limitations on reporting troop movements and other matters clearly related to military security. In addition, there was a blanket prohibition of any discussion of allied air power, and it was now forbidden to make any criticism of the UN war effort or "any derogatory comments" about UN troops or commanders. The unprecedented scope of censorship seemed to be intended to prevent criticism of policy and to protect the reputations of military leaders.

Penalties for violations ranged from a temporary suspension of privileges to expulsion from the Korean theater. In extreme cases, MacArthur's command warned, reporters would be subject to trial by court martial.[20] Although that threat was never carried out, the sense of intimidation was omnipresent. Those who had encountered MacArthur during World War II and during the postwar years when he commanded U.S. forces in Japan were especially unlikely to seek a confrontation. Phillip Knightley notes, "No correspondent dared ask whether MacArthur had overextended his forces by miscalculating China's reaction and the strength of her intervention, probably because the supreme commander had already expelled some seventeen reporters from Japan for having criticized his policies."[21]

According to Knightley, the military's censorship system was probably unnecessary. Critical reporting, which had been sparse at best during the early months of the conflict, virtually disappeared after the Chinese intervention. Correspondents who continued to attempt to send anything but laudatory accounts of the war discovered that editors and publishers back home thought that "it was time to 'get on side' and stop helping the Reds."[22] Probably the most devastating admission came from Robert Miller of the Associated Press. Miller, who viewed the press as an important ally of government in the global battle against communism, conceded, "There are certain facts and stories from Korea that editors and publishers have printed that are pure fabrication. Many of us who sent the stories

51

knew they were false, but we had to write them because they were official releases from responsible military headquarters and were released for publication even though the people responsible knew they were untrue."[23]

In Knightley's judgment, the prospect that the Korean War would be reported fully and fairly "receded rapidly, under a variety of pressures, foremost among which was the political atmosphere in the United States at the time." Crucial events in the Korean War "were either not reported at all or were not given proper attention—the proposed use of the atom bomb, disunity among the allies, the amazing behavior [collaboration] of the allied POWs, and the farcical conduct of the peace talks." Knightley concludes that one "cannot escape the conclusion that although [correspondents] showed admirable professional courage on the battlefield, they failed to show equal moral courage in questioning what the war was all about."[24]

The atmosphere of conformity persisted throughout the remainder of the 1950s and extended far beyond battlefield reporting. The spirited and wide-ranging debates on the Republic's foreign policy that had marked earlier eras were noticeably absent; an obsession with "loyalty" dominated the political culture of the nation. Although the activities of Sen. Joseph McCarthy (R-Wis.) and his admirers were the most visible examples of the demand for conformity on defense and foreign policy issues, they were hardly the only ones. McCarthyism was merely the most extreme manifestation of a pervasive attitude. The equation of dissent with disloyalty and the insistence that Washington's Cold War policy should be beyond criticism both predated McCarthy's rise to prominence and would last long after his political downfall. The spectrum of permissible positions in the debate on foreign policy during the 1950s was extraordinarily narrow—essentially ranging from moderately interventionist to stridently interventionist.

Much of the conformity was not the result of blatant governmental restrictions. Instead, it was a response to subtler signals—expressions of official approval of "patriotic" accounts and vaguely ominous indications of disapproval of critical stories. Most U.S. policymakers sought to enlist the media in the crusade against communism much as they had previously in the crusades against the Kaiser and the fascists. As it had in those earlier episodes, the bulk of the opinion-shaping sector responded willing; the press was not so much suppressed as it was seduced, or at least cowed. Many journalists seemed to view their mission much as they would in wartime, even though the United States was technically at peace, and they appeared more concerned about advancing U.S. policy objectives than about a quest for the truth. Lester Markel, Sunday editor of the *New York Times*, typified that attitude. Because of the urgency of Cold War conditions, he stated, "The question of how much news . . . shall be released and when, must be left largely in the hands of the government."[25] As political scientist Dan D. Nimmo described the situation in the mid-1960s, journalists and government operatives both assumed " 'responsible leadership' to mean an agreement between government and press leaders that certain matters can be publicized in the 'national interest' while others must remained unrevealed, hidden or overlooked."[26]

Typical of that incestuous relationship was the campaign by CBS founder David Sarnoff to create a media-government partnership in the anti-Soviet struggle. The centerpiece of his effort was a 42-page memorandum, "Program for a Political Offensive against International Communism," that he submitted to President Eisenhower in April 1955. Sarnoff's memo not only envisioned an extensive use of radio, television, and other forms of communication to disseminate U.S. government propaganda worldwide, it railed against left-wing media outlets that were not inclined to cooperate in such an effort.[27] The implication was that it was disloyal to not enlist in the Cold War crusade.

The result of the de facto media-government partnership on foreign policy issues that developed during the Cold War was a dearth of critical media scrutiny of the government's stewardship of foreign policy. As media historian J. Fred MacDonald observes,

> Reporters clearly identified with the United States. They spoke consistently of "our bloc," "our side," "our power," and "our policy." This was journalism as advocacy. Reporters spoke as partisans and viewers were hard pressed not to support "our position" on any given issue.[28]

The tendency that MacDonald detected has not disappeared with the passing of the Cold War. Media critic Jim Naureckas cited ABC News's *Nightline* host Ted Koppel's habitual use of the term "we" in connection with U.S. policy during the Panama invasion and the

Persian Gulf crisis as indicative of the continuing problem. "Koppel's first person plural is not atypical of the way the media identifies in such moments with the U.S. government, particularly the U.S. military." Naureckas provided other examples from coverage of the Panama episode: " 'We haven't gotten him yet,' NBC's Tom Brokaw said of Noriega on the first day of the invasion. *MacNeil/Lehrer's* Judy Woodruff reported that 'not only have we done away with the PDF [Panamanian Defense Forces], we've done away with the police force.' " Naureckas noted that foreigners are acutely aware of that bias, which is "almost invisible to most Americans." Unfortunately, a press "that unselfconsciously identifies itself and its audience with the U.S. military helps to promote such a mindset."[29] Pressure to identify with the national cause is particularly potent in wartime. In an account that excoriated the government's stifling of the news media in the gulf war, Walter Cronkite nevertheless conceded, "It is drummed into us, and we take pride in the fact, that these are 'our boys (and girls),' 'our troops,' 'our forces,' in the gulf. They are, indeed, and it is our war."[30]

Far more chilling was the attitude of syndicated columnist Harry Summers, a retired U.S. Army colonel. Summers not only denounced correspondent Peter Arnett for reporting from Baghdad during the gulf war but chastised CNN's Bernard Shaw for claiming that he was "neutral" on the war. "I believe strongly that newsmen, like every other American citizen, are bound by the Preamble to the Constitution to 'provide for the common defense.' And if they choose to abdicate that responsibility, then they have no claim to rights under the First Amendment of that Constitution."[31] It would be difficult to imagine a more succinct summary of the belief that journalists have a moral obligation to be allies of the national security bureaucracy.

A reflexive media identification with the foreign policy mission of the U.S. government produced especially corrosive results during the Cold War. It led to, among other things, the lack of journalistic curiosity that permitted the Eisenhower administration's accounts of coups against Iranian prime minister Mohammed Mossadegh, Guatemalan president Jacobo Arbenz Guzman, and Congolese premier Patrice Lumumba to go unchallenged. Washington depicted those events as indigenous uprisings, when in fact the Central Intelligence Agency's fingerprints were all over the three supposed coups.

It would be years before American reporters bothered to dig for the truth. Most press reports of those episodes so blindly reiterated administration statements that they might as well have been written by State Department or White House officials. Government officials exploited media passivity for all it was worth. After the successful CIA operation in Iran, the U.S. ambassador in Tehran, Loy Henderson, urged his superiors in Washington to launch a major propaganda campaign. Both government and "private American news dissemination channels," he recommended, should be used to promote the idea that the victory of the shah was the result of the "will of the Iranian people."[32]

The prevailing attitude among columnists and correspondents seemed to be that they did not want to know about covert operations. Walter Lippmann, James Reston, and other writers even chastised the government for either bragging or lying about such missions, not because the conduct itself was reprehensible, but because leaks and revelations made it difficult for the press to turn a blind eye. As Lippmann put it, "When a government goes into a political black market [i.e., covert operations] it must learn to keep its mouth shut."[33]

A similar mindset was evident in the reaction of the mainstream press to the U-2 spy plane incident in 1960. When the plane piloted by Francis Gary Powers disappeared over Soviet territory on May 1, the Eisenhower administration released a "cover" story that Powers had become "lost" and strayed into Soviet airspace while on a weather reconnaissance mission for the National Aeronautics and Space Administration and the U.S. Air Force Weather Service. That story was thoroughly discredited a few days later when the Soviet government announced that it had captured Powers and he had confessed that he was a CIA spy.

The behavior of the U.S. government in the U-2 episode was troubling. Historian Clarence Wyatt justifiably asks,

> From whom was the cover story about the U-2 designed to keep the truth? Key members of Congress, the leaders of allied nations providing bases for the U-2, important news organizations, and even the Soviets had known about the flights from their beginning on July 4, 1956. No, once the plane was down, the attempt to maintain the fiction surrounding it had only one target—the American people—and only one purpose—to shield the Eisenhower Administration and the Republican Party from political embarrassment.[34]

Wyatt's assessment may be a little too harsh. It is possible that the administration was concerned that a public revelation of U.S. espionage flights would force the Kremlin to adopt a confrontational policy to preserve its international prestige. Nevertheless, the U-2 cover-up must be viewed in the context of the government's habitual effort to conceal policy blunders and other embarrassing information from the American people. If the government's conduct was reason for concern, the performance of the press was even more worrisome. Up to the time when Moscow provided irrefutable evidence that the Eisenhower administration had lied, most U.S. media outlets presented Washington's story without the slightest expressions of doubt. Indeed, on the morning that the Kremlin sprang its trap, an editorial appeared in the *New York Times* accusing Soviet leader Nikita Khrushchev of having "misrepresented the facts" of the incident for crude propaganda purposes.[35] Such an apparent lack of skepticism would have been bad enough if it had merely reflected gullibility. But several prominent journalists, including at least two affiliated with the *Times*, already knew about the existence and real purpose of the U-2 flights.

According to historian Michael R. Beschloss, as early as the summer of 1958, *New York Times* military affairs correspondent Hanson Baldwin had reportedly confronted Robert Amory, the CIA official in charge of the U-2 program, and indicated that he was going to publish the story. Amory not only begged Baldwin not to do so, but CIA director Allen Dulles prevailed on *Times* publisher Arthur Ochs Sulzberger to kill Baldwin's story.[36] Consequently, when the *New York Times* published its May 7 editorial embracing the administration's story and accusing Khrushchev of lying, it knew that the Kremlin leader's statement was true—unless one assumes that neither Baldwin nor Sulzberger informed the editorial writer, which is unlikely. In all likelihood, the *Times* was a willing participant in the U.S. government's disinformation campaign.

The *Times* was not alone. Nearly a dozen journalists associated with other outlets had learned about the U-2 program by the spring of 1960 yet chose not to reveal it. The reason for that silence, according to one of their number, Chalmers Roberts of the *Washington Post*, was that "we knew the United States needed very much to discover the secrets of Soviet missilery."[37] Roberts and his colleagues identified so closely with U.S. foreign policy objectives that they were willing to suppress their normal inclinations as journalists.

Such voluntary restraint persisted in some quarters even after the administration's story was thoroughly blown. Although a number of publications denounced administration officials for lying, many others seemed more upset that the administration had been so inept in developing and announcing its cover-up.[38] The implication was that they wanted the press and the public to be kept in the dark. The editors of the *Nation* rightly criticized the mainstream press for its apparent collective belief that "it was just too bad we got caught." If that characterization accurately reflected media and public opinion, the *Nation* went on, it was apparent that the Cold War had conditioned the American people to a peculiar and cynical moral climate.[39]

The apparent wish of the mainstream media to be deceived was more than a little distressing, for they accepted without scrutiny or reservation the government's contention that all of its actions were vital to the nation's security. Such passivity would seem to be almost as corrupting of journalistic integrity as press-government cronyism, against which Lippmann had earlier inveighed. One of the crucial functions of a free press is to make independent determinations; it should not accept the national security bureaucracy's justifications at face value. Journalists as well as an alert public must recognize that the Pentagon, the CIA, the State Department, and the National Security Council have institutional incentives to regard all of their actions as noble and essential—even if specific initiatives may in fact be dubious, self-serving, or even nefarious. Those journalists who adopted the Lippmann-Reston "hear no evil, see no evil, speak no evil" rationale were so eager to be good soldiers in the Cold War struggle against communism that they forgot the healthy skepticism that is essential to the monitoring of government policy.

Government "requests" to soften or suppress a story frequently produced eager cooperation. When the State Department asked the radio and television networks to downplay Nikita Khrushchev's visit to the United States in 1959, only ABC and the Mutual radio network protested the government's action. The others not only remained mute but appeared to comply with the State Department's wishes. Journalist Edward R. Murrow subsequently denounced both CBS and NBC for failing to defend their First Amendment rights.[40]

The servile response of the broadcast media was understandable, however. Given the fact that they must be licensed by the Federal

Communications Commission, defying a government "request" on a matter of "national security" entailed some risk. It would not be all that difficult for FCC officials to determine that a recalcitrant station had failed to serve the public interest within the definition of the Federal Communications Act and revoke the offender's license at a later date, when it would be difficult or impossible to prove retaliation. An overt threat to do so was rarely necessary; the mere existence of the authority to revoke licenses was usually sufficient to ensure cooperation from the radio and television industry.

The government was not above employing direct threats, however, if the more subtle approach failed. FCC chairman Newton Minnow's May 1961 speech in which he described television programming as a "vast wasteland" had ominous foreign policy overtones. A major theme of that speech was that broadcasters must "serve the nation's needs," and he warned that "in today's world, with chaos in Laos and the Congo aflame, with Communist tyranny on our Caribbean doorstep and relentless pressure on our Atlantic alliance," television was not fulfilling its national duty.[41] The timing of Minnow's comments was not accidental. Such remarks would have been unnerving under any circumstances, but in the midst of a concerted campaign by President John F. Kennedy to encourage self-censorship by the press on national security issues, they were especially menacing. An even more brazen attempt to use the FCC licensing process to silence critics of U.S. foreign policy was made during the Nixon and the Reagan administrations (see chapter 4).

Far less understandable than the broadcast media's timidity was the deferential attitude of print journalists. Within a year of the U-2 spy plane incident, which had demonstrated both the extent of CIA activities and the willingness of the government to lie, the *New Republic* accepted "without question" President Kennedy's request to not run an article on CIA activities among Cuban refugees in preparation for the Bay of Pigs invasion.[42] Indeed, Gilbert Harrison, publisher of the magazine, had obligingly sent galleys of the article to the White House for review. Presidential assistant Arthur Schlesinger Jr. described Harrison's willingness to pull the story as "a patriotic act which left me oddly uncomfortable."[43] The *New York Times*, also responding to White House blandishments, greatly watered down a story by Tad Szulc on the CIA's training of Cuban exiles.

The complicity of the press could not be justified on legitimate national security grounds. Aside from the question of whether a CIA-orchestrated assault on a small country was really necessary to defend the United States, the planning for the invasion and the CIA's involvement were open secrets in Guatemala, where the training missions were taking place. The project was also widely discussed in Miami's Cuban exile community. Fidel Castro was clearly not ignorant of the operation. Not only did he have agents in the training camps, but Radio Havana repeatedly broadcast stories about an impending invasion. Although the mission was supposedly covert, James Reston later conceded, "It was about as secret as opening day at Yankee Stadium." He added, "Even if all the reporters had been drowned at dawn three weeks before the inglorious landings, the bearded legions in Havana and their Russian accomplices would not have been denied much information."[44]

Moreover, neither the *New Republic* story nor the original version of Szulc's article would have disclosed the date or location of the planned invasion. The traditional argument against stories that disclose "troop movements" (and in this case the troops were not even U.S. military personnel) did not apply. Yet the government used that argument to persuade its friends in the press to soften or kill stories that merely disclosed general information about a dubious mission that was already common knowledge to the target. As was the case with the U-2 incident, an important underlying goal appeared to have been to keep the American public ignorant of a controversial component of U.S. foreign policy.

Kennedy's own views on the role of the press were quite apparent when he addressed the American Newspaper Publishers Association shortly after the Bay of Pigs fiasco. He stressed the need for the media's commitment to self-censorship on defense and foreign policy issues, and the impact of the precedents and attitudes established during the two world wars was alarmingly apparent in his thinking.

> In time of war, the Government and the press have customarily joined in an effort, based largely on self-discipline, to prevent unauthorized disclosure to the enemy. In times of "clear and present danger," the courts have held that even the privileged rights of the First Amendment must yield to the public's need for national security.
>
> Today no war has been declared—and however fierce the struggle may be, it may never be declared in the traditional

59

fashion. . . . If the press is awaiting a declaration of war before it imposes the self-discipline of combat conditions, then I can only say that no war has ever posed a greater threat to our security. If you are awaiting a finding of "clear and present danger," then I can only say that the danger has never been more clear and its presence has never been more imminent.

It requires a change in outlook, a change in tactics, a change in mission by the Government, by the people, by every businessman and labor leader, and by every newspaper.[45]

One could scarcely imagine a more blatant expression of a garrison state thesis applied to the First Amendment. Moreover, the context of Kennedy's call for regimentation must be kept in mind. He was upset by negative press coverage of the Bay of Pigs operation—an ill-conceived and ineptly executed invasion of a small country. Yet he acted as though the press had disclosed the most sensitive information on the U.S. strategic nuclear arsenal. According to Kennedy's logic, any geopolitical maneuver by the United States or its arch rival, no matter how minor, was vital to national security, and the press should, therefore, exercise rigorous self-censorship.

This nation's foes have openly boasted of acquiring through our newspapers information they would otherwise hire agents to acquire through theft, bribery or espionage; that details of this nation's covert preparations to counter the enemy's covert operations have been available to every newspaper reader, friend and foe alike. . . .

The newspapers which printed these stories were loyal, patriotic, responsible and well-meaning. Had we been engaged in open warfare, they undoubtedly would not have published such items. But in the absence of open warfare, they recognized only the tests of journalism and not the tests of national security. And my question tonight is whether additional tests should not now be adopted. . . .

I am asking the members of the newspaper profession and the industry in this country to reexamine their own responsibilities—to consider the degree and nature of the present danger—and to heed the duty of self-restraint which that danger imposes upon all of us. Every newspaper now asks itself with respect to every story: "Is it news?" All I suggest is that you add the question: "Is it in the interest of national security."[46]

As journalist James Aronson noted, "Rarely has a government official in the United States—and in this case the nation's highest official—expressed more clearly the concept that the press should voluntarily become an arm of the government. Despite all the pious words about the First Amendment that larded the President's speech, it was a call for abdication by the press of the guarantees— and the responsibilities—of the First Amendment."[47]

At the very least, Kennedy was asking the press to voluntarily impose restrictions that had previously applied only in wartime. The "abnormal" wartime standards now threatened to become the norm. The most disturbing aspect of Kennedy's rationale was that, unlike previous wars that lasted only a few years, the Cold War had no prospective termination date. He expected the media to operate on a wartime footing for what might well be decades. The troublesome point the president failed to address was whether healthy, independent news media could survive such a prolonged period of constraints.

Ironically, it was former vice president Richard M. Nixon who offered the most trenchant rebuke to Kennedy's call for press restraints. "The whole concept of a return to secrecy in peacetime demonstrates a profound misunderstanding of the role of a free press as opposed to a controlled press," he argued. Kennedy's demand for media self-restraint would "inevitably encourage government officials to further withhold information to which the public is entitled." Moreover, "the plea for security could well become a cloak for errors, misjudgments and other failings of government."[48] Needless to say, Nixon took a very different view of such matters when he became chief executive. But his warning was prophetic. Indeed, one would be hard-pressed to find a better epitaph for his administration.

Kennedy's speech to the newspaper publishers was not his only effort to co-opt the press on national security issues. He also called Byron Price and his World War II deputy Theodore F. Koop, director of the Cold War era's "standby" censorship program (see chapter 5), to the White House for a meeting. Price and Koop explored with Kennedy's top aides the feasibility of a "voluntary" censorship system of some sort. Price and Koop both argued against the proposal, contending that neither the journalistic community nor the public would accept such a system in peacetime.

Kennedy and his subordinates were still not willing to abandon the idea of voluntary censorship. The president next called in seven top news executives to discuss the issue. Only when those executives expressed their unanimous opposition, stating that in the absence of a declared national emergency they would not accept any new security restrictions on the publication of information, did the administration finally back off.[49]

The resistance of the media to Kennedy's co-option strategy was a refreshing contrast to the usual response during much of the Cold War period. Too often, journalists not only obediently echoed the government's line on controversial foreign policy initiatives but helped officialdom to discredit their more independent-minded colleagues. When members of the Saigon press corps began producing accounts critical of U.S. policy in Vietnam during the early and mid-1960s, the Kennedy and Johnson administrations successfully called on their friends in the media to counter such reports with stories favorable to Washington's position and laced with nasty innuendoes about the judgment and patriotism of critics. Similarly, when *New York Times* correspondent Harrison Salisbury began reporting from Hanoi and exposing the civilian casualties inflicted by U.S. bombing raids, establishment journalists immediately came to the government's rescue. Chalmers Roberts, for example, blasted Salisbury's articles as a new North Vietnamese ploy, "one as cleverly conceived as the poison-tipped bamboo spikes [Ho Chi Minh's] men implanted underfoot for the unwary enemy."[50] Roberts's slur was virtually identical to the Pentagon's depiction of Salisbury as a communist stooge.

Historian Clarence R. Wyatt contends that Roberts's and other establishment journalists' hostility toward Salisbury's dispatches was partly due to the fact that the press in Washington had for over a year and a half "accepted without skepticism or doubt the official characterization of the bombing's accuracy and effectiveness." Consequently, Salisbury's series disturbed other members of the press by "making abundantly clear its dependence on the United States government for information about the war."[51] Wyatt could have added that in this case at least the information was inaccurate and misleading.

The identification of many mainstream journalists—especially those who had gained prominence during World War II and the early Cold War—with the government's views on foreign policy issues was sometimes extraordinary. Even Salisbury's colleague at the *Times*, Hanson Baldwin, stated in a lengthy memo to his superiors that what bothered him about the reports from Hanoi was how sharply Salisbury's assertions differed from the government's.[52] Although the government's propensity to lie may not have been as obvious in 1966 as it would become a few years later, Baldwin's failure to even consider that possible explanation of the contrast was revealing.

Some members of the press were not merely seduced into maintaining a discreet silence about dubious foreign policy enterprises or even becoming propagandists for those activities; they went considerably further in their collaboration. A number of journalists lent their talents and names to specific government projects. Others willingly took government posts for a period of time and then returned to their news organizations.

Such prominent television journalists as Chet Huntley and Walter Cronkite narrated films produced by the Department of Defense. Huntley, for example, narrated "The Ramparts We Watch," a 30-minute DoD film that praised the cooperative efforts of the various branches of the armed forces and their mission of guarding the "free world." At the time the film appeared (1960), Huntley was coanchor of NBC's *Huntley-Brinkley Report*, the top-rated television evening news program. A few years later, he narrated another DoD film, "The United States Navy in Vietnam," a 30-minute Navy production praising the service's role in the Vietnam War. J. Fred MacDonald notes that engaging in such activities involved an inherent compromise of professional objectivity. "At a time when millions of Americans watched Chet Huntley week nights on NBC for a better understanding of the war in Southeast Asia, he was contracting with the Pentagon to appear on camera and narrate its patently propagandistic motion pictures."[53]

The "revolving-door" phenomenon was exemplified by Edward R. Murrow, who left CBS to head the United States Information Agency, and by John Chancellor, who left NBC to become director of the Voice of America in 1965 and returned to the network after several years in that post. A similar revolving-door pattern was followed by NBC correspondent Bernard Kalb, who served a stint at the State Department in the 1970s; ABC diplomatic correspondent

John Scali, who was ambassador to the United Nations; columnist William Safire, who worked as a presidential speech writer; and NBC correspondent Ron Nessen, who was presidential press secretary, to mention just a few prominent examples.

An event that underscored the incestuous relationship between the national security bureaucracy and the media was the hiring of former Pentagon spokesman Pete Williams as a correspondent for NBC News in April 1993. In his capacity as assistant secretary of defense for public affairs, Williams had developed and executed strategies to impede independent press coverage of the Panama and Persian Gulf military operations (see chapters 7 and 8). Although many portions of the journalistic community—including the news departments of the television networks—had criticized Williams for mugging the First Amendment, NBC's hiring decision undermined the credibility of such objections. It strengthened the image of a "cooperative" tame press on defense and foreign policy matters.

Corporate executives in the news industry also had some questionable governmental or quasi-governmental affiliations. CBS president Frank Stanton, for example, served as a trustee and chairman of the RAND Corporation, a government-supported think tank that was (and is) virtually a research arm of the Pentagon. Stanton also accepted an appointment by President Lyndon Johnson to head the Committee on Information Policy, an advisory group charged with offering suggestions on ways to strengthen the government's overseas propaganda efforts. Robert Kintner, president of NBC in the 1960s, accepted an appointment as special assistant to the president when he left the network.

The problem is not that such individuals were unethical or even that they consciously compromised their professional independence when they went to work for the government. The corrupting effects were more subtle. Even the most committed journalist would find it hard to be critical of policies adopted by men and women who had been friends and coworkers only a short time before. It would be even more difficult to criticize policies that the journalist had helped to formulate or had defended in his capacity as a government official. By serving on both teams, such people inevitably blurred the roles of press and government, transforming what should be an adversarial relationship into one of tacit, if not active, collaboration on foreign policy issues. That is quite likely what government leaders had in mind when they offered prestigious appointments to leaders of the press.

Several journalists did not merely cooperate with the government; they apparently became active participants in intelligence-gathering and covert political operations while remaining members of the news media. The most notorious example was *New York Times* reporter Kennett Love's conduct during the 1953 CIA-orchestrated coup that restored the shah of Iran to his throne. Love later wrote one of the most detailed and revealing accounts of U.S. activity on behalf of the shah's cause during those crucial days in the summer of 1953. Unfortunately, that account never appeared in the pages of the *New York Times* or any publication until investigative journalist Jonathan Kwitny surreptitiously obtained a copy and quoted portions of it in his book *Endless Enemies*.[54] Love did not write his account for public consumption; it was later found in the files of CIA director Allen Dulles.

Not only did Love's report recount in great detail the extent of CIA and U.S. embassy involvement in the coup that ousted Prime Minister Mossadegh, it described his own role during the critical phase.

> I myself was responsible, in an impromptu sort of way, for speeding the final victory of the royalists. After the radio station fell I went up there to obtain permission to broadcast a dispatch. All commercial telegraphic and telephonic communications had been interrupted. . . . A half-dozen tanks swarming with cheering soldiers were parked in front of the radio station. I told the tank commanders that a lot of people were getting killed trying to storm Dr. Mossadegh's house and that they, the tank commanders, ought to go down there where they would be of some use instead of sitting idle at the radio station. They declared my suggestion to be a splendid idea. They took their machines in a body to Kokh Avenue and put the three tanks at Dr. Mossadegh's house out of action after a lively duel with armor-piercing 75-millimeter shells.[55]

Kwitny commented wryly on the spectacle of "the Iranian correspondent for the *New York Times* directing the successful tank attack on the home of the Iranian prime minister, overthrowing the government, [and] fixing one-man rule in Iran."[56]

Love denied that he was ever a CIA employee, and the *New York Times* likewise denied any knowledge of such a connection. But whether Love was an official intelligence operative is really beside the point. Even if he was not, he had been thoroughly co-opted by the government's foreign policy apparatus. It is difficult to conclude that he could, at the same time, be both a participant in a major covert operation and fulfill his responsibility as a journalist to report accurately and completely on the events surrounding the Iranian coup. Most significant, Love's articles in the *Times* described the situation as though it were a struggle between indigenous Iranian factions. Love gave his readers no inkling of the extensive U.S. interference, about which he knew more than a little.

That is precisely how the co-option of members of the press is designed to work. During the early years of the Cold War, coopera-tive journalists did not print stories that might place U.S. foreign policy in an embarrassing light. The American people, in turn, remained largely ignorant of the less savory aspects of that policy and were inclined to not question any aspect of America's global Cold War strategy. Their lack of awareness suited those who formu-lated and executed that strategy.

One should certainly not assume that Love was the only individual to become involved in foreign policy operations while employed as a journalist. In its investigations of U.S. intelligence agencies, the Senate Select Committee chaired by Frank Church (D-Idaho) uncov-ered numerous other incidents in which the CIA had used journalists for intelligence-gathering and other operations. Indeed, the commit-tee determined that some 50 news personnel had actually been on the CIA payroll. In examining the CIA's use of the U.S. media, the committee found two major causes of concern: "The first is the potential, inherent in covert media operations, for manipulating or incidentally misleading the American public. The second is the damage to the credibility and independence of a free press which may be caused by covert relationships with U.S. journalists and media organizations."[57]

Exploitation of the news media by U.S. intelligence agencies should not be surprising. After all, the CIA had recruited business-men, university professors, union officials (especially members of the AFL-CIO's American Institute for Free Labor Development), and even members of the National Students Association.[58] It would be naive in the extreme to suppose that members of the press were exempt from such governmental seduction.

Even after the Church committee's revelations, prominent members of the national security bureaucracy insisted that there was nothing unhealthy about a close relationship between the CIA and journalists. Most surprising, Stansfield Turner, director of central intelligence under President Jimmy Carter and normally sensitive to the deleterious effects of the national security state on constitutional liberties and democratic institutions, clung to that view. Turner bemoaned the fact that during his tenure at the CIA, the news media "had come to believe that they should have nothing to do with American intelligence." That attitude, he noted wistfully, was "a complete reversal from less than a decade before, when the CIA and the media cooperated closely. On foreign posts the CIA station chief and the bureau chief of a wire service or an American newspaper would usually be colleagues."[59]

The Church committee's disclosures, Turner contended, led "to an overreaction. Most newsmen refused to share information with the station chiefs or anyone else at the CIA."[60] His complaint underscored the habitual attitude of foreign policy officials that journalists should be part of the U.S. foreign policy team. Although he conceded that an independent press was essential to a healthy democracy, Turner insisted that media aloofness from the intelligence community "belie[s] that we are both working for the good of our country and have compelling common interests."[61] He dismissed the contention of some reporters that known or even suspected affiliation with the CIA would jeopardize not only their professional credibility but their safety. "Those views were not persuasive to me, and frankly I couldn't believe that journalists took them seriously either. Most knowledgeable foreigners, especially those in countries without a free press—and many of our allies can be counted among them—assume that the American press and the CIA work together."[62]

Despite Turner's attitude, he came under pressure from the media and civil liberties organizations to provide a written directive disavowing any CIA attempt to recruit or otherwise compromise news personnel. It was a measure of the public disillusionment that followed the Watergate revelations and the disclosures of the Church committee that Turner's predecessor, George Bush, a man not known as a great partisan of a critical press on national security issues, had made an oral disclaimer to that effect. "The CIA will not enter into any paid or contractual relationship with any full-time or part-time news correspondent accredited by any United States news service, newspaper, periodical, radio or television network or station."[63] Turner resisted pressure for a written affirmation of Bush's assurance. The most Turner would do was to issue a regulation limiting CIA use of media personnel to acquiring information only "in exceptional circumstances," a standard that seemed dangerously vague to many civil libertarians.

Turner's attitude exemplified a pervasive problem throughout the Cold War. Even the most enlightened officials were unwilling to acknowledge that the role of an independent press was fundamentally incompatible with journalists' being members of the U.S. foreign policy team. Worse still, many journalists did not comprehend the inherent conflict of interest.

Consequently, throughout much of the Cold War, the American people often read what the government's foreign policy apparatus wanted them to, even when the official version of events bore little resemblance to reality. Reporters who allowed themselves to be co-opted contributed in a fundamental way to a comprehensive campaign of disinformation. Unfortunately, as the media coverage of the Persian Gulf War and the crises in Somalia and Bosnia demonstrate, that problem has not disappeared with the end of the Cold War.

3. The Cult of Secrecy

The foundation of the national security bureaucracy's ability to dampen criticism of its foreign policy is the secrecy system—the power to classify information and put it off limits to the public. That power greatly increases the ability of officials to conceal evidence that might discredit or at least raise doubts about their stewardship of foreign affairs. At the very least, the secrecy system enables sitting administrations to stifle or skew the public debate on important foreign policy issues. At worst, it fosters both arrogance on the part of officials and institutional corruption. It is one of the most potent of the government's tactics to weaken the media's monitoring of U.S. foreign policy.

In some respects, the unsavory consequences of secrecy do not represent a new problem. James Madison understood the close connection between a secretive foreign policy and the undermining of constraints on arbitrary power. As he wrote in a letter to Thomas Jefferson, "The management of foreign relations appears to be the most susceptible to abuse of all the trusts committed to a Government, because they can be concealed or disclosed, or disclosed in such parts and at such times as will best suit particular views."[1] Although it may have been a problem in Madison's day and succeeding decades, the menace of excessive secrecy has grown much worse since World War II.

The Growth of the Secrecy System

Almost as soon as World War II ended, initial steps were taken by both the executive branch and Congress to strengthen the government's control of information. As one might expect, support for a rigorous secrecy system focused first on a dramatic new development in the arena of national security, the atomic bomb. In September 1945, less than a month after the bombings of Hiroshima and Nagasaki, several bills were introduced in Congress to establish controls over atomic weapons, energy, and research. On August 1, 1946, President Harry S Truman signed legislation sponsored by Sen.

Brien McMahon (D-Conn.), chairman of the Special Atomic Energy Committee, into law. The McMahon Act (or Atomic Energy Act), among other provisions, mandated a strict secrecy regime for atomic research.[2] In essence, anything written on the subject by scientists who worked on atomic energy projects was "born classified." The act marked the first peacetime occasion on which an entire category of information related to national security was deemed to be automatically too dangerous for public access. Although it applied to just one "special" category, the McMahon Act was an omen of the obsession with secrecy that would soon prevail.

One of the most important consequences of the Cold War for press freedoms was the exponential increase in the number of classified documents. Before the Cold War, only information that was deemed to have a direct relevance to military operations was considered outside the public domain in peacetime. The emergence of the national security state during the Cold War changed that standard dramatically. Officials soon demonstrated that they had an extremely broad definition of national security, and "when in doubt, classify" became their guiding principle. The inevitable result was overclassification. Even worse, the classification system was perverted to conceal—on bogus grounds of "national security"—evidence of incompetence, deceit, and even criminal behavior. Perhaps the most brazen statement of intent came from Arthur Sylvester, assistant secretary of defense for public affairs, in December 1962. In a foreign policy crisis, Sylvester said, the government had an inherent right to lie "to save itself."[3] An especially notable feature of that statement was that Sylvester's rationale for lying was not that the nation's survival was at stake or even that lesser security interests were imperiled; government could justifiably lie *to save itself*. Sylvester expressed candidly the arrogance of power that was becoming commonplace in the national security bureaucracy.

Writing in the mid-1960s, James Russell Wiggins, onetime editor of the *Washington Post*, described the crucial connection between the secrecy system and the government's ability to manipulate or control the news.

> One of the worst consequences of secrecy is the license it confers on deceit. Where the access to facts about government is open and unobstructed, where the sources of intelligence are numerous and unrestricted . . . misrepresentation is perilous. The possibility of contradiction then rises as a constant

threat to authority. But when there are no independent means of verifying official accounts of public transactions, an invaluable check is removed. It then becomes relatively easy for authority to publish such a version of an event as lends the most luster to government, or the least discredit. Even when outright falsehood or deceit is not involved, less flagrant misrepresentation may occur. The temptation to sugar-coat each disaster and gild every triumph will prove almost irresistible to officials who are secure against contradiction. Government then can manage the news to its tastes. It will speak with one voice and, however much that voice may err, there will be none to say it nay.[4]

The temptation of officials to use the national security claim to justify concealing information for more mundane reasons became evident even during the earliest stages of the Cold War. For example, in 1947 the Security Advisory Board of the State Department–Army–Navy–Air Force Coordinating Committee recommended a classification scheme that would, among other things, have forbidden the media to use information that might cause "serious administrative embarrassment."[5] Samuel R. Gammon, executive director of the American Historical Association, had that misuse of power in mind when he quipped, "While proverbial doctors are able to bury their mistakes, bureaucrats merely overclassify them."[6]

The misuse of secrecy can, indeed, have unfortunate, even fatal, consequences. A recently declassified memorandum indicates that in 1947 the government classified information on radiation experiments and atomic weapons testing because it feared the public's reaction. The memo, from a military official to the Atomic Energy Agency, stated, "It is desirable that no document be released which refers to experiments with humans and might have [an] adverse effect on public opinion or result in legal suits." It went on to say that three such documents were set for declassification but should be reclassified "secret."[7] The *New York Times Magazine* commented, "This may be the clearest example so far of the false piety of government secrecy. National security was not even mentioned as a reason for classification. The sole purpose in this case was the manipulation of public opinion."[8]

The pervasive veil of secrecy around Washington's nuclear program enabled officials to conceal alarming information from residents of areas where atmospheric nuclear tests were conducted.

Throughout the 1950s and early 1960s, the Atomic Energy Agency issued press releases assuring Americans that such tests were safe. But in secret documents compiled by scientists who built the first atomic bombs, there were voluminous references to the effects of radiation—leukemia, cancer, genetic damage, and even death. Associated Press correspondent Robert Dvorchak offers the stinging but accurate indictment that "again and again the government issued blithe assurances that there was no reason to fear nuclear experiments—even as their secret and classified communications suggested that there was every reason to fear."[9] Even if the press had been inclined to warn the public of the peril (which at that stage of the Cold War is doubtful), the government's sequestering of the pertinent information made that task impossible—to the detriment of thousands of Americans whose health, and perhaps lives, were put in jeopardy.

Efforts to restrict the media's sources of information on defense and foreign policy issues—with the notable exception of data on atomic energy—were sporadic in the post–World War II period until the onset of the Korean War. During that conflict, President Truman formalized a sweeping classification system. He issued Executive Order 10-290 authorizing all federal agencies to mark information that they considered sensitive "top secret," "secret," "confidential," or "restricted." Truman's order proved extremely unpopular with journalists, who argued that it was far too vague and would lead to massive overclassification. David Lawrence, the editor of *U.S. News & World Report*, called the executive order an American version of the Iron Curtain. He offered the prophetic warning that the only information the public was likely to get officially would be "that which the President and his political advisers deem good for the Administration's political fortunes."[10] The American Society of Newspaper Editors and other press organizations condemned the move for a variety of reasons, including the following: it extended what was essentially a military classification system to such nonmilitary agencies as the State Department; it failed to define the criteria for the various classification designations; it provided no system for reviewing the decisions of classifying officials (who might be low-level bureaucrats); and it established no appeal system for challenging the decisions of such officials.[11]

Republican activists also denounced Truman's action. On October 2, 1951, Sen. Styles Bridges (R-N.H.) and 24 of his colleagues issued a statement of their determination to resist any attempt to conceal information on any subject, including defense and foreign policy issues, from the American people. "We shall defend to the utmost the fundamental right of free, unlimited discussion of controversial questions in government."[12] The following year the staff of the Republican Policy Committee of the U.S. Senate issued a report, "The Growth of Federal Censorship under 20 Years of Democratic Administration," that denounced Truman's order. In addition, the 1952 GOP platform pledged "not to infringe by censorship or gag order the right of a free people to know what their government is doing."[13] Such criticisms are most interesting in light of the obsession of subsequent Republican presidents with restricting information in the name of protecting national security.

Reacting to complaints about Truman's classification system, President Dwight D. Eisenhower issued a new executive order in 1953 that reduced the number of categories to three (abolishing "restricted") and curtailed the number of agencies that could classify information. That order also allowed the press to appeal to a higher authority a lower level official's decision to deny access to specific information. Nevertheless, the standards remained vague, and the reforms failed to impress critics in the media. An assessment by the American Civil Liberties Union was caustic but essentially accurate when it concluded, "Actually all this new Eisenhower order did was to placate some of the editors, temporarily, and eliminate a few of the more glaring absurdities in President Truman's directive."[14]

Certainly, the plague of overclassification did not abate during the 1950s and 1960s. William G. Florence, a former Defense Department security classification specialist who spent four decades working for the government as a military officer and a civilian analyst, bluntly told a congressional committee in 1971, "I sincerely believe that less than one-half of one percent of the different documents which bear currently assigned classification markings actually contain information qualifying for even the lowest defense classification."[15] More than a decade later, Edward Teller, a prominent nuclear scientist and conservative Cold War hawk, conceded that the secrecy system had gotten completely out of hand. In his view, it was not only encouraging abuses of power by federal officials but was retarding progress in many branches of science. Teller made a provocative observation and offered an equally provocative proposal.

> My firm belief is that it is useless to try to keep secrets from
> the Soviets for longer than one year. Therefore, I propose that
> classified material should be automatically and completely
> declassified after that period. There may be a few exceptions,
> but they should be exceedingly few and of clearly demonstra-
> ble importance.[16]

Secrecy and CIA Covert Operations

Overclassification was not the only problem associated with the
secrecy system. Keeping information from the press and the public
was also a crucial component of Washington's growing array of
covert operations overseas. As we saw in chapter 2, many journalists
preferred to remain ignorant of the Central Intelligence Agency's
various covert enterprises, voluntarily killed stories when they did
come across pertinent information, or were themselves involved in
covert missions. Even when a reporter might have been inclined to
break a story on a particular CIA initiative, getting reliable information often proved to be exceedingly difficult.

CIA covert operations ran the gamut from subtle political meddling to clandestine acts of war against foreign states. Activities
included surreptitiously providing funds to friendly political forces
in other countries, orchestrating clandestine "black propaganda"
disinformation campaigns to disrupt or discredit foreign political
parties or movements deemed hostile to U.S. interests, placing foreign government officials on the CIA payroll, attempting to create
economic instability in other countries, and organizing military
coups to overthrow unfriendly regimes.[17]

Until revelations of CIA misdeeds both at home and abroad
erupted in the mid-1970s, the executive branch had been quite successful in concealing most agency missions from public—and even
congressional—scrutiny. As Gregory Treverton emphasizes, however, the use of the secrecy system to prevent disclosures of CIA
covert operations entailed a serious political cost that went to the
heart of America's democratic system.

> If the United States is to have a Clandestine Service, especially
> one that engages in covert action, tension between account-
> ability and operational necessity cannot be resolved. . . .
> Covertness—secrecy—requires limiting the number of peo-
> ple informed of an operation. Accountability requires broad-
> ening the circle. It means broadening it to include people

whose perspectives and political interests differ from those
[of the people] who manage covert operations—especially
if the circle includes Congress.[18]

The dilemma is much more acute when it involves the disclosure of
covert operations in the news media, thereby bringing the American
public directly into play. National security officials would, of course,
prefer to keep the public (and Congress) in the dark. That would
simplify matters greatly from an operational standpoint. It is not
coincidental that covert-operations enthusiasts often wax nostalgic
about the first two decades of the Cold War when most missions
did remain secret. They contend that the United States was able to
deal great blows to the international communist adversary—helping
noncommunist forces to win elections in several West European
countries in the late 1940s, neutralizing pro-Soviet insurgent movements in emerging Third World nations, and helping to oust pro-
Soviet regimes in key countries. Conversely, they attribute Moscow's
geopolitical successes in Central America, southern Africa, and elsewhere during the 1970s and early 1980s, at least in part, to the
"crippling" of the CIA's covert capabilities. The latter development
they attribute, in turn, to statutes enacted in the mid-1970s requiring
congressional oversight of CIA operations, which led to massive
leaks of information that ended up on the front pages of newspapers
and on television news programs.

Those who cite the obvious contradiction of attempting to conduct
effective covert operations in public view have a point. But even if
it were desirable to return to the practices of the 1950s and 1960s
when the government was able to keep such information out of the
public domain and journalists cooperated—or at least acquiesced—
in that policy, it would probably not be possible to do so. It is far
more difficult to maintain secrecy today. Decades of authorized and
unauthorized government leaks have led to an entirely different
attitude on the part of members of the media as well as government
employees toward breaching secrecy, and the sources of disclosure
have multiplied. "In the 1980s and 1990s, large secret operations
almost inevitably will spill into print at some point," Treverton
concluded.

Not only are American investigative journalists more active than
they were two or three decades ago, and the sources of leaks in
Washington more extensive, but even if an administration could

control the information spigot, secrecy would not be guaranteed. If a leak does not originate in Washington, "the American press overseas will pick up the scent—even if, as in 1986 [the Iran-Contra scandal] the first article is published in Beirut in Arabic." Third World media outlets are much more active and sophisticated than they were during the early stages of the Cold War. "Moreover, leaders and media in the third world may have a powerful incentive to reveal a U.S. covert operation, especially if their nation is its target."[19]

More important is the issue of accountability, raised by Treverton and others, which cannot be dismissed with the facile reasoning that if covert missions require secrecy, then secrecy must somehow be maintained. That logic undoubtedly serves the institutional interests of the national security bureaucracy, but it is not at all clear that it serves the best interests of the American people or that it is even compatible with a healthy democratic political system. That dilemma has become increasingly acute with the breakdown of the foreign policy consensus that existed during much of the Cold War. In the future, Washington's international policy objectives may often be as controversial and divisive as domestic policy initiatives tend to be. Attempting to conceal operations merely because there might otherwise be significant opposition suggests a "Big Brother knows best" mentality that is inconsistent with any reasonable definition of democracy.

During the first two decades of the Cold War, most Americans probably would have supported the bulk of Washington's covert activities had they become public knowledge. The sense that the Soviet Union posed a massive threat to America's security was so pervasive that concern about violations of international law or even serious lapses of ethical behavior were winked at. A public that supported bloody military interventions in Korea and in Vietnam, at least initially, and accepted the risk of nuclear war to prevent Soviet expansion into Western Europe or East Asia was unlikely to become fainthearted about meddling in the political processes of other nations or even overthrowing regimes that Washington considered pro-Soviet. (The timely circulation of reports that the CIA was funding a favorite political party and otherwise interfering in the political processes of a friendly democratic country such as Japan, however, might have raised a few eyebrows.)[20]

Only when it was revealed that the CIA and other agencies were targeting American citizens inside the United States did a sizable portion of the media and the public became uneasy, sensing a threat to domestic liberties. The new hostility toward covert operations and the secrecy system that supported them arose in the context of the failed Vietnam crusade, which finally raised questions about the efficacy and wisdom of Washington's overall foreign policy strategy. Even then, most members of the press and public embraced the largely fallacious rationale that the CIA was, in Sen. Frank Church's memorable phrase, a "rogue elephant"—an agency out of control pursuing its own foreign policy and domestic policy agenda. The reality was actually much more disturbing: the CIA (and other intelligence agencies) had been, by and large, obediently carrying out the agendas of political leaders in the executive branch.

In more recent times, the tension between operational security and information disclosure has become more pronounced. The public has been far less supportive of many covert operations, as evidenced by reports of such missions in the news media. There was, for example, considerable resistance to initiatives taken during the 1980s under the rubric of the "Reagan Doctrine" to assist anti-communist insurgencies against leftist regimes in Nicaragua, Angola, and elsewhere in the Third World. That is not to say that all so-called covert operations were controversial. Some missions, such as sending military hardware to help the Afghan *mujaheddin* resist the Soviet army of occupation, leaked reports of which appeared in the press, were widely, though not universally, supported in the United States.

On the more controversial initiatives, however, the issue of the public's right to know kept surfacing—and that issue is at the center of the concept of democratic accountability. The problem was most apparent with the Iran-Contra affair. Both components of that episode—the decision to trade arms to the Iranian government in exchange for Tehran's assistance in freeing Americans being held hostage in Lebanon and the diversion of profits from the enterprise to fund the Contra forces attempting to unseat Nicaragua's Sandinista regime—should have been disturbing to the American people.[21] Controlling the initiative through National Security Adviser John Poindexter and National Security Council staff member Lt. Col. Oliver North was a blatant attempt at an end-run around congressional restrictions on covert CIA operations. Even more troubling were allegations that Poindexter and CIA director William Casey regarded the program as the initial stage of an effort to create an independent, self-sustaining fund, outside the normal appropriations channels mandated by the Constitution, for covert missions.[22]

In some respects the "Iran" phase of the incident was more worrisome than the "Contra" phase. At least voters were aware that Reagan and his advisers strongly supported U.S. aid to the Nicaraguan rebels. That the administration would try to circumvent congressional prohibitions of such assistance in an underhanded fashion was annoying but not entirely shocking. The public had no inkling, however, that the administration contemplated sending arms to Iran. Indeed, administration officials' rhetoric about Iran had been uniformly hostile and confrontational. The question then arises: how can the populace in a democratic system of government pass judgment on the wisdom or the morality of a policy that they have no idea even exists—and that in fact runs directly counter to everything they have been led to believe? And if they have no ability to judge such a policy, how do we avoid having the concept of the accountability of elected officials become meaningless?

The cult of secrecy also inevitably fosters attitudes of omnipotence and omniscience on the part of policymakers. Even Secretary of State George Shultz was struck by the arrogance of some of his colleagues' reactions to the Iran-Contra revelations.

> I was amazed that despite the revelations and the immediate uproar in the country, in Congress and in the press, Poindexter and the White House–National Security Council staffs were apparently intent on plowing ahead with what sounded to me like *more* "arms-for-hostages" swaps. In his cable, Poindexter was oblivious to and unconcerned about the uproar in the press and seemed convinced that an operation of enormous significance was under way. He seemed to feel that the administration could simply "stonewall" the press, Congress, and the public about the arms-for-hostages swap despite revelations indicating that we had violated two of the president's most important policies.[23]

The undermining of political accountability is the fundamental problem not only with covert operations but with the entire secrecy system that undergirds it. As Morton Halperin and Daniel Hoffman observed, "The First Amendment rights of petition, free speech and freedom of the press can scarcely be meaningfully exercised if the public is kept ignorant of vital facts and policy decisions of life—taxes, military service, war and peace. In principle, the secrecy system is inimical to First Amendment values."[24] A healthy democratic government requires a free flow of information so that members of Congress and the public can consider and debate important issues of public policy—including foreign and defense policy. Covert operations, whether conducted by the CIA or by another agency, and secret executive agreements to defend other countries (which were widely rumored to exist with respect to Yugoslavia and China during portions of the Cold War and are generally thought to still exist with respect to such countries as Saudi Arabia) are inconsistent with that requirement.

National security officials may regard disclosures of such secrets by the news media as the functional equivalent of treason, but journalists often provide information without which the notion of democratic accountability would become farcical. Disclosures may well undermine the foreign policy objectives of incumbent administrations (and may arguably have even damaged Washington's interests overseas on occasion), but the alternative—the passivity or collaboration of journalists that marked the media's performance during the first two and a half decades of the Cold War—was far worse. Not coincidentally, it was during that era that the worst abuses—the coups in Iran and Guatemala, the destabilization of Chile's elected government, and Washington's support of right-wing autocrats throughout the Third World—took place, to the Republic's lasting shame.

Those practices have apparently persisted despite the end of the U.S.-Soviet struggle. Even as American troops occupied Haiti to restore the government of elected president Jean-Bertrand Aristide in the autumn of 1994, reports surfaced that the CIA had helped fund the right-wing paramilitary organization, the Front for the Advancement and Progress of Haiti (FRAPH), a major supporter of the military junta that had ousted Aristide from the presidency. Although FRAPH had been implicated in numerous political murders and other atrocities, the CIA had the organization's president, Emmanuel Constant, on its payroll for more than two years. By no stretch of the imagination could Washington cite the danger of Soviet machinations in Haiti to justify that operation. The subsidy of

FRAPH was purely a matter of meddling in Haiti's internal politics because Bush administration officials disliked Aristide's leftist views and policies.[25]

Attempts at Reform

Although most presidents have sought to perpetuate or even strengthen the secrecy system in the name of national security, Congress has made periodic efforts to the opposite end. The most significant early measure to strengthen press access to government information on defense and foreign policy matters was the Freedom of Information Act (FOIA) of 1966. (The statute actually went into effect the following year.) For the first time journalists, scholars, and policy analysts gained a statutory right to press the government for the review of classified material and to have that material declassified if it did not pose a threat to national security. As it turned out, however, the change was more theoretical than substantive.

Journalists who attempted to take advantage of FOIA found themselves frustrated by a variety of obstructionist tactics. The act exempted nine categories of information, including records "specifically required by Executive Order to be kept secret in the interest of the national defense or foreign policy." That was a huge loophole that national security bureaucrats exploited to the utmost. Those who hoped for a more open system were dealt a further blow by the U.S. Supreme Court in *Environmental Protection Agency v. Mink* (1973).[26] That case involved an effort to secure information about the environmental impact of a planned underground atomic test in Alaska. The Court held that the national security exemption meant whatever the executive branch determined, since in passing FOIA Congress had not intended the courts to review the propriety of particular classifications. Even when a decision to classify appeared to be "cynical, myopic, or even corrupt," the federal courts were obligated to respect the executive branch's determination and exempt the document from disclosure under the act.

In addition to limitations of FOIA itself and the other roadblocks imposed by such a crabbed judicial ruling, journalists frequently encountered difficulties in getting the government to even make a pretense of acting in good faith on FOIA requests. For example, officials demanded that search requests be phrased in such a way that the material could be found without undue effort. The statute directed executive branch officials to make materials "promptly available" to any person who submitted a "request for identifiable records."[27] In practice that meant that failure to ask exactly the right question or to identify the requested material with nitpicking precision would often result in the reply that no such material could be found. When that stratagem was impractical, officials resorted to the time-honored practices of bureaucrats everywhere—delaying (or even losing) processing requests, delaying searches for relevant materials, and the like.[28] Officials typically interpreted the "make promptly available" standard very loosely. In addition, FOIA procedures were often expensive and time-consuming even for such major media outlets as the *New York Times*; they were usually prohibitively so for smaller publications—much less individual scholars or free-lance journalists.[29]

The publication of the leaked Pentagon Papers, which revealed the duplicity that characterized the formulation of Washington's Vietnam policy, and mounting charges that the government routinely covered up information that reflected poorly on the wisdom of its foreign policy actions led to additional reforms. Under intense pressure, President Richard M. Nixon issued Executive Order 11652 in 1972 placing further limits on the number of agencies (and individuals within those agencies) that were authorized to classify materials. That order was also supposedly designed to speed up declassification. In reality, the benefits were meager.

The abuses of power associated with the Watergate scandal, however, led to other changes. Prodded by the increasingly aggressive media to correct at least the more egregious abuses of the secrecy system, Congress passed several amendments to the Freedom of Information Act in 1974. Among other things, the legislative branch sought to ease burdens on information seekers by clarifying the "identifiable records" requirement to mean any request that "reasonably describes" the material in question. It also sought to greatly curtail the application of the Supreme Court's *Mink* ruling by providing that applicants could now request a judge to inspect in camera documents denied them by an agency on national security grounds. Another amendment expressly authorized the federal courts to make sure that documents "are in fact properly classified," if a dispute arises, although that requirement was softened slightly by language directing the court making a de novo determination to give "substantial weight" to an agency's affidavit concerning the status of classified material. President Gerald R. Ford vetoed the changes, but Congress overrode his veto, and the amendments formally became part of the act the following year.[30]

Although the 1974 amendments theoretically represented significant reforms, the actual benefits proved to be relatively modest. Agencies still had considerable latitude in determining whether a search request "reasonably" described the sought material. Some of the same frustrations and delays that journalists and scholars had encountered in trying to get the government to release information under the original FOIA continued. National security bureaucrats merely had to be more subtle in their obstructionism.

Even the limited effectiveness of FOIA was too much for President Ford and other cold warriors. In his memoirs, Ford railed against the statute.

> Until 1975 the CIA could withhold documents by stressing their importance to "national security." Then the courts ruled that the agency had to comply with the requirements of the Freedom of Information Act. Not long ago, I'm told, an official of the Polish embassy in Washington wrote a federal agency to request specific information. The agency had no choice under the FOIA: it had to tell the Pole what he wanted to know. Presumably, if an agent of the KGB wrote the Defense Department to request some of its files, it too would have 10 days to respond. That's ridiculous.[31]

"Ridiculous" more accurately describes Ford's interpretation of the act and its impact. Instead of opening the floodgates to the disclosure of information, the FOIA amendments merely made a closed and frustrating system slightly more tolerable. Journalists and scholars still complain about interminable delays and apparently arbitrary rejections of requests on the grounds of national security, with little or no evidence offered by the classifying agency to justify its decision. Such tactics have rendered FOIA of marginal use to the press. Michael J. Singer, an expert on FOIA, noted that "although the news media were instrumental in persuading Congress to enact the FOIA, they have rarely made direct use of it in the news gathering process." The principal reason: "Typically, there is insufficient time to pursue the formal procedures of access."[32]

My own experience is replete with examples of governmental delays and obstructionism. While doing research for my Ph.D. dissertation in the late 1970s, I filed numerous requests that State Department, Defense Department, National Security Council, and CIA documents from the late 1940s relevant to my study be declassified and released. In a distressing number of cases, decisions were anything but timely. I continued to receive a trickle of documents as late as 1983—some three years after the dissertation was completed and five to six years after the original requests were made. Such delays were primarily annoyances in the production of a historical work, but they could have far more serious effects on time-sensitive journalistic investigations.

A surprising number of my requests for declassification were denied. The notion that the release of documents that were then nearly four decades old would jeopardize national security boggles the mind. That agencies would resort to such an implausible and shopworn justification is additional evidence that the "national security" label is frequently used to conceal any information the authorities do not want disclosed for any of a multitude of reasons. Unfortunately, my experience in connection with other research projects in the late 1980s and early 1990s indicates that the situation has not improved; if anything, it has grown worse.

Secrecy and Abuses of Power

Other foreign policy writers have encountered similar problems. Indeed, the State Department and other national security agencies have apparently become so intent on advancing their policy agendas and protecting their institutions' historical reputations that even *Foreign Relations of the United States*, the venerable series that is supposed to give a complete and accurate record of U.S. policy in past decades, has come under fire from scholars for serious gaps and inaccuracies. So many documents have been withheld or "sanitized" that a misleading impression is created about the motives and purposes of American foreign policy and the actions based thereon during critical phases of the Cold War. For example, the 1953 volume on U.S. Middle East policy makes no mention of the CIA's role in restoring the shah of Iran to power, even though former U.S. and British intelligence officers have written about their roles in the mission and other analysts have described it in profuse detail.[33]

Indeed, the documents selected for inclusion give the false impression that the United States was not involved. Similarly, the 1954 volume on Latin America offers scarcely a hint of the U.S.-orchestrated effort to overthrow the Arbenz government in Guatemala.[34] Anger at such ham-handed attempts to conceal unsavory aspects of U.S. policy led the State Department's advisory committee of scholars, which is supposed to review and verify the accuracy of the historical record, to resign en masse in 1990.[35]

Governmental hostility toward and obstruction of FOIA and the entire concept of information disclosure received a considerable boost from the Reagan administration. There were numerous signs of an obsession with maintaining secrecy and controlling the flow of information to protect policies and reputations from criticism. One example was the March 1983 issuance of National Security Decision Directive 84, which required more than 100,000 government employees to take a lifetime censorship oath. All officials who had access to "sensitive information" were required to submit books, articles, or speeches they gave on subjects that might relate to such information to the government for prior review.

In theory, of course, the government was only to deny publication (or insist on the deletion of certain passages) if the material involved classified information. In practice, the directive gave a sitting administration considerable power to gag any former official whose writings or speeches might embarrass—or even merely contradict—current policymakers.[36] NSDD 84 greatly expanded the technique used by the CIA against such dissident former agents as Frank Snepp and Victor Marchetti, who dared to criticize the agency and revealed some of its less savory activities. The federal courts upheld the inclusion of lifetime censorship oaths in CIA employment contracts, in *Marchetti* among other cases, accepting the government's claim that the president, acting in his capacity as commander in chief, had the authority to prevent disclosures by CIA employees not only to prevent "grave and irreparable harm" but whenever "disclosure may reasonably be thought to be inconsistent with the national interest."[37] The Reagan administration moved to expand the coverage of the *Marchetti* and *Snepp* precedents to many other departments and agencies, especially those dealing with defense or foreign policy issues.

The administration's primary attack, however, was directed against FOIA and the release of classified information. Almost immediately after taking office, the new president and his attorney general, William French Smith, sought unsuccessfully to limit the scope of FOIA; among other things, they tried to exempt the CIA and the Federal Bureau of Investigation entirely from its coverage. The principal modification of the classification system since Eisenhower's revision came the following year with Reagan's issuance of Executive Order 12356 on April 2, 1982.[38] Unlike the earlier executive orders on classification matters, the 1982 order focused intently on national security information. Reagan's edict unmistakably reflected the times—especially the extraordinarily tense state of U.S.-Soviet relations in the aftermath of the Red Army's invasion of Afghanistan—and the administration's view of the press as an enemy of its foreign policy agenda.

In addition to drastically slowing (and in some cases indefinitely postponing) the already snaillike pace of declassification, Reagan's order lowered the minimum standard for each level of classification and required that all doubts be resolved in favor of secrecy. It also discarded any notion that potential harm to national security be balanced against the public's interest in the release of information. Perhaps most insidious, the administration reversed a Carter era provision that forbade retroactive classification of a document after a FOIA request for it had been filed, sought to control the dissemination of private scientific research, and ordered the reclassification of millions of previously declassified documents.

Indeed, the Reagan administration went beyond reclassifying documents that had been declassified. The catalyst was the publication in 1982 of James Bamford's book on the National Security Agency.[39] (The NSA was an entity so supersecret that for many years government spokesmen refused even to acknowledge its existence, which led wags to suggest that the acronym stood for "No Such Agency.") Angered by Bamford's revelations about the NSA's extensive participation in domestic spying operations in the 1960s and 1970s, the government took an unprecedented step. It moved to retroactively classify material Bamford had consulted in collections at the George Marshall Library, even though the material—letters from the private papers of William F. Friedman—had never before been classified (despite an earlier NSA review of their contents) and had in fact

been available to researchers for years.[40] That was an alarming precedent, since the potential for arbitrary, retroactive classification of
information on national security grounds would seem to be virtually
unlimited. Indeed, the following year, federal officials reclassified
documents that historian Barry Rubin had used in *Paved with Good
Intentions: The American Experience with Iran* (1980), his highly critical
account of U.S. policy toward Iran since the 1940s.[41]

Since the end of the Cold War there have been conflicting trends
in the treatment of classified materials. Tucked away in the State
Department's reauthorization bill for fiscal year 1992, signed into
law by President Bush in October 1991, was a section requiring the
government for the first time to make public as a matter of course
records that are more than 30 years old. In theory, that requirement
should prevent the distortions of history that result from the withholding or sanitizing of documents. How much actual liberalization
will result remains to be seen. The bill did allow exceptions for
especially "sensitive" documents, and that loophole may be all creative bureaucrats need to eviscerate the statute. Operationally, the
people who are going to decide what documents are unusually
sensitive will be the same officials who have been concealing information all along and have every incentive to continue doing so.
Nevertheless, the congressional action should help prevent the blatant politicization of the *Foreign Relations of the United States* series
and may give journalists and other writers greater access to pertinent
information.

During the final year of the Bush administration, there were other
promises of greater openness about information on defense and
foreign policy issues. (That was somewhat ironic coming from an
administration that had previously shown little concern for press
freedoms in its conduct of foreign affairs.) Even the CIA pledged
to be more open in its dealings with press and public. Such promises
ought to be viewed skeptically, however; no better reminder is
needed than that the 15-page CIA "Task Force Report on Greater
CIA Openness" was initially classified "Secret."[42]

President Clinton also expressed his support for reducing government secrecy early in his administration. Presidential Review Directive 29, issued on April 26, 1993, ordered a sweeping review of Cold
War era classification rules by an interagency task force with the
goals of speeding the declassification process and preventing the

overclassification of new documents. Clinton stated that "with the end of the Cold War, we should reevaluate our security classification and safeguarding systems . . . to ensure that they are in line with the reality of the current, rather than the past, threat potential."[43] The president's goals may be worthy, but critics quickly pointed out that previous presidents—with varying degrees of sincerity—had issued similar directives with similar stated objectives. Functionaries in the national security bureaucracy by and large ignored such orders. Moreover, as a *New York Times* editorial observed, "Mr. Clinton may be seeking answers from the wrong people—those who have presided over the secrecy system."[44]

That is precisely the problem. Sociologist Max Weber observed long ago that secrecy is a disease endemic to bureaucracy. Officials typically view secrecy as essential protection against outside interference with their activities. The preference for secrecy is reinforced in the case of foreign policy personnel by the belief that national security will benefit by keeping as much information as possible from foreign governments. Halperin and Hoffman emphasize the inherent institutional interest in maximizing the scope of the secrecy system. "When bureaucratic interests can be enhanced by leaking information . . . officials have often done so and will continue to do so in the future. But informing the public on a systematic and principled basis is not a central purpose of any vested interest in the national security bureaucracy."[45] Consequently, expecting members of that bureaucracy to adopt practices that would actually shrink the secrecy system is as naive as expecting defense contractors to advocate lower military budgets or members of the public education bureaucracy to endorse proposals to privatize the schools. They are not inclined to do so, because such changes would run directly counter to their institutional and career interests.

Despite periodic pledges to open government records to greater public scrutiny, the trend for the past half century has clearly been toward mounting secrecy. A General Accounting Office report released in June 1993 found that there were more than 304 *million* pages of documents awaiting declassification. Of that number, some 270 million pages came from the Pentagon and a substantial portion of the remainder from the State Department and the intelligence agencies.[46] In other words, the overwhelming majority of backlogged documents in the declassification system were generated by the national security bureaucracy. The most startling aspect of the GAO report is that the figures refer only to documents that are at least 30 years old and are awaiting decisions about declassification. Apparently no one knows how many newer classified documents exist. According to Steven Garfinkel, director of the Information Security Oversight Office, the federal agency that administers the classification system, they are "a huge mountain, perhaps billions."[47]

The results of the declassification decisions made during fiscal year 1992 offered little comfort to those who hoped that the government's obsession with secrecy might abate with the end of the Cold War. According to the GAO, more than half of the declassification decisions in FY92 were open-ended (i.e., there was no set date for declassification). That means that defense and foreign policy documents may still remain outside the public domain for decades, long beyond the time they could have the slightest relevance to national security. (Indeed, according to acting national archivist Trudy Peterson, some documents from the World War I era remain classified.)[48]

The results for FY93 appear to confirm those assessments. Various agencies reviewed 9 million pages of documents—some 1.6 million fewer than in 1992—and declassified only 6.6 million pages—3 million fewer than during the previous year. Figures on the creation of new secrets revealed a similar pattern. Agencies classified more than 6.4 million documents, with the Defense Department accounting for 58 percent, the CIA 25 for percent, and the State Department for 3 percent of that total. Each day during FY93 the government cranked out an astonishing 17,558 pages of classified material. An Associated Press story concluded dryly, "Try as it might, the government has a problem letting go of its secrets."[49]

Despite the Clinton administration's rhetoric about the need for greater openness and the truthful treatment of the history of U.S. foreign policy, there has not been a marked movement to open files on the Cold War period—especially on Washington's more controversial actions. "So much is being released by the Soviet and Chinese sides on the deepest, darkest aspects of cold war history that you have to wonder what the rationale is for keeping secrets on our side," historian John Lewis Gaddis wonders.[50] It would be difficult to find a national security rationale for keeping those files closed, but the national security bureaucracy is greatly concerned about protecting its historical reputation (and by extension, its current credibility) by preventing potentially embarrassing disclosures.

That is especially true when it comes to evidence of CIA dirty tricks or Washington's long-time association with such autocrats as the shah of Iran, Philippines dictator Ferdinand Marcos, and Nicaraguan dictator Anastasio Somoza. The national security bureaucracy's reluctance to release aging information to the public not only makes a farce of declassification, it indicates a continuing determination to guard institutional reputations and prerogatives.

Members of the media as well as historians and other scholars should expose and undermine such behavior. Michael Gartner, former president of NBC News, has articulated the attitude the media should strive to adopt.

> If you have information, print it. If it discloses state secrets, so be it. If the reporter learned them, chances are the enemy— whoever the enemy of the month happens to be—also knows them. But regardless, the newspaper's role in America is to tell the public what's going on. Newspapers aren't supposed to keep secrets; they're supposed to disclose secrets.[51]

With narrow exceptions, such as disclosing information about military deployments in a combat setting or disclosing the identities of intelligence agents operating in the field, the media play a questionable role when they become accomplices in preserving government secrecy. That action is more likely to be a disservice than a service to the public, for it maximizes the ability of officials to conceal information about unwise or disreputable actions.

Above all, journalists and scholars must recognize that the missions of national security bureaucrats and the incentives to which they respond are inherently in conflict with widespread dissemination of information on defense and foreign policy issues. To expect those bureaucrats to react otherwise is to expect them to undermine their personal and institutional interests. But, as American Historical Association executive director Samuel R. Gammon reminds us, "The national interest is not the self-interest of a bureaucracy in hiding its errors in the time capsule of perpetual secrecy."[52]

By using incantations of national security to disarm or intimidate those who favored a more open system, the priests of America's secrecy cult were frequently able to keep relevant information out of the public domain during the Cold War. Unfortunately, those habits show only grudging and limited signs of changing. The Clinton administration, which is supposedly committed to greater openness about national security issues, is increasingly acting like its predecessors. For example, despite the noble sentiments expressed in Presidential Review Directive 29, no new classification order had been issued by the autumn of 1994, and some people who had hoped for a meaningful change in the government's information policies were accusing the administration of either incompetence or deception. The lack of a new order "was embarrassing [for the White House] six months ago," charged Steve Aftergood of the Federation of American Scientists. "Now it's just pathetic."[53]

A more troubling indication of the administration's growing enthusiasm for secrecy was the White House's attempt in March 1994 to exempt the National Security Council from the record-preservation laws that are applicable to all government agencies. The administration submitted a brief to the U.S. Court of Appeals for the D.C. Circuit, arguing that the NSC's only function is to advise the president and that it is therefore not a federal "agency" within the meaning of the preservation laws. As Georgetown University law professor Philip Schrag noted, "Designating the NSC as something other than an 'agency' would make it possible for an administration to shred sensitive NSC records rather than preserve them for eventual historical research, or for use by future grand juries or congressional committees investigating possible wrongdoing."[54]

The administration's legal argument is most disturbing, especially since the NSC does far more than "advise" the president: it is one of the most influential bodies in the formulation and execution of U.S. foreign policy. Moreover, the administration's logic is reminiscent of the arguments used by previous administrations that were committed to highly restrictive policies on the flow of information. The cult of secrecy, with all its corrupting tendencies, appears to be as strong as ever.

4. The Iron Fist: Dealing with Critics

The government has employed a variety of tactics to intimidate recalcitrant members of the press during and after the Cold War. Two of those tactics—impugning the loyalty of critics and using classification powers to keep vital information from the media and the public—have been especially popular.

Innuendoes of disloyalty have been used so often that they have become part of the larger context of press-government relations. David Halberstam recalled that he had to become inured to such slurs when he dared criticize the course of U.S. policy in Vietnam. "I can't tell you how many times when I was a reporter there, I had my patriotism, my courage or even my manhood challenged."[1]

It might be tempting to attribute allegations of disloyalty to the overwrought emotions of government officials who are committed, both personally and institutionally, to the policy that is being attacked. That all-too-human response to criticism undoubtedly plays a role in many cases. But the systematic and sometimes cynical nature of the campaign to discredit critics of U.S. foreign policy suggests that other factors are also at work. Members of the national security bureaucracy have learned that impugning the patriotism of journalists and others who challenge official policy is one of the quickest and most reliable strategies for victory. Unfortunately, that strategy also poisons the atmosphere in which the debate about foreign policy is conducted. Although it may serve the narrow purposes of foreign and defense policy bureaucrats, it damages the quality of democratic discourse and impedes the ability of the public to make intelligent decisions about vitally important matters.

Dissent Equated with Disloyalty

Journalists (as well as other Americans) who dared challenge the conventional wisdom were not only subjected to innuendoes of lack of patriotism during the Cold War, they were frequently victims of more substantive witch-hunts. For example, in the late 1940s the Army arbitrarily revoked the credentials of 11 reporters and denied them to 50 others, thus preventing them from covering military activities. In early 1948 Secretary of Defense James Forrestal sought to require all reporters seeking credentials to pass a stringent loyalty test similar to that required of government employees. Only a tidal wave of criticism from the journalistic community compelled him to shelve that plan, but the military still investigated the backgrounds of journalists who sought to cover military events.[2]

Such tactics became routine features of a loyalty crusade, which some historians have termed the "Second Red Scare," that culminated in the excesses of McCarthyism. The basic features of that crusade were evident even before the Wisconsin senator made his celebrated 1950 speech in Wheeling, West Virginia. Indeed, the Truman administration had openly fostered efforts to impugn the loyalty of critics of its Cold War policies, just as the Roosevelt administration had smeared opponents of its policies in the months before Pearl Harbor.

The resulting atmosphere of hysteria and intolerance began to frighten even some administration officials—especially as it became increasingly evident that the administration's conservative Republican opponents were seizing control of the loyalty issue for partisan gain. Stephen Spingarn, an assistant to presidential adviser Clark Clifford, expressed his concern forcefully.

> Since the end of World War II there has been an ominous trend in the United States toward the curtailment of freedom of expression and opinion. . . . It is one thing for a nation to take basic counter-espionage and security measures necessary to protect its existence. It is another thing to urge or tolerate heresy hunts at every stump and crossroads to smoke out and punish nonconformists. . . . I'm afraid we are moving in that direction.

Spingarn added that the "consuming fear of communism has led many sincere persons into the belief that loyalty and orthodoxy are synonymous." He concluded that with "the possible exception of the days of John Adams and those of A. Mitchell Palmer, the situation is becoming more dangerous today than at any other period in American history."[3]

Intolerance of foreign policy critics increased as the Cold War continued. Throughout the 1950s and early 1960s the federal government conducted elaborate and frequently intrusive surveillance of such critics, primarily through the Federal Bureau of Investigation's COINTELPRO (counterintelligence) program. Although that program was supposedly designed to monitor the activities of individuals affiliated with the Communist Party USA (on the theory that they were potential espionage threats), the FBI cast a very wide net and, in the process, spied on Americans who had no communist leanings, much less any connection with a hostile foreign government.[4]

When bitter divisions over Washington's policy in the Vietnam War replaced the stifling conformity of views that had characterized the foreign policy "debates" of the Eisenhower and Kennedy years, the government's hostility toward critics intensified. From as early as the summer of 1965 on, officials systematically sought to discredit opponents of the war. Initially, officials adopted the patronizing attitude that anti-war activists were naive, uninformed, or excessively idealistic and not conversant with the unpleasant realities of international power politics. The implicit message was that the ignorant rabble should be silent and let the members of the foreign policy priesthood pursue policies necessary for the defense of the nation.

As the strength of the opposition mounted, however, the tone of beleaguered officials became increasingly shrill and nasty. They denounced their tormentors as "anarchists," "calamity hawkers," "Communists," "nervous Nellies," and "damned fools," to cite the more printable epithets.[5] In addition to the name-calling, there were repeated innuendoes about the motives and loyalty of war critics. A favorite ploy was to argue that opponents deliberately exaggerated the inadvertent errors of the United States and its South Vietnamese ally while ignoring the calculated atrocities of the communist forces. In July 1966, for example, President Lyndon B. Johnson sarcastically scored dissidents for being so eloquent in their denunciation of air strikes against Hanoi and Haiphong but so "strangely silent" about Vietcong attacks on a U.S. naval hospital near Da Nang. The following March he similarly argued that "tens of thousands of innocent Vietnamese civilians have been killed and tortured and kidnapped by the Vietcong. . . . Yet, the deeds of the Vietcong go largely unnoted in the public debate." He concluded, "It is this moral double bookkeeping which makes us sometimes get very weary of our critics."[6]

Although some anti-war activists were undoubtedly guilty of hypocrisy, the president's campaign to tar the entire anti-war movement with that brush (and similar efforts by his subordinates) seemed calculated to create the impression that all opponents of the war were, at best, communist dupes or, at worst, outright traitors. A similar purpose was evident in the government's constant refrain that criticism of the war encouraged Hanoi to believe that it could outlast the United States. Returning from his second stint as ambassador to South Vietnam in 1967, Henry Cabot Lodge declared bluntly, "Disunity in America prolongs the war." Vice President Hubert Humphrey similarly observed, "The hope for victory for the enemy is not in his power but in our division." And Secretary of State Dean Rusk asked a Los Angeles audience, "How do we prevent [North Vietnam's] misunderstanding the news that forty or fifty thousand people are demonstrating in front of the Pentagon?"[7] Gen. William Westmoreland was less oblique. Speaking to a gathering of newspaper editors during a visit to the United States in April 1967, the general denounced an earlier anti-war demonstration in New York, adding that he and his men were "dismayed" by "recent unpatriotic acts here at home."[8]

Such a crude slur was too much even for the mild, mainstream critics of the war effort. Sen. J. William Fulbright (D-Ark.), who had turned against the war in the years since he guided the Gulf of Tonkin Resolution through the Senate, charged that the Johnson administration was equating dissent with treason. Sen. George McGovern (D-S.D.) responded that, far from aiding the enemy, dissenters had exposed the contradictions and falsehoods that surrounded administration policy.[9] A few newspapers chided Westmoreland for impugning the patriotism of opponents of the war, but at least as many expressed agreement with the general's comments.[10]

As F. M. Kail, an expert on the government's rhetoric during the Vietnam War, observed, even when officials stated that they had no doubts about the sincerity or motives of opponents, "to maintain that their impact was to dishearten U.S. soldiers and encourage those of the Vietnamese could not help but awaken such doubts in others. And despite the disclaimers, the impression that the opposition was engaged in un-American activities was fostered and reinforced, heightened by official commentary verging on vilification that transcended any reasonable standard of 'fair exchange.' "[11]

The government did not confine expression of its hostility toward dissent to overheated rhetoric. The Johnson and Nixon administrations launched programs to harass and disrupt the opposition. Not only did Washington have the FBI monitor critics of the war, but both the Central Intelligence Agency—through its Operation CHAOS—and the U.S. Army were assigned to spy on anti-war individuals and groups.[12] That activity was in blatant violation of the CIA's charter as well as other laws prohibiting domestic espionage. Moreover, with stunning impartiality, the national security apparatus amassed dossiers on critics and drew into its surveillance web not only those few who endorsed violent tactics but the far more numerous individuals who were entirely peaceful in expressing their dissent from U.S. policy in Southeast Asia. By the early 1970s the CIA had compiled files on more than 10,000 Americans, including a number of journalists.[13] Counterintelligence agents sometimes went beyond mere spying by infiltrating anti-war organizations and acting as agents provocateurs, sowing dissension and even encouraging law breaking that might help discredit such groups. Although journalists were not the primary targets of the government's surveillance, the tactic itself clearly demonstrated an intent to chill dissent from all quarters.

The government's hostility toward those who opposed its foreign policy escalated as its political and military fortunes in the Vietnam conflict declined. Kail notes,

> By the late 1960s Washington had served notice that dissent was a hindrance, a source of frustration, and attempted by aspersion more than argument to minimize its force. Critics were charged with being something less than loyal and little more than fools. Criticism was dismissed as misinformed and misguided, as well as potentially dangerous. The First Amendment, which insured what was in theory the central and absolute American freedom, was, as applied to opponents of the Vietnam war, becoming an increasingly empty and peripheral abstraction.[14]

Journalists were not exempt from the government's attempt to discredit critics of the war. Those who raised even the mildest doubts about the official version of events or the wisdom of U.S. policy frequently found themselves accused implicitly or explicitly of un-American conduct. Correspondents such as Harrison Salisbury of the *New York Times*, who dared defy the State Department's travel ban and reported from North Vietnam, were openly castigated as traitors (see chapter 6).

An incident involving CBS correspondent Morley Safer illustrates how the government responded to critical accounts of the war effort. Safer and a cameraman covered the Marine assault on the village of Cam Ne in August 1965; their report contained graphic footage of Marines setting 150 huts ablaze using everything from flame-throwers to their cigarette lighters. Safer's reports on subsequent evenings focused on South Vietnamese civilian casualties resulting from U.S. military operations and candid interviews with young Marines about the difficulty of telling friend from foe and combatants from noncombatants in the Vietnam conflict.

Assistant Secretary of Defense Arthur Sylvester immediately con-tacted the president of CBS News, Fred Friendly, to have Safer recalled. Among other things, Sylvester charged that Safer, a Cana-dian, "would have no interest" in the success of the U.S. effort in Vietnam. He added that "Canadian military friends of mine" who were familiar with Safer "tell me that he has long been known as a man with a strong anti-military bias."[15] On this occasion, Sylvester encountered surprisingly tenacious resistance from a news execu-tive. Friendly rejected Sylvester's account as "a matter of pure and simple character assassination." The contention that an American journalist would have offered a more balanced and "sensitive" report, Friendly dismissed as "tantamount to saying that an Ameri-can would be more sympathetic" to the official line. He concluded,

> The essence of our dispute is quite simple. You don't want anything you consider damaging to [U.S.] morale or [the U.S.] world-wide image reported. We don't want to violate purely *military* security with reports which could endanger the life of a single soldier but, by the same token, we must insist upon our right to report what is actually happening despite the political consequences.[16]

Friendly's rebuff of Sylvester was an early indication that the incestuous relationship of press and government during the Cold War was beginning to ebb. The government did not confine its efforts to attempting to get Safer reassigned, however. Johnson, certain that Safer must be a Communist, immediately ordered the

FBI to run a detailed background investigation, which turned up nothing incriminating.[17]

The equation of dissent with disloyalty continued beyond the Vietnam War era. During the 1980s the Reagan administration had the FBI (and perhaps other agencies) repeatedly spy on and harass critics of U.S. policies in Central America. Although the FBI insisted that such monitoring had ended in 1986, evidence indicated that it continued.[18] The administration also went after journalists whose accounts of atrocities being committed by the U.S. client government in El Salvador and the U.S.-backed Contra forces in Nicaragua undermined Washington's policy agenda. For example, officials reportedly pressured the *New York Times* to recall correspondent Raymond Bonner from El Salvador, arguing that he was a communist dupe. (In fact, subsequent investigations by the United Nations as well as private human rights organizations confirmed most of Bonner's atrocity stories.) Although *Times* officials still deny that the decision to reassign Bonner to the United States had any connection with government pressure, the administration's attempt was disturbing. The administration did not confine its smear tactics to efforts to discredit opponents of U.S. policy in Central America. Sometimes government-orchestrated campaigns to impugn the integrity and patriotism of foreign policy critics extended even to those who dared question the administration's policy on nuclear weapons or the wisdom of Reagan era levels of military spending.[19]

The FBI continued to cast an extremely wide net in its efforts to monitor American citizens who might harbor unorthodox foreign policy views. Even the most inoffensive conduct tended to attract the agency's attention. Americans who merely corresponded with people in Communist bloc countries or who subscribed to newspapers or magazines published in those countries frequently found themselves subjected to FBI surveillance or "interviews." Grade school students in New Jersey and Indiana who wrote letters to the Soviet embassy in connection with a school project were visited by FBI agents. A 73-year-old grandmother—a subscriber to *Soviet Life*—also received a visit from the FBI.[20] Even members of Amnesty International ran afoul of the FBI's counterespionage programs as they investigated human rights abuses in the eastern bloc and wrote letters of protest to communist regimes. The mere act of corresponding with such governments was considered cause for suspicion by

U.S. authorities. As late as 1989, during the waning months of the Cold War, Paul Hoffman, chair of the board of directors of Amnesty International, USA, testified that the organization's members had reported numerous visits by FBI agents.[21]

During congressional hearings on the agency's practices, Rep. F. James Sensenbrenner (R-Wis.) noted that several witnesses "alluded to their occasional feelings of intimidation when the FBI contacted them." He conceded that "a certain amount of intimidation is unavoidable by the mere fact that the FBI visits you." Yet Sensenbrenner epitomized the mentality of supporters of the national security state in his defense of the practices. "Contacts by U.S. citizens with foreign countries is a very likely source by which to develop important intelligence. It's possible that only 1 in 1,000 individuals interviewed by the FBI would have any kind of information which would be beneficial to the FBI, but nevertheless, that one individual might provide a key intelligence link to that country." Defending the refusal of the agency to disclose its reasons for interviewing targeted individuals, Sensenbrenner placidly accepted the FBI's insistence that it could not do so "without disclosing classified information."[22]

It is probable that the FBI's surveillance and investigation activities were at least partly the result of generic institutional pressures to generate work to justify the agency's mission, budget, and personnel. It is a little hard to believe, for example, that even the most paranoid members of the national security bureaucracy actually thought that school children were Soviet moles or that they would have useful information about Moscow's intelligence and propaganda apparatus. Nonetheless, the FBI's "visits" must be viewed in the total context of government efforts to maintain foreign policy orthodoxy and discourage even mild public dissent. Highly publicized agency visits reminded all Americans, particularly actual or potential foreign policy critics, that Big Brother was watching *everyone*.

Even the end of the Cold War has not eradicated the national security state mentality. It certainly has not halted attempts by political leaders to smear as traitors those who dare question the major tenets of U.S. foreign policy, especially in times of crisis. Peter Arnett, one of the Vietnam era correspondents, received the same treatment as Harrison Salisbury had in the 1960s when he continued to report from Baghdad during the Persian Gulf War. Sen. Alan Simpson (R-Wyo.), one of the Bush administration's closest political allies, led a vitriolic attack on him. Simpson not only suggested that Arnett was a propaganda stooge for Iraqi dictator Saddam Hussein, but he dredged up allegations that the journalist may have been supportive of Hanoi's cause during the Vietnam conflict. According to Simpson, the reporter "is what we used to call a sympathizer. . . . He was active in the Vietnam War and he won a Pulitzer Prize largely because of his anti-government material. And he was married to a Vietnamese whose brother was active in the Viet Cong."[23] Arnett hotly denied the "sympathizer" label as well as the characterization of the politics of his ex-wife's brother. (Perhaps he should merely have responded that one's politics are rarely influenced positively by the views held by one's brother-in-law.)

Simpson's allegation was far-fetched on several counts. Evidence to support his accusation was totally lacking, and the equation of printing "anti-government" material with being pro-communist was a smear. It was also bizarre to raise the loyalty issue in the context of the gulf war. Even if one suspected that Arnett had favored North Vietnam's cause, why would that have translated into sympathy for Saddam Hussein, who was not even arguably a Communist? But the senator's accusation was not meant to be a model of logic. Like other examples of the politics of loyalty, it was an exercise in character assassination, designed to discredit critics of the government's policy in the minds of Americans who were not likely to dig for the truth.

Simpson's recycled McCarthyism was only the most egregious example of the campaign of smears and innuendoes directed against critics of the gulf war. The rhetoric used by Bush administration officials and congressional supporters of military action against Iraq routinely implied that their opponents were "unpatriotic" in refusing to endorse Washington's policy. It was an old, if disreputable, tactic, and it unfortunately proved to be as effective as always.

Harassment Techniques

The government has used a host of other measures to deter or at least annoy critics. In the late 1940s the State Department adopted a policy of denying passports to reporters whose overseas travels were deemed "not in the interests of the United States."[24] That restriction was merely one component of a comprehensive effort to intimidate or harass opponents of Washington's embryonic Cold

War strategy. Foreign visitors were prevented from speaking in public without approval of the government, and alien critics of U.S. foreign policy repeatedly discovered that such approval was not granted. Passport restrictions were not confined to members of the Communist party or left-wing fringe elements. The State Department denied a passport to left-liberal congressman Leo Isaacson (D-N.Y.) in 1948, and for a time U.S. officials even considered applying that sanction against Truman's most persistent foreign policy critic, former vice president Henry Wallace.[25]

Hostile journalists had to deal with passport restrictions well into the 1950s. Moreover, general restrictions on travel to certain countries such as China, Cuba, and North Vietnam usually applied to reporters as well as other American citizens. Such restraints manifestly reduced the ability of news personnel to obtain stories that might have challenged aspects of U.S. foreign policy toward those countries.

On other occasions, executive branch functionaries have threatened to revoke the White House press privileges of hostile reporters—a penalty that would place the victims at a significant disadvantage in the highly competitive news-gathering business. The government has also attempted to limit press access to important foreign policy events to reward its friends and punish its critics. For example, the White House carefully selected the news organizations whose reporters accompanied President Nixon on his historic trip to China in 1972. Although the administration obviously could not exclude the television networks or major metropolitan newspapers (as much as presidential aides might have wished to do so), the power of selection did skew the press delegation to ensure maximum friendly coverage.[26]

Indeed, the government has repeatedly tried to restrict or exclude journalists whom it views as hostile to Washington's foreign policy agenda. A more subtle version of the "loyalty test" trial balloon of the late 1940s emerged in the mid-1980s following the invasion of Grenada. Media anger at the government's exclusion of the press from covering that invasion (see chapter 7) led to proposals to create a national media pool—supposedly to facilitate more "organized" coverage of future military operations. Not only did the Pentagon attempt to gain authority to specify which news organizations would be allowed to contribute journalists to the standby pool, it wanted the right to accredit all pool reporters in advance. Refusal of accreditation, for whatever reason, would have apparently barred a journalist from pool membership. Even worse, military officials wanted to make U.S. citizenship a requirement for all pool correspondents. That provision, critics pointed out, would have prevented such journalists as Peter Jennings (a Canadian) and Peter Arnett (a citizen of New Zealand) from covering the Vietnam War for American news outlets.[27]

Harassment of critics has assumed a variety of other forms. Radio and television stations are especially vulnerable to pressure, since they do not have the secure legal tenure of the print medium but exist at the sufferance of the Federal Communications Commission and its licensing process. Government retaliation for criticizing U.S. policy is not a new danger. Theodore F. Koop noted that although he and Byron Price favored a voluntary censorship system for broadcasting as well as print journalism during World War II, "always in the background was the threat of complete government regulation." He observed further,

> The fact that radio programs were heard far beyond the borders of the United States might have furnished a legal argument for advocates of compulsory rather than voluntary censorship of broadcasting stations. Might it not have been contended that these programs actually were international communications, under the language of the First War Powers Act, and therefore subject to the censors' "absolute discretion"? Enforcement of such an interpretation would have meant, at the very least, a corps of censors in every broadcasting studio and, at the most, complete government operation of the industry. And there was nothing the broadcasters could have done about it.[28]

Fortunately, that chilling, worst-case scenario did not materialize, but as Koop conceded, "Withdrawal of a station's license was a ready-made penalty, entirely apart from the stiff penalties of the First War Powers Act."[29]

That danger did not disappear with the end of World War II. During the Nixon years, White House officials floated a scheme to get political allies to challenge the license renewals of stations owned by the *Washington Post*, a constant critic of the administration's foreign policy. The Reagan administration mounted a more limited but nonetheless menacing campaign of harassment. In December 1984 NBC News acceded to a "request" from Secretary of Defense Caspar Weinberger that it suppress stories about an impending flight of the space shuttle on grounds of national security. As on so many other occasions, there appeared to be no reasonable basis for the government's position. The military purpose of the flight had been common knowledge for months. That a number of newspapers and magazines published pieces on the shuttle mission—in marked contrast to NBC's timidity—was indicative of the electronic media's uneasiness about placing FCC licenses in jeopardy.

An even more unsettling incident occurred in 1985 when the CIA filed an FCC complaint about an ABC News story unflattering to the agency.[30] One federal agency—especially an organization as influential as the CIA, which was directed during this period by Reagan confidant William Casey—submitting a complaint to associates at another federal agency was bound to make broadcasters more nervous than a routine complaint by Jane Doe in Podunk about bad language on the airwaves. Such incidents remind broadcasters in a none-too-subtle fashion that the government can threaten the very existence of valuable assets if it decides to retaliate against foreign policy critics.

The harassment potential of another government entity emerged in early 1988 when the U.S. Information Agency, invoking previously obscure regulations, labeled an American film critical of U.S. policy in Nicaragua "propaganda." Four other films, including one hostile analysis of the military's use of herbicides during the Vietnam War, also received that dubious designation. The action was not of merely academic interest. Under a 1948 treaty, films so labeled by the USIA are not eligible for duty-free importation into most countries, and in some cases the import taxes can be extremely high. The result is a severe decline in potential foreign sales, which can jeopardize the overall economic viability of a film project. Although USIA spokesmen contended that politics "have never been a part" of the agency's review process, it is noteworthy that no film favorable to U.S. foreign policy objectives has ever been branded propaganda.[31]

Leaks and the Threat of Prosecution for Espionage

Even more significant threats to freedom of the press can be found in three government tactics: threatening to prosecute the press for disclosing classified information; physically preventing media coverage of controversial foreign policy (especially military) enterprises; and reserving the option of invoking formal censorship in the case of some vaguely defined "national emergency" or, in the alternative, creating a de facto version of Britain's Official Secrets Act that would effectively gag the media. Critics of U.S. foreign policy have already been victimized by the first two measures, and the third is an omnipresent sword of Damocles.

Few things arouse the ire of political leaders more than discovering classified information in the press—unless, of course, they have leaked the information. Such leaks occur frequently as high-echelon officials promote the administration's agenda—or their own personal agenda. It is also not unusual for key members of the national security bureaucracy to knowingly plant false stories in the press as part of a sophisticated global disinformation campaign. For example, during the summer of 1986 the National Security Council, apparently on the orders of NSC adviser Adm. John Poindexter, leaked supposedly top-secret information suggesting that the United States was planning further military reprisals against Libya because of Col. Muammar Gadhafi's continuing terrorist plotting. In reality, no firm plans for military action existed, nor was there any evidence of Libyan complicity in terrorist schemes after the U.S. bombings in April. Yet stories based on that false information appeared in the foreign press and at least one major domestic newspaper, the *Wall Street Journal*.[32]

The cynical covert disclosure of classified or erroneous information has been standard operating procedure for every administration since World War II. "Authorized" leaks are an essential component of any effort to manipulate the news media to further foreign policy objectives—or advance political reputations. Former CIA director Stansfield Turner describes the ubiquitous nature of calculated leaks of information in Washington.

> The White House staff tends to leak when doing so may help the President politically. The Pentagon leaks, primarily to sell its programs to the Congress and the public. The State Department leaks when it's being forced into a policy move that its people dislike. The CIA leaks when some of its people want to influence policy but know that's a role they're not allowed to play openly.[33]

There is empirical evidence to support Turner's cynicism. In a survey of current and former senior government officials conducted in the mid-1980s, 42 percent acknowledged having deliberately leaked information to the press.[34] Calculated leaks by high-level officials are considered part of the unofficial political system in Washington and are at least tacitly tolerated by all parties. Political scientist Gregory Treverton recalls that he and his colleagues in the Carter administration joked that "the ship of state is like no other for it leaks from the top."[35] Such authorized leaks tend to be highly selective in two ways. First, only information or disinformation that advances the administration's policy agenda is revealed. Second, only "friendly" journalists receive such classified material—a reward for their cooperative attitudes.[36]

It is the *unauthorized* leak, usually originating at a lower level of the national security bureaucracy and frequently containing information embarrassing to the administration, that generates governmental threats to investigate the matter and punish not only the source but possibly the offending media outlet as well. Henry Cabot Lodge, U.S. ambassador to South Vietnam during the mid 1960s, epitomized the elitist attitude of senior policymakers toward subordinates who leak information without approval. "Leaking to the press is one of the prerogatives of the president and his duly appointed representatives," Lodge asserted, and "whoever takes it upon himself to leak, therefore, is, in effect, usurping a presidential prerogative and taking the conduct of foreign relations into his own hands."[37]

The desire to plug unauthorized leaks has sometimes led the government to adopt repressive, even blatantly unlawful, measures. Many of the abuses associated with the broadly defined Watergate scandal in the early 1970s arose from attempts to discover the source of leaks about U.S. foreign policy initiatives. Such actions included the White House–authorized burglary of the office of Dr. Lewis Fielding, whom Daniel Ellsberg—principal leaker of the Pentagon Papers—had been seeing for psychiatric treatment. National Security Adviser Henry Kissinger even approved wiretapping the phone of one of his own deputies at the NSC, Morton Halperin, because he feared Halperin had been divulging sensitive information to the press. Kissinger also apparently transmitted the names of reporters whose phones were to be tapped to William Sullivan, the assistant director in charge of domestic intelligence operations at the FBI.

Among the prominent journalists who were reportedly snared in that surveillance net were Hedrick Smith and Marvin Kalb.[38]

The use of investigations to attempt to intimidate the media was most pronounced during the Nixon era, but the tactic hardly originated with Nixon. In 1963 Hanson Baldwin, then military affairs editor for the *New York Times*, reported that the FBI was being used to track down leaks to the media from the Defense Department and other federal agencies. (The incident was ironic since Baldwin was a thoroughly mainstream Cold War journalist and extremely receptive to the government's national security claims.) A few years later a Washington correspondent reported that the DoD had established an investigative unit to track down the sources of unfavorable news stories and in at least one case had investigated the reporter as well as potential sources.[39] Even such a pro-military journalist as ABC's John McWethy was apparently investigated more than once by the FBI and other security agencies as a result of reports that allegedly damaged national security.[40]

Such tactics have continued in the post–Cold War era. When Massachusetts Institute of Technology scientist Theodore A. Postol published an article in the quarterly journal *International Security* highly critical of the performance of the Army's Patriot missile in the gulf war, the Army responded by launching an investigation alleging that he had used classified materials. Postol heatedly denied the accusation, but investigators dropped their probe only after Postol complained to Rep. John Conyers Jr. (D-Mich.), chairman of the House Committee on Government Operations, who in turn decided to hold hearings on what he termed the Pentagon's attempt at "post-publication classification." Even then, the military's goal of intimidating and inducing self-censorship on the part of writers who deal with defense topics was alarmingly transparent. Although she stated that, after a review of the article by "technical experts," the Army had decided not to pursue the matter against Postol, Deputy Assistant Secretary for Counterintelligence and Security Countermeasures Nina Stewart added that Postol's experience with national security issues "should have led him to conclude that a security review by the government before publication would be most prudent."[41]

For the most part, threats of prosecution have centered around the provisions of the Espionage Act of 1917. But that legislation, especially as interpreted by the federal courts, has been a somewhat ineffective vehicle for coercing the press in peacetime—at least until recently. The law bars disclosure of "information relating to the national defense," *not* (with the narrow exception of codes or electronic intercepts) "classified information." That distinction is crucial, for when the government seeks to bring criminal charges it must prove that a classified document in fact pertained in a significant way to the nation's defense. As David Wise observes,

> If the possession or publication of classified information was illegal per se, the law would be an invitation and a license to the government to classify anything and everything it pleased. Under such a system, the government's control over information would be total, and the First Amendment reduced to nothing.[42]

In addition to the requirement that the government prove that revealed information is relevant to national defense, the Espionage Act specifies that unlawful disclosure must be "with intent or reason to believe that the information is to be used to the injury of the United States, or to the benefit of any foreign nation." Although that provision is somewhat vague, the Supreme Court has construed it in a manner beneficial to press freedoms. In *Gorin v. United States* (1941), the Court held that the government must prove that an accused party "acted in bad faith."[43] Moreover, a jury was to decide whether bad faith existed and whether disclosure adversely affected national defense. Merely stamping a document "secret" did not automatically demonstrate that it pertained to national defense as specified in the act. The Court reaffirmed the latter point in *U.S. v. Drummond* (1965). In sum, the government bears a considerable burden of proof—especially in trying to gain the conviction of a member of the press whose "bad faith" is unlikely—under the Espionage Act.

Only once in the post–World War II era did the government arrest journalists for alleged violation of the espionage laws. In June 1945 the FBI raided the offices of *Amerasia*, a small left-wing magazine specializing in Asian affairs, and confiscated a large number of classified State Department documents that apparently had been passed by government officials.[44] *Amerasia*'s editor, Philip J. Jaffe, and another associate eventually received light fines for conspiracy to receive government property illegally, but any attempt to push the more serious espionage allegations was vitiated because the government had obtained evidence unlawfully.

Although the *Amerasia* case has been unique, the possibility of prosecution for espionage remains an omnipresent threat both to government employees who leak classified documents and to journalists who receive and publish them. On several occasions, especially during the Nixon years, the government considered seeking indictments of reporters who printed stories based on classified information that were hostile to the incumbent administration's foreign policy. The Reagan administration also flirted with that menacing strategy.[45] In late 1984 both Secretary of Defense Weinberger and CIA director Casey accused the *Washington Post* of giving "aid and comfort" to the enemy by publishing a story concerning the space shuttle's deployment of a military spy satellite and threatened to prosecute the newspaper for espionage.[46] Their accusation was especially chilling, since the phrase they used (whether intentionally or not) was the constitutional definition of treason.[47] The administration's intolerance became evident again the following year when Casey threatened to prosecute NBC News, the *Washington Post*, and other media outlets for printing or broadcasting "sensitive" information connected with the Ronald Pelton spy case. Casey reportedly met with *Post* editors over drinks and warned them, "If you publish this, I would recommend that you be prosecuted under the intelligence statute."[48] Lt. Gen. William E. Odom, director of the National Security Agency, subsequently recommended that the government prosecute news organizations that revealed details of intelligence gathering.[49]

The news media could perhaps have dismissed government blustering about applying the Espionage Act had it not been for the unprecedented action taken by the Reagan administration in the case of Samuel Loring Morison, grandson of the renowned naval historian Samuel Eliot Morison. The younger Morison, a civilian analyst of Soviet naval systems for the U.S. Naval Intelligence Support Center, surreptitiously obtained three satellite photographs of a Soviet aircraft carrier under construction at a Black Sea shipyard. He then sent them along with a memorandum compiled from various intelligence reports, not to the KGB, but to *Jane's Defence Weekly*, an authoritative British journal on military affairs to which Morison occasionally contributed. Morison's motives seemed to be mundane and personal—he apparently hoped to impress the editors and secure a prestigious, full-time job with the journal.

Nevertheless, the Reagan Justice Department chose to prosecute Morison just as though he had covertly delivered classified information to the Soviet Union. Department officials made it clear that it did not care who received the documents. "Foreign agents read that magazine," stated one government attorney.[50] The government's allegations of espionage were especially dubious in Morison's case. Obviously, the Soviet navy was familiar with the characteristics of its own aircraft carrier, so the substance of Morison's purloined information was of little use. Even the more plausible contention of prosecutors that a careful examination of the photo might yield important insights into the capabilities and limitations of American satellite technology failed to withstand scrutiny. Such information would have been exceedingly difficult to glean from a relatively low resolution picture in a magazine; a careful examination of the original photo might have been another matter, but Russian analysts had no access to it. The Soviets had in fact seen similar photos before, and they were well acquainted with the capabilities of U.S. spy satellites. Roland S. Inlow, who had long been the CIA's in-house expert on spy satellites, testified at Morison's trial that the leaking of the photographs had caused "zero damage" to the security of the United States.[51] Inlow's conclusion was especially persuasive, since the manual for the KH-11 spy satellite, which had taken the photo of the shipyard, had been sold to the KGB by a CIA defector in 1978.[52]

In marked contrast to previous espionage cases, the administration also insisted that it did not have to prove subversive intent. In other words, the government now argued that the delivery and publication of classified material were a form of espionage. The absence of any hard evidence that the disclosure actually damaged U.S. security and a total lack of any intent by the defendant to harm the United States or aid a foreign power were deemed irrelevant. Investigative journalist Mark Hertsgaard concludes, "What made the Morison case so significant was the government's implicit argument that passing harmless information to the press was as bad as sharing state secrets with the enemy, and should be punished just as severely."[53]

A federal district court judge in Baltimore embraced the Reagan administration's revolutionary legal theory in March 1985, ruling that the Espionage Act did apply to dissemination of classified information to recipients other than foreign governments, and a jury convicted Morison of espionage the following October. That verdict may well have been returned because of the espionage hysteria sweeping the United States in the wake of the Walker family naval spy ring scandal, the arrest of FBI agent Ronald Miller for passing secrets to the KGB through his Russian lover, and other incidents. Indeed, the Justice Department probably timed the Morison prosecution to take advantage of the charged public atmosphere. The verdict was subsequently upheld by the Fourth Circuit Court of Appeals, and in October 1988 the U.S. Supreme Court declined to review that ruling. Morison then began serving his two-year prison sentence.

The significance of the *Morison* case cannot be overstated. Morison was the first American convicted of espionage for leaking classified documents to the press. The Reagan administration thereby succeeded, where the Nixon administration had failed, in establishing a landmark legal precedent. Former Defense Department official Daniel Ellsberg and RAND Corporation analyst Anthony Russo were indicted in 1973 for leaking the Pentagon Papers to the *New York Times* and the *Washington Post*, but the case was dismissed by federal district judge Matthew Byrne because of rampant government misconduct during the investigation. The Justice Department then abandoned its efforts at prosecution. Nevertheless, the mere attempt should have been cause for concern. As Halperin and Hoffman point out, "This was the first espionage indictment in American history that failed to allege that the defendants had the intent, or even the reason to believe, that the material would be used to the injury of the national defense or to the advantage of a foreign power. It was also the first case that did not involve the alleged transfer of information to foreign agents or spies."[54]

The successful prosecution of Morison, even more than the attempted prosecution of Ellsberg and Russo, threatened to chill press coverage of controversial defense and foreign policy issues. In a direct manner, the government sought to dry up irreplaceable sources of information by employing harsh criminal sanctions against individuals who disclosed classified materials to the media. It also endeavored to intimidate reporters and their employers in an indirect fashion. If the person who provides classified information is guilty of espionage, the legal theory implies that the person who receives the material and the publication that prints it could be charged with the same offense. Although the government has not yet been bold enough to take such a step, the threats expressed by Weinberger, Casey, Odom, and other officials—and the *Amerasia* precedent—remind journalists that the danger is not merely theoretical.[55]

Although the Clinton administration seems distinctly more friendly to press freedoms on national security matters than either of its predecessors, that situation should offer only minimal comfort to those alarmed about the results of the *Morison* case. A dangerous legal precedent has been established that can be used by a future hard-line administration. The danger may be dormant at the moment, but it has not disappeared.

Indeed, the outcome of *Morison* highlights a more fundamental problem than the motives or impulses of any particular administration. America's espionage laws—primarily the Espionage Act of 1917 and the Internal Security Act of 1950—are sufficiently vague that they invite an administration to use them against anyone who dares to undermine the government's control of the information flow on national security issues. Former CIA chief counsel Anthony Lapham, testifying before the House Intelligence Committee in 1979, offered a troubling perspective.

> What has never been sorted out is whether these statutes can be applied, and would be constitutional if applied, to the compromise of national security information that occurs as a result of anonymous leaks to the press. I cannot tell you with any confidence what these laws mean in these contexts. I cannot tell you, for example, whether the leak of classified information to the press is a criminal act, or whether the publication of that information by a newspaper is a criminal act, or whether this conduct becomes criminal if committed with provable intent to injure the United States, but remains noncriminal if committed without such intent.[56]

The vague scope of the espionage laws creates the temptation for ambitious officials to interpret them in a manner that would create the equivalent of a comprehensive official secrets act—a measure that would effectively eviscerate the First Amendment as it applies to national security issues. That temptation has existed for decades, as U.S. political leaders have viewed with envy the vast powers enjoyed by their British counterparts. The *Morison* case was merely another installment in the quest for an official secrets act and other censorship powers.

5. The Quest for Peacetime Censorship Authority

The ultimate weapon the government can employ to silence foreign policy critics is overt censorship. We have seen that censorship mechanisms were fully operative during both world wars, but many Americans may not realize that "standby" authority to censor the press was a reality throughout most of the Cold War era. Such authority was included in executive branch mobilization plans to be activated in case of a "national emergency"—a sword of Damocles poised over a free press.

Ominous signs that the censorship mentality that justified press restrictions during World War II might carry over into peacetime emerged almost immediately. In the autumn of 1945, just weeks after V-J Day, President Harry S Truman appointed the Censorship Planning Commission to operate on a "strictly confidential basis" and to be financed from the president's discretionary funds.[1] Before leaving his post in August, Byron Price, the outgoing director of censorship, had recommended a continuity of policy from wartime to the postwar period. "I ask for your particular attention to the proposal that censorship planning be resumed without delay, and that a continuing Commission be appointed to carry forward that responsibility," Price stated in a letter to Truman. "Censorship is an indispensable part of war and planning for it should keep pace with other war plans. I strongly recommend that this form of preparedness not be permitted to lapse as it did for long periods after the First World War."[2]

In many ways, though, Price exhibited a restraint and idealism that seem touchingly naive from the perspective of the 1990s. He asserted that "the first and last principle to be remembered ... is that censorship will come into being solely as an instrument of war. It must charge itself only with contributing to the success of armed combat." He also offered a prophetic warning:

111

> There will be those who believe ... that the censor should
> operate according to a broader totalitarian philosophy; that
> he should undertake to suppress criticism of the government
> and conceal governmental blunders and delinquencies; that
> he should make fishing expeditions into private affairs hav-
> ing no possible connection with war; that he should withhold
> from the American people, for policy reasons, information
> known to be available to the enemy.[3]

Even without an operational censorship code, administrations
throughout the Cold War—and during the initial post–Cold War
period—have committed every one of those offenses.

Both the plan suggested by Price in 1945 and the more comprehensive version adopted by the National Security Resources Board
(NSRB) in 1949 as part of its emergency planning effort contained
disturbingly vague conditions under which censorship could be
invoked. For example, the 1949 measure provided, "Whenever in
time of war or of national emergency proclaimed by the President
and found by him to arise from the use or threat of force by a foreign
power the President shall deem that the public safety demands it,
he may cause to be censored under such rules and regulations as
he may from time to time establish," a variety of communications.[4]
It would be difficult to envision a more sweeping grant of power
to the executive.

Although advocates of censorship habitually insisted that it would
only be invoked during wartime, the guidelines contained no such
limitation. A declaration of war was not required; merely a declaration of emergency arising from a perceived foreign menace was. (In
addition, article 606 of the Communications Act of 1934 specifically
gave the president the authority to confiscate all broadcasting facilities in time of national emergency.) Such carte blanche authority
was especially disturbing, since before enactment of the National
Emergencies Act of 1976, there was no provision for congressional
oversight or termination of declared national emergencies.[5] Essentially, the president could declare a national emergency for any
reason he deemed sufficient and keep it in effect for as long as he
considered necessary. It was also instructive that the NSRB plan did
not require the actual existence of hostilities to trigger emergency
censorship; the mere "threat of force" (whatever that might mean)
by a foreign power was enough. Equally disquieting was the opinion

expressed by Price and later censorship planners that while formal congressional legislation granting censorship authority was desirable, a case could be made that the president already had such authority in his constitutional capacity as commander in chief.[6]

A full standby censorship code was developed during the Eisenhower years, and in 1958 President Dwight D. Eisenhower appointed Theodore F. Koop, the former director of CBS News in Washington, to head a secret 26-member censorship board. Koop, who had served as deputy director of the World War II agency under Byron Price, continued in that post throughout the 1960s when censorship planning became the mission of the Office of Emergency Preparedness.[7] Following press revelations of the existence of a standby Office of Censorship, President Richard M. Nixon changed the agency's name to the less inflammatory Wartime Information Security Program (WISP) and reduced the board from 26 members to 8. On substantive matters, though, virtually nothing changed. In the event that the president declared a national emergency, press censorship would go into effect and several thousand "executive reservists" would report to locations across the country to censor all mail, cables, telephone calls, and other communications (including press dispatches) entering or leaving the United States.

The powers WISP could exercise were as dangerously vague as those of previous incarnations of the government's standby censorship authority. For example, the 1971 Department of Defense directive describing both the military and the civil components of WISP stated that the program's objective would be to prevent not only the disclosure of information that might assist the enemy but of information that "might adversely affect any policy of the United States."[8] The guidelines did provide that WISP restrictions would be enforced "only for reasons of military import" and would not be used to "act as a guardian of public morals, to enforce civilian statutes unconnected with the war effort," or to suppress information "other than in the interest of national security or defense."[9] The last "restriction" on WISP authority was essentially meaningless, however. Any reasonably creative bureaucrat could always formulate a plausible case that censoring an offending item was in the interest of national security or defense.

Supporters of WISP and its predecessors stressed that in all likelihood censorship would be invoked only in the event of an attack on the American homeland, not a limited conflict involving U.S. troops elsewhere in the world. Since authorities did not use censorship powers on the home front during the Korean or Vietnam conflicts, there is no reason to doubt the sincerity of those assurances. Nonetheless, the plan in operation during the Vietnam War specifically stated that censorship could be imposed in cases of "limited war, or conflicts of the 'brush fire' type, in which U.S. forces are involved elsewhere in the world on land, sea, or in the air." The 1971 version merely assumed that the president would activate the censorship system "in case of war," presumably meaning declared or undeclared, total or limited. Another portion of that DoD directive stated that the armed forces component of WISP could be imposed in peacetime, if specifically directed by the president or the secretary of defense—something less than ironclad protection for freedom of expression.[10]

Moreover, on at least one occasion—shortly after the Bay of Pigs invasion—the executive branch apparently did contemplate imposing formal censorship in peacetime. Koop reportedly discussed the possibility of instituting a censorship program with White House aides Theodore Sorensen and Pierre Salinger. What is especially alarming is that such a step could have even been considered in the absence of any dire threat to U.S. security; President John F. Kennedy was simply miffed about newspaper stories that had hinted that an invasion of Cuba might be forthcoming.[11]

The mere existence of such a censorship plan was unhealthy in a society that valued the freedoms guaranteed by the First Amendment. As author David Wise concluded after congressional probes of the subject in the early 1970s, "That there should exist in America a shadow group of censors, surrounded by secrecy, that the conditions under which the unit might be activated by the President of the United States—and its mode of operation—are at best imprecisely defined, surely cannot be regarded as a comforting state of affairs in a democracy."[12]

The shroud of secrecy is a matter of particular concern. Even though the House and Senate Appropriations Committees voted to eliminate funding for WISP military reserve units in 1974, and by April 1977 the Army (the last branch of the service to have such units) abolished them, one ought to be cautious about concluding that the executive branch no longer has a comprehensive standby

censorship plan. In the absence of compelling evidence to the contrary, one should instead assume that WISP or some other incarna-
tion of the censorship plan probably still exists. The constant presence of such planning as part of emergency preparedness measures
from the mid-1940s to the mid-1970s suggests that government officials may not have abandoned the scheme. Since the matter remains
classified, however, it is impossible to determine even the existence,
much less the scope, of any censorship plans. Advocates of an unfettered press must remain alert to the danger that some future president involved in a difficult or unpopular military enterprise may
not exhibit his predecessors' restraint but may instead decide to
stifle annoying press criticism of his foreign policy by activating a
formal censorship system.

Standby censorship plans have not been the only example of government efforts to gain broad powers to suppress foreign policy
critics. U.S. officials have attempted to go beyond the apparent limitations of the Espionage Act and forge a broader legal theory that
could be used to squelch embarrassing disclosures in the press about
national security matters. The most prominent example of that drive
was the 1971 Pentagon Papers case.

Following the appearance of the initial installment of documents
pertaining to America's Vietnam policy during the 1960s in the *New
York Times* and *Washington Post*, the Nixon administration sought
an injunction to prohibit the publication of additional classified material. The administration's action was unprecedented in two respects.
It was the first time that the federal government had gone to court
to censor a newspaper before publication. Moreover, the Justice
Department based its request, not on provisions of the Espionage
Act, but on a broad claim of injury to the government and "grave
and immediate danger to the security of the United States."[13]

In seeking injunctive relief and fashioning a vague legal theory
beyond the scope of any specific statutory authority, the Nixon
administration overreached itself. Prior restraint ran directly counter
to nearly two centuries of American constitutional tradition; in large
measure the First Amendment's provision for freedom of the press
was explicitly designed to prevent such restraint. Even during the
world wars, the government had generally avoided actions (except
for the denial of mailing privileges to certain radical publications)
that smacked of prior restraint. That was equally true during the

Cold War. Even in the Internal Security Act of 1950, the high-water mark of Cold War era anti-subversive legislation, Congress stated explicitly that nothing in the act should be construed as authorizing prior restraints. Only in the Atomic Energy Act had Congress made provision for court injunctions against disclosure, and that provision was not invoked until the *Progressive* case in the late 1970s. A number of Supreme Court decisions, most notably *Near v. Minnesota* (1931), also stressed that any governmental agency bore an extraordinary burden of proof when it attempted to engage in prior restraint.[14]

Two federal district courts and the Court of Appeals for the District of Columbia held that the government had failed to meet that burden with respect to the Pentagon Papers. In a six-to-three decision issued on June 30, 1971, the Supreme Court affirmed the lower courts' judgment, noting that "any system of prior restraints on expression comes to this Court bearing a heavy presumption against its constitutional validity."[15] Thus ended the Nixon administration's attempt to fashion a legal theory to justify the censorship of critical stories based on classified material.

The Supreme Court's rejection of the Justice Department's strategy appeared to strike a blow for freedom of expression as it pertained to national security issues. But there were some disquieting aspects to the outcome. First of all, the six majority justices could not agree on an opinion; instead six separate opinions were issued. Some of them, notably the ones by Hugo Black and William O. Douglas, emphatically rebuked any attempt at censorship. The opinions of William Brennan and Thurgood Marshall were also relatively solid on that issue. But two members of the majority, Potter Stewart and Byron White, stressed that their objections to the government's case were confined to the matter of prior restraint. White, for example, conceded that revelation of the documents would do "substantial damage" to the national interest. More ominous, he emphasized that "failure by the Government to justify prior restraints does not measure its constitutional entitlement to a conviction for publication. That the Government mistakenly chose to proceed by injunction does not mean that it could not successfully proceed in another way."[16]

White's comment and similar passages in Stewart's opinion constituted a virtual invitation to the Justice Department to file criminal charges against the *Post* and *Times* for publishing classified material. The attitudes of those justices, combined with the views of the three dissenters who were even receptive to considering at greater length the Nixon administration's objective of prior restraint on coverage of national security issues, indicated that the Supreme Court's action in the Pentagon Papers case was less than an unalloyed endorsement of press freedoms. Indeed, it suggested that had the government sought to punish the offending newspapers after publication rather than seeking an injunction, a majority of the Court might well have upheld such action.[17]

One of the most worrisome aspects of the Pentagon Papers decision was the willingness of White, Stewart, and the three dissenting justices to accept the government's unsupported claim that revelation of the documents would do serious damage to U.S. national security. For example, Justice Harry Blackmun agreed with a district court judge that publication of some of the material "could clearly result in great harm to the nation," defined as "the death of soldiers, the destruction of alliances, the greatly increased difficulty of negotiation with our enemies, the inability of our diplomats to negotiate." Blackmun added the factors of "prolongation of the war and of further delay in the freeing of United States prisoners."[18]

The government has employed the specter of damage to national security throughout the Cold War and since to justify suppressing information on controversial foreign policy matters. In the case of the Pentagon Papers, that allegation was overblown if not utterly fanciful. Contrary to the claims of the Nixon administration and the fears of Blackmun and other credulous justices, the projected calamities did not occur. Indeed, nearly two decades later, Erwin N. Griswold, who as solicitor general had presented the government's case, conceded that he had "never seen any trace of a threat to the national security from the publication" of the Pentagon Papers.[19]

Revelations of the documents may have embarrassed the authors of America's disastrous intervention in Vietnam, for the material exposed the flawed logic, puerile arguments, and pervasive deceit that went into the formulation and execution of that policy. For example, the documents disclosed that at the same time Lyndon Johnson was castigating Barry Goldwater, his opponent in the 1964 presidential campaign, for wanting to deepen U.S. involvement in the war, virtually all of Johnson's own advisers—including the Joint Chiefs of Staff—had already concluded that extensive U.S. military intervention would be necessary to prevent a communist victory in

South Vietnam. The documents also revealed that, far from being a response to North Vietnamese attacks on U.S. naval vessels, the Gulf of Tonkin Resolution had been prepared months in advance by the administration. Other portions of the Pentagon Papers indicated that Saigon had been extremely reluctant to approve the introduction of American combat forces and submitted its "request" only after intense pressure from U.S. envoy Maxwell Taylor. As Morton Halperin, who in his capacity as deputy assistant secretary of defense from 1967 to 1969 had general supervisory responsibility for compiling the Pentagon Papers, later concluded, "Clearly, proposals that the United States send troops in over the objections of the Saigon government would have provoked a major debate within the United States. The administration avoided that controversy by keeping the facts secret."[20]

There was little doubt that publication of the papers bruised sensitive bureaucratic egos and deflated some reputations, but that was hardly a legitimate reason for keeping such information secret. Halperin's assessment makes that crucial distinction.

> The Pentagon Papers reveal a consistent pattern of deception by the administration, centered on withholding from Congress and the public vital information that raised devastating questions about the effectiveness and propriety of administration policies and the credibility of responsible officials. It is not hard to understand why, given the policies and rationales to which the government was committed, the Pentagon Papers had to be kept secret.
>
> We should take note . . . of some things the Papers did not contain: There was nothing in the nature of weapons or electronic design information, identities of secret agents still in the field, or other material of the sort that could be of great value to foreign governments while of little relevance to public concern. The secrecy of the study could not be justified on such straightforward grounds.[21]

Most important, disclosure of the Pentagon Papers did not damage the nation's well-being, much less produce the "grave and immediate danger to the security of the United States" about which the Nixon administration had warned. That discrepancy between prediction and outcome should give pause to anyone inclined to believe alarmist government rhetoric about dangers to national security in the future.

118

Both the Pentagon Papers case and the more recent *Morison* case represent attempts by the government to create the judicial equivalent of Britain's infamous Official Secrets Act. That legislation, along with associated measures such as the laws of confidence, empowers the British government to enjoin the press from printing any story based on classified information and to punish violators once a story has appeared. There is no requirement to show that the material was essential to national security or even that it was properly classified. The government has the power to declare secret and withhold from the public whatever it wants to. U.S. officials have long hungered for similar authority.

Britain's Official Secrets Act

The history of Britain's Official Secrets Act demonstrates that the tension between ambitious foreign policy objectives and press freedoms is not unique to the American experience. The first version of the act was introduced by the government of Prime Minister Lord Salisbury in 1888 and received parliamentary approval the following year. Salisbury's enthusiasm for the legislation sheds considerable light not only on the motives for the act but on the desire of officials in all countries for censorship authority. As foreign secretary a decade earlier, Salisbury had suffered acute embarrassment when Charles Marvin, a minor official in the Foreign Ministry, leaked details of a secret agreement between Britain and Russia to the London *Globe* on the eve of the Congress of Berlin. Challenged in the House of Lords, Salisbury dismissed the press report as wholly inaccurate, whereupon the official provided the *Globe* a copy of the full text of the treaty. The evidence convinced virtually everyone that Salisbury had deliberately misled the House of Lords, which put his political career under a serious (albeit temporary) cloud. As is so often the case, the leak of information did not adversely affect the nation's security; it merely revealed duplicity and unethical behavior on the part of a high-ranking official.

To Salisbury's frustration, attempts to prosecute Marvin for larceny foundered when he was able to show that he had not stolen the actual document but merely copied its contents. Since there was no legislation prohibiting a government official from disclosing information to the newspapers, Marvin went free. When Salisbury became prime minister, he quickly took steps to prevent such leaks in the future, and the result was the Official Secrets Act.

Spokesmen for the Salisbury government were less than candid about the scope and the implications of the proposed legislation. They repeatedly stressed that the bill was aimed at deterring espionage, barely mentioning that the statute would prohibit unauthorized disclosure of official information by a government employee to any party (including newspapers) whether or not damage was done to the public interest.[22] Although the 1889 measure did not apply to newspapers that published leaked information, the purpose of the legislation was to cut off an increasingly inquisitive press from its sources inside the government.

Targeting the press itself for similar restrictions was the logical next step, although it was not until 1908 that a government dared to attempt it. The new bill not only proposed to strengthen the espionage provisions of the 1889 act but sought to prohibit the unauthorized "receipt" of official information (thus bringing newspapers into the web of potential criminal offenses). The bill also attempted to extend criminal sanctions to cover any member of the public, not merely government employees. In marked contrast to the failure of the press and public to appreciate the full import of the 1889 legislation, this time the proposed restrictions encountered such vehement opposition in Parliament and the press that the government ultimately withdrew the bill.

The battle against the erosion of press freedoms was not over, however. Another alleged foreign policy crisis gave government leaders a new opportunity for victory. A series of revelations concerning espionage activities in Britain by German agents in 1909 (the so-called German spy scare) created an atmosphere verging on public hysteria. That mood was reinforced a few months later with the onset of the Agadir crisis—Berlin's clumsy attempt at geopolitical coercion by deploying a gunboat off the coast of Morocco—which fanned fears of a general European war. The government of Prime Minister Herbert Asquith moved to exploit the public's apprehension by reintroducing the 1908 proposals—this time packaged as urgently needed measures to protect national security. As historian Clive Ponting notes, "The advantages of linking protection against disclosure generally with the aim of protection against espionage had been evident since the relatively trouble-free passage of the first secrecy law in 1889. The experience of 1908 demonstrated that attempts to widen the law might well run into serious trouble unless carefully presented."[23] That strategy paid off when Parliament approved the Official Secrets Act of 1911 with minimal opposition.[24]

The system of information control established by the Official Secrets Act was expanded greatly during World War I with the adoption of the stringent Defence of the Realm regulations that created a comprehensive system of censorship. Although those temporary wartime measures lapsed when the fighting ceased, the government was loathe to give up the additional restrictions. It soon proposed measures to strengthen the 1911 act so that the new peacetime version more closely resembled the wartime censorship regime. With passage of those amendments in 1920, the legal framework for pervasive government secrecy was in place.

Although the Official Secrets Act became the centerpiece of the British government's system of information control, it was not the only measure that could be used against a troublesome press. A closely related device was the so-called D-Notice procedure—a carryover from the censorship of both world wars. D-Notices, issued in the post–World War II period by the government's Defence, Press and Broadcasting Committee, provided detailed guidelines to the media about publishing stories on defense-related issues.

America's first secretary of defense, James Forrestal, apparently entertained notions of setting up a similar arrangement. He advocated creating a "security advisory council" of six media representatives to help him establish standards for the publication of information relating to national security. Forrestal eventually abandoned the idea when he was unable to get the journalistic community to see either the necessity or the feasibility of such a scheme.[25] (It is not exactly comforting that a British expert on press coverage of national security issues in both countries contends, "The D-notice is, in effect, an institutionalized way of doing what is done in the United States through informal government-press contacts.")[26]

Although the British D-Notice system was supposedly voluntary, and therefore dependent on cooperation by editors and publishers, the government made it clear on more than a few occasions that failure to heed a D-Notice restriction could result in prosecution under the Official Secrets Act.[27] Indeed, the D-Notice system was initiated in 1912 to guide editors away from the potential pitfalls of the Official Secrets Act.[28] It was clear that the restrictions were not designed solely to protect national security. One attempted D-Notice in the early 1960s, for example, would have allowed only officially released information on military weapons and equipment to be published—thereby blocking criticism of rising costs and increasing delays, both of which had reached scandalous proportions.[29]

Applications of the Official Secrets Act throughout the Cold War period concentrated on intimidating and punishing sources of information rather than the media outlets that published the stories. Two of the most famous episodes show that the British government was less concerned with thwarting "espionage" than with punishing "leakers" who revealed incidents of official deceit or misconduct. The first occurred in 1983 when the *Guardian* published details of the government's plans, outlined in a secret document, for handling parliamentary and public statements about the arrival of the first U.S. Cruise missiles at Greenham Common, an extremely controversial and sensitive political issue at the time. The *Guardian* story suggested that the government of Prime Minister Margaret Thatcher was being less than candid in its official statements and was engaged in a concerted campaign of disinformation.

The government went to court to force the *Guardian* to hand over the document, which the authorities ultimately traced to Sarah Tisdall, a 23-year-old clerk in the foreign secretary's private office. She was then charged with violating section 2 of the Official Secrets Act. Tisdall plead guilty but defended her actions as an attempt to expose the government's duplicity and its effort to avoid parliamentary accountability. For its part, the government in its official damage assessment for the prosecution did not even attempt to argue that the disclosed information was useful to the Soviet Union or other foreign enemies. Instead, it merely suggested that the disclosure "might" have led to some erosion of allied confidence in Britain as a partner in confidential exchanges. Nevertheless, the government asked that Tisdall serve time in jail for her offense, and the judge complied, sentencing her to six months' imprisonment. He stressed the need to make an example of the case to show that "in these days" a plea that no harm had been done to the nation's security or even that the disclosure had been in the public interest would not be accepted as a valid defense.[30]

If the *Tisdall* case suggested the British government's willingness to use the Official Secrets Act as a weapon against critics who dared expose duplicitous policies, the *Clive Ponting* case the following year confirmed that growing arrogance. The *Ponting* case arose from the sinking of the Argentine cruiser *General Belgrano* by HMS *Conqueror* during the Falklands War. That sinking was the most controversial episode of the war, not only because it involved the loss of 386 lives, but because it occurred when diplomatic efforts to settle the conflict were at a delicate and promising stage.

The version of events given to both press and Parliament by the Thatcher government was misleading in numerous respects; most notably, it gave the impression that the *Belgrano* had been sailing toward rather than away from the British fleet at the time it was torpedoed. (There are parallels between that cover-up and the U.S. government's official explanation of the circumstances surrounding the shooting down of an Iranian airliner in 1988—perhaps another case in which Washington took a leaf from London's book on how to manage disagreeable and potentially damaging news.) Efforts to get at the facts drifted inconclusively until July 1984 when Ponting, a senior civil servant in the Ministry of Defence, sent two documents to Tom Dalyell, a Labour member of Parliament, showing that Dalyell and the Foreign Affairs Select Committee were being misled.

The incident immediately became a cause célèbre, especially when Ponting was indicted for violating section 2 of the Official Secrets Act. For the first time an official had been indicted for disclosing information to a member of Parliament. Ponting used a vigorous "public interest defense," made all the more credible by the virtually irrefutable evidence that the Thatcher government had repeatedly lied about the facts of the *Belgrano* episode. Most of the British press supported Ponting, as did the trial jury, which defied the blatantly pro-prosecution instructions given by the presiding judge and returned a verdict of not guilty.[31]

An alternative to using the Official Secrets Act to strike at critics of the government has been to use the civil law to impose prior restraint. Under British law a High Court judge may issue an injunction against publication if it appears that a forthcoming news story is based on confidential information. Using the civil law of confidence has several advantages from the government's point of view. A temporary injunction can be obtained, often without notice to the other side, in a private hearing before a judge. It is disturbingly easy to then convert a temporary injunction into a permanent ban against publication. Finally, an injunction against one publication applies with equal force to all media.[32]

Although the British press chafed for years under the restraints imposed by the Official Secrets Act and the other measures used to intimidate critics of the government, it did not openly rebel until 1987 when Thatcher's government not only barred publication of Peter Wright's book *Spycatcher* but tried to ban the publication of excerpts from, or reports about, it. Wright, a former member of Britain's intelligence service, contended, among other things, that high-ranking officials in the service during the 1960s considered Prime Minister Harold Wilson a Soviet "mole" and sought to undermine him. The Thatcher government's invocation of the laws of confidence to squelch press accounts of such revelations underscored the potential for abuse that was inherent in the British secrecy system. Wright's book was freely available throughout the Western world, and the press of numerous countries commented on it. Yet the Thatcher government treated the British press and public as children who were incapable of evaluating such information for themselves. Suppressing debate in the name of protecting "national security" had reached absurd levels, and members of the British press began clamoring for the same protection afforded their American counterparts under the First Amendment.[33]

The Thatcher government resisted such calls, as it did similar pressure to enact a British version of the U.S. Freedom of Information Act. Instead, it merely offered to reform the Official Secrets Act. How Thatcher and her associates defined "reform" soon became all too apparent, and the result of their "reforms" may have left freedom of expression on defense and foreign policy issues in an even more precarious state. Indeed, the new legislation adopted in 1989 appeared to tighten rather than to ease the whole system of restrictions. The most odious provision was one that introduced the new, more specific criminal offense of "unauthorized publication." There was no longer any need to demonstrate that a classified document had even changed hands; the mere publication of a news story based on secret information originating in a government agency would expose a media outlet to prosecution. Moreover, the new legislation severely restricted possible grounds for defense. It was no longer possible for an official or journalist to argue that disclosure was justified because it exposed corruption, misconduct, or negligence.[34]

The Official Secrets Act of 1989, in short, continues the system that makes the British press the least free of any press in the Western world on matters relating to defense and foreign policy. The provisions of the so-called reform measure belie the comforting assurances of *New Republic* editor Andrew Sullivan—a British expatriate—that the Thatcher government "is the first since 1911 actually to reform the Official Secrets Act in a clearly liberal direction."[35] It is also more than a trifle disquieting that many prominent current and former U.S. officials seem to regard the repressive British system as a model for the United States.

Attempts to Secure a de Facto U.S. Official Secrets Act

Just as the British press envies America's formal guarantees of freedom of expression, American proponents of an interventionist foreign policy have long wanted to stifle embarrassing media revelations through a U.S. version of the Official Secrets Act and other components of London's information control system. Secretary of State Dean Acheson, for example, openly advocated the adoption of such legislation in the late 1940s, and after the leak of the Pentagon Papers in 1971, he reiterated his call for "a severe Official Secrets Act to prevent irresponsible or corrupt transfer of secret papers from the government to publishers."[36]

During the Eisenhower administration that option was discussed on several occasions. The summary of a discussion conducted at a November 1953 session of the National Security Council indicated both the desire for such legislation and the caution induced by an appreciation of political realities.

> The Attorney General stated that the chief problem with respect to a revision of the internal security legislation was whether or not the United States should have a counterpart to the British Official Secrets Acts. With respect to espionage our statutes cover much the same ground as the British, but the British coverage is much broader with respect to the unauthorized disclosure of classified information. We would certainly need guidance, said the Attorney General, on *just how far we want to go, for example, in punishing a newspaper man who deliberately publishes classified information.*
>
> The President commented that . . . he doubted we should now attempt to emulate the British. Exasperating as the many recent leaks had proved, *the present climate of the country* was

anything but the right setting for an American equivalent to these British laws.

Mr. Dodge queried whether it would not at least be desirable to have a draft of such an American Official Secrets Act ready for consideration in the event that it should later appear desirable.[37]

The NSC endorsed Budget Director Joseph M. Dodge's suggestion, agreeing to "have in readiness" a revision of the U.S. espionage statutes "to correspond generally to the British Official Secrets Acts."[38]

Perhaps most disturbing was the attitude of presidential adviser Harold Stassen. Not only did he express the hope that "it might be possible to sit down with the publishers and agree on the main points that such a law should cover," the ultimate in a co-option strategy, he offered the chilling observation that "in many cases when one informs the American people, one automatically informs the enemy."[39] The inescapable conclusion to be drawn from Stassen's position was that the press should be free to disclose to the American people only information on defense and foreign policy matters that was of no value to Washington's superpower adversary.

Interventionists have been consistently eager to get an American official secrets act. When *Aviation Week* published a story in its October 21, 1957, issue disclosing that U.S. monitoring installations in Turkey had provided detailed information on Soviet missile tests since 1955, Eisenhower administration officials reacted vehemently, even though the account was based largely on unclassified sources. Robert Cutler, Eisenhower's national security adviser, stated that publication of the story was clearly "in a category of things prejudicial to our nation and its people in the free world struggle for survival."[40] Cutler later told a congressional committee investigating the government's information policy that he hoped the incident "would lead your committee and the Congress to examine existing law with a view to determining whether it effectively protects the people of the United States from public disclosure of information helpful to an opponent dedicated to destroying our individual liberties."[41] The import of his remarks was that the United States should move beyond the existing restrictions in the Espionage Act toward something resembling the British system. On other occasions, Cutler also hinted that the British model might be appropriate for restricting the disclosure of information relevant to U.S. security.

Cutler was not the last prominent member of the national security bureaucracy to entertain such objectives. In October 1966 the CIA's assistant general counsel, John D. Morrison Jr., reportedly prepared a lengthy secret study in which he argued that the Espionage Act was insufficient to prevent the revelation of classified information. He urged the agency to press for legislation that would make it a crime to disclose any classified material and allow the CIA director to obtain injunctions preventing publication. The proposed statute, Morrison stressed, would "substitute the judgment of the director of Central Intelligence for that of a jury."[42] In other words, the government would no longer have to prove either that the information was important to national defense or that the accused party intended to injure the United States or aid a foreign power.

More recently, Michael A. Ledeen, a former special adviser to the secretary of state and consultant to the NSC, enthusiastically advocated a censorship system based on the restrictive British and Israeli models. Citing journalist Bob Woodward's book *Veil*, an exposé of CIA dirty tricks, as an example of how unrestricted press freedoms can jeopardize U.S. security interests, Ledeen stated bluntly, "Such a book ought not to have been published." With an American official secrets act, it would not have been, and in Ledeen's view, that system "might actually help the policy process."[43] Whether it would help the values of democracy and limited government, of course, is a different matter.

Despite the wishes of Acheson, Cutler, Ledeen, and many other advocates of censorship, Congress has repeatedly rebuffed efforts to create an official secrets act. Even in the aftermath of the Pentagon Papers episode, the legislative branch explicitly declined to act on the Nixon administration's request for such a statute. Indeed, the administration's tactic appeared to backfire; a very different focus was apparent in the hearings that were called to consider the matter by the House Government Operations Committee and, later, by three subcommittees of the Senate Judiciary and Government Operations Committees. They concentrated on the problem of excessive government classification of information and took the first step leading to amendments liberalizing the Freedom of Information Act.

The closest proponents of an official secrets act came to success was in 1957 when the Commission on Government Security, reflecting the

127

wishes of the Eisenhower administration, recommended a statute based on the British measure. Reaction in Congress and the nation's press was extremely negative, and the proposal was rejected. Again in 1972 the staff of a Senate subcommittee drafted a passage in the · proposed revision of the federal criminal code that would have made any disclosure of classified information a felony, but that provision was omitted from the bill when it was introduced.[44] Similar proposals have surfaced periodically since the early 1970s, all without success.

One limited exception to the record of congressional resistance did occur in 1982 when Congress passed the Agents Identities Protection Act, a statute prohibiting the deliberate and systematic revelation of the identities of CIA and other intelligence agents.[45] Although that measure has some potential to chill investigative reports on abuses committed by U.S. intelligence agencies, protecting agents in the field from assassination is a reasonable goal. Moreover, the legislative history makes it clear that the act was designed to ban the publication of agents' identities simply for the purpose of exposure. The logic, according to two constitutional experts, was essentially that "the gratuitous listing of agents' names in certain publications goes far beyond information that might contribute to informed public debate on foreign policy or foreign intelligence activities. That effort to identify U.S. intelligence officers and agents in countries throughout the world and to expose their identities repeatedly, time and time again, serves no legitimate purpose."[46] Such a narrow statute falls far short of a comprehensive official secrets act.

Thwarted in its broader legislative attempts to gag the press, the national security bureaucracy has attempted to achieve the same result in the federal courts. That was the intent and meaning of the Pentagon Papers case. Although the Nixon administration seemed especially determined to obtain a judicial equivalent of the Official Secrets Act, actions of subsequent administrations have also indicated a similar desire. One of the most important episodes occurred in March 1979 when the Justice Department obtained an injunction against *Progressive* magazine, prohibiting it from publishing a story by Howard Morland on the design and manufacture of hydrogen bombs.[47]

There were several worrisome aspects to the *Progressive* case. There was, for example, the assumption of Federal District Judge Robert Warren that "the question before the Court is a basic confrontation between the First Amendment right to freedom of the press and national security." With the issue framed in that fashion, it was not surprising that Warren ruled that the First Amendment would have to give way. When national security was involved, the judge held, press freedoms had to be curtailed. If the *Progressive* were allowed to publish its article, the way could be paved "for the thermonuclear annihilation for us all. In that event, our right to life is extinguished and the right to publish becomes moot."[48]

Warren's reasoning was national security hysteria at its worst. The Pentagon Papers episode (along with many others) demonstrated that the government invariably trots out a parade of horribles to buttress its argument that serious harm will occur if its bid for censorship is rejected. In the overwhelming majority of cases, the negative consequences prove to be far less calamitous than projected—frequently they do not materialize at all. Yet Warren accepted the government's contention that an article in an obscure leftist magazine would lead to Armageddon. Even a cursory assessment would have cast doubt on that nightmare scenario. The one hostile state capable of annihilating the United States already had a large, sophisticated arsenal and certainly did not need to peruse the pages of the *Progressive* for information.

Even the more realistic fear that an existing nonnuclear state or a terrorist movement might find valuable information in the article was vastly overdrawn. Morland's piece contained nothing that thousands of engineers and nuclear physicists did not already know; it contained no "cutting edge" data. Terrorist regimes or movements were more likely to be stymied by the problem of obtaining plutonium or enriched uranium for a bomb than by any conceivable engineering difficulties. After all, nuclear technology was already more than three decades old. It was the height of hubris to assume that only a few advanced industrial countries had the technical sophistication to build a bomb. Thus, the *Progressive* piece was "old news" and hardly a menace to national security.

Although the Carter administration ultimately abandoned its effort to bar publication, it did so only when confronted with irrefutable evidence that the story was based entirely on unclassified sources. Furthermore, the Justice Department succeeded in delaying publication for seven months. That delay, compared to the speed with which the *Washington Post* and the *New York Times* had vindicated their right to publish the Pentagon Papers, suggests how the government may be able to harass and intimidate publications that lack the legal or financial resources of the media giants. In this case an extended delay in publication did not greatly affect the importance or timeliness of the article, given the nature of the topic. But what if the government had succeeded with regard to an article on a more "time sensitive" topic? In some instances, mere delay could serve the government's policy purposes as effectively as an outright ban on publication.

Perhaps most worrisome, the government sought to advance the argument that information on certain subjects was "born classified." Under the Atomic Energy Act of 1945, the government insisted, *all* data—including lawfully obtained information—on the design or manufacture of nuclear weapons is restricted. According to that thesis, it was irrelevant whether the government generated the information or whether the information was ever in the government's possession. As the *Progressive* pointed out in its brief appealing the district court's restraining order, "A journalist's 'original work product,' a private scientist's independent research, [or] a university professor's deductive reasoning can all be 'classified at birth.' "[49] At least with regard to atomic energy issues, that represented a blueprint for censorship at least as expansive as that embodied in the British Official Secrets Act. If the Justice Department had prevailed with its argument in the *Progressive* case, it would have set an extraordinarily dangerous precedent—one that might not have been confined to the field of atomic energy.

Where the Nixon administration failed in the Pentagon Papers case and the Carter administration failed in the *Progressive* case, the Reagan administration succeeded in the *Morison* case, securing a major judicial precedent in the campaign to create a de facto official secrets act.[50] As legal scholar Steven Burkholder concluded, "Justice Department attorneys, in effect, had persuaded a court to legislate what Congress had refused to legislate for seventy years: a law approaching Great Britain's Official Secrets Act."[51] The meaning of the *Morison* verdict is that the government may prosecute anyone who divulges classified information to any recipient, not merely a foreign government. There is no need to show that the information was properly classified or that disclosure was in fact harmful to the security of the United States; mere assertion of the latter point now seems to be sufficient. That rationale comes perilously close to the

130

logic of the Official Secrets Act, and those who leak information without the authorization of high-level officials are now probably as vulnerable to prosecution as their British counterparts. Tom Wicker correctly concluded that the government had scored a worrisome victory. "If it is a crime to make classified information available to the public, as the Morison precedent suggests, the Government's ability to conceal *any* information is greatly increased. Just classify it, whether secrecy is warranted or not."[52] True, federal authorities have not yet moved to prosecute a media outlet for publishing classified material—the other feature of the Official Secrets Act— but one wonders how long it will be before such an attempt is made. It does not offer much comfort that when the *Morison* case was being litigated, a high-level Justice Department official stated on a not-for-attribution basis that "neither the Government officials who do the leaking, nor the news publications at the receiving end . . . should consider themselves immune from prosecution under the Espionage Act."[53]

The far-reaching significance of the *Morison* decision was aptly described by civil liberties columnist Nat Hentoff.

> On October 19, 1988, few newspapers—and none of the television networks—carried the news that for the first time in American history, the press and employees of the Federal Government were subject to an Official Secrets Act. This did not come about because Congress passed a new law. It was the result of a decision by the U.S. Supreme Court that it would not review the espionage conviction of Samuel Loring Morison.[54]

The *New Republic* observed that the *Morison* verdict "leaves far too much power in the hands of the government to curb free debate on military issues, and endangers the ability of the press to report the news."[55] That was an understatement: seeking a de facto official secrets act is only one of many things the government has done to curb dissent on foreign policy.

6. Losing Control: The Vietnam War

The cozy relationship that existed between government and most of the press on national security issues during World War II and the first two decades of the Cold War began to unravel during the Vietnam War. The estrangement was gradual, however. Most media accounts in the initial years of the conflict were supportive of U.S. policy and optimistic about the prospects for success. Some aspects of Washington's policy, though, did come under unaccustomed scrutiny as early as 1962 when critical stories about South Vietnamese president Ngo Dinh Diem's repressive practices created widespread revulsion in the United States. The contrast between the media's treatment of Diem and their earlier placid acceptance of an equally authoritarian U.S. client, South Korea's Syngman Rhee, was noticeable.

A handful of young reporters, including many in their late 20s or early 30s such as David Halberstam, Neil Sheehan, and Malcolm Browne, was in the forefront of early efforts to produce more realistic accounts of the Vietnam struggle, even if that entailed blunt criticism of U.S. policy. At least initially, their conduct seemed motivated by a desire to clear away distortions in the belief that more accurate information would help the United States to succeed in its mission. As late as 1964 Halberstam, for example, still contended that as a "strategic country in a key area, [Vietnam] is perhaps one of only five or six nations in the world that is truly vital to U.S. interests."[1] Only much later would Halberstam and some of his colleagues focus on the deeper and darker deficiencies of U.S. foreign policy.

The generally pro-interventionist sentiments of the Saigon press corps accurately reflected the overall perspective of the American news media on the Vietnam intervention. When the United States launched its bombing raids against North Vietnam in August 1964 following the Gulf of Tonkin incident, it did so with overwhelming press support. Of the 27 editorials excerpted in the August 7 edition of the *New York Times*, 24 endorsed the bombing without reservations, 2 expressed minor reservations, and 1 was noncommittal.[2]

Moreover, the media showed little inclination to question the Johnson administration's version of the murky events in the Gulf of Tonkin. They placidly accepted the administration's contention that North Vietnamese patrol boats attacked two U.S. destroyers, the *C. Turner Joy* and the *Maddox*, without provocation in international waters.

Years later congressional investigators and other skeptics finally amassed evidence that painted a rather different picture. The second "attack" may never have occurred at all; jittery crewmen apparently reacted to a phantom threat. Moreover, although the first incident may have been real, it was hardly an unprovoked attack. The U.S. ships had been on an intelligence-gathering mission, which included sailing into North Vietnamese territorial waters to test Hanoi's coastal radar defenses.[3]

Although it would have been virtually impossible for the media to have uncovered that information in time to have had an impact on the congressional votes approving the Gulf of Tonkin Resolution— given the unseemly haste with which both chambers voted to give Johnson a blank check to use military force in Southeast Asia—even reasonably diligent digging by journalists might have debunked the administration's story in weeks or months rather than years. Compelling evidence that Johnson and his advisers had been less than honest with the American people might have, in turn, produced greater public skepticism (and realism) about Washington's Vietnam policy. The press, however, was too busy acting as cheerleader for the administration's actions.

That attitude changed very slowly. When CBS News produced a series of "Vietnam Perspectives" for broadcast in August 1965, the network invited numerous administration officials to participate— including Secretary of State Dean Rusk, Secretary of Defense Robert McNamara, National Security Adviser McGeorge Bundy, Gen. Maxwell Taylor, and U.S. ambassador to the United Nations Arthur Goldberg—but not a single critic of the war. CBS also gave the officials the opportunity to review and edit tapes of their comments before broadcast.[4] Such solicitude at the very least blurred the distinction between the press as independent observer and the press as a mouthpiece for the government.

Unfortunately, CBS's performance was all too typical of radio and television coverage of the early war effort. As J. Fred MacDonald observes,

134

> In the early years of the American slippage into the Vietnam
> War, television journalists failed to offer informed rebuttal
> or even healthy doubt when the government explained the
> imperatives for a military commitment in Southeast Asia.
> ... [T]here were no opposing voices urging a full exposure
> of the issues in Vietnam, a weighing of all sides, a full national
> debate of the advisability of the American actions, or an
> adherence to constitutional processes in the expanding mili-
> tary role of the United States in Southeast Asia.[5]

The media's credulous acceptance of Washington's explanations
did not decline greatly until the communist Tet offensive of January
1968 fatally undermined the Johnson administration's credibility—
and provoked a split within the American political elite. At the
beginning of 1968, when the *Boston Globe* surveyed editorial opinion
among 39 major newspapers with a combined circulation of 22 million, not 1 of those newspapers favored the withdrawal of U.S.
troops, although a few were becoming frustrated or disillusioned
with the progress of the war effort.[6] The retrospective myth that
there were numerous vocal media critics of U.S. policy before 1968
is just that, a myth. A more accurate assessment came at hearings
before the Senate Foreign Relations Committee in August 1966, when
Sen. J. William Fulbright (D-Ark.) mused, "It is very interesting that
so many of our prominent newspapers have become almost agents
or adjuncts of the government; that they do not contest or even raise
questions about government policy."[7]

Well-Intentioned Critics

The actions of the Saigon press corps must be viewed in the context
of such general media passivity. American military and diplomatic
leaders in Vietnam did not appreciate even well-motivated devia-
tions from the government's version of events. Browne, the Associated Press correspondent in Saigon, ran afoul of both U.S. and South
Vietnamese authorities in March 1962 when he sent a dispatch com-
plaining that U.S. officials had concealed the extent to which American servicemen were involved in combat operations. At that stage
of the U.S. intervention, U.S. military personnel were supposedly
in Vietnam solely as "advisers"—a fiction that Washington
attempted to maintain for another two years.[8] Indeed, American
officials in both Saigon and Washington went to great lengths to

highlight South Vietnamese military successes and to play down the U.S. role. That practice was formalized in a February 1962 directive (cable 1006) from the State Department to the mission in Saigon stressing that "it is not in our interest" to have stories "indicating that Americans are leading and directing combat missions against the Vietcong."[9] The Army's official history of media relations during the Vietnam War was quite candid about the principal reason for that directive: "By limiting the American public's knowledge about what was happening in South Vietnam, it would help defuse any adverse domestic reaction to U.S. risk-taking in Southeast Asia."[10]

Pursuant to cable 1006, Ambassador Frederick Nolting and his staff promptly classified most documents concerning the U.S. military role in South Vietnam. They also tried to exclude reporters (or more accurately to get the Saigon government to exclude them) from covering military operations in which the extent of the American combat role would be evident. Neither tactic worked particularly well. Indeed, such stonewalling was counterproductive. As historian Clarence Wyatt points out, reporters needed independent and reliable information, and when U.S. officials shut off the flow, enterprising journalists turned to the rank-and-file troops in the field. However, the closer one got to the action, "the farther one got from the official optimism of Washington and Saigon."[11] When correspondents became increasingly angry about the transparently false nature of official statements on the matter, the response of U.S. officials "was to claim that this deception on the American public was necessary, that the Communists had to be stopped . . . and to appeal to the correspondents' patriotism not to damage the national interest."[12] Such appeals had some impact, but they gradually became less and less effective.

The Kennedy administration responded to Browne's breach by redoubling efforts to reassert control over how the counterinsurgency mission in Vietnam was being portrayed. As it had in previous wars, the government recruited a respected journalist to help keep his colleagues in line. In this case, the State Department arranged for John Mecklin, *Time*'s bureau chief in San Francisco, to take a leave of absence for government service and sent him to Saigon to straighten out the "press mess." Mecklin was the perfect choice for collaborator. Indeed, he was so enthusiastic about the U.S. crusade to keep South Vietnam out of the clutches of international communism that he shared the government's perception that inquisitive reporters were undermining the war effort. "In Vietnam," he wrote later, "a major American policy was wrecked, in part, by unadorned reporting of what was going on."[13]

Mecklin was not the only newsman who collaborated with the government at the expense of the truth. So close was the cooperation back home that some editors and Washington correspondents became little more than boosters for the Kennedy administration's Vietnam policies. Phillip Knightley notes that the administration's seduction techniques were so effective that "many an editor, unable to reconcile what his man in Saigon was reporting with what his man in Washington told him, preferred to use the official version."[14] Thus even the cautious and well-meaning efforts of the Saigon press corps to report accurately what was going on in Vietnam were undermined. The media-administration collaboration reached its apogee in September 1963, when *Time* managing editor Otto Fuerbringer, a close friend of several high-ranking administration officials, orchestrated a piece attacking the competence and the veracity of the Saigon correspondents—including the magazine's own correspondent, Charles Mohr. David Halberstam made the scathing observation, "It read as if written by a high Pentagon PIO [public information officer]."[15]

The reasons for such a puff piece on Washington's Vietnam policy were not hard to discern. Part of the problem, as Halberstam observed, was that *Time*'s executives viewed their publication "not just as a magazine of reporting, but as an instrument of policy making. Thus, what *Time*'s editors *want* to happen is as important as what is happening. In Vietnam, where U.S. prestige was staked against a Communist enemy, and the government was Christian and anti-Communist, *Time* had a strong commitment to Diem."[16] That inclination was reinforced by the "old boy" network within Washington's political community. Thus, when the Kennedy administration sought assistance from its journalistic allies in discrediting the disturbing stories coming from the Saigon press corps about the Diem regime's corruption and incompetence and the impending failure of U.S. policy, it found a receptive audience in the editorial offices of *Time*. Indeed, *Time* publisher Henry Luce was unusually susceptible to Kennedy's blandishments. "He seduces me," Luce reportedly conceded on one occasion. "When I'm with him, I feel like a whore."[17]

The problem of co-option was hardly confined to the relationship between the Kennedy administration and one mass circulation news magazine. It had been typical of the press-government connection throughout the Cold War and would persist into the late 1960s. During an informal session with reporters in Saigon in the summer of 1965, Assistant Secretary of Defense for Public Affairs Arthur Sylvester expressed his disgust that critical dispatches about the war were being written "while American boys are dying out there." He then stated contemptuously, "I don't even have to talk to you people. I know how to deal with you through your editors and publishers back in the States."[18] Given the Fuerbringer incident and many similar episodes throughout the Cold War, it was no wonder that Sylvester believed the government could bring the Saigon press contingent to heel.

The Kennedy administration also enlisted the aid of highly respected reporters and special correspondents (including Joseph Alsop and other prominent figures from the World War II and early Cold War periods) to travel to Vietnam and file stories countering the negative impressions being created by the younger press representatives on the scene. With virtual unanimity, those visitors concluded that the war effort was going well, that Diem's government was solidly in control and committed to reform, and that Washington's cause was certain to prevail.[19] Alsop, for example, compared the Saigon press corps with journalists who had hailed Mao Zedong and Fidel Castro while criticizing Chiang Kaishek and Fulgencio Batista. He denounced the "reportorial crusade" against Diem, whom he described as "a courageous, quite viable national leader."[20] Six weeks later, that "viable" leader was overthrown by a military coup.

The irony of the government's campaign to discredit the Saigon press "rebels" was that most of those correspondents were in fact supporters of the war effort. They did not question either the wisdom or the morality of the U.S. intervention, merely whether it was effective. Halberstam, Sheehan, Mohr, and others who would later become heros to a growing anti-war faction disagreed primarily with the government over strategy and tactics—especially Washington's stubborn enthusiasm for the Diem government despite mounting evidence of the regime's corruption, brutality, and ineptitude. Mohr, for example, was somewhat chagrined when in the late 1960s anti-war groups cited his 1963 decision to resign from *Time* in protest of the magazine's diatribe against the "negative" treatment of the war by the Saigon press corps as an anti-war act. "Everyone thought I left because I was against the war. I just thought it wasn't working. I didn't come to think of it as immoral until the very end."[21]

Halberstam was even more hawkish. On the eve of the drastic escalation of the U.S. military involvement in Vietnam in 1964–65, he took an extremely dim view of any suggestion that the United States cut its losses and withdraw from Vietnam.

> What about withdrawal? Few Americans who have served in Vietnam can stomach this idea. It means that those Vietnamese who committed themselves fully to the United States will suffer the most under a Communist government, while we lucky few with blue passports retire unharmed; it means a drab, lifeless and controlled society for a people who deserve better. Withdrawal also means that the United States' prestige will be lowered throughout the world, and it means that the pressure of Communism on the rest of Southeast Asia will intensify. Lastly, withdrawal means that throughout the world the enemies of the West will be encouraged to try insurgencies like the one in Vietnam. Just as our commitment in Korea in 1950 has served to discourage overt Communist border crossings ever since, an anti-Communist victory in Vietnam would serve to discourage so-called wars of liberation.[22]

That defense of U.S. objectives in Vietnam could just as easily have been written by Lyndon Johnson, Dean Rusk, or Robert McNamara. The image of Halberstam and his Saigon colleagues as left-wing ideologues trying to promote a communist victory in Southeast Asia—or conversely as perceptive, early opponents of a disastrous war—was postdefeat historical revisionism at its most imaginative.

As Washington's policy in Vietnam turned increasingly sour, U.S. officials on the scene intensified their pressure on news personnel to promote the official version of events and cooperated with the Saigon government in censoring "negative" stories and preventing them from leaving the country. Halberstam noted "the almost psychotic preoccupation of Diem and his family with the Western press—the one element operating in Vietnam, other than the Vietcong, which they did not control."[23] One newsman later contended that getting such stories back to editors in the United States during the 1961–64 period "became a major smuggling operation." U.S.

officialdom's collaboration with the Saigon government's attempts to suppress hostile reports was especially pronounced during the period when Nolting served as ambassador. Nolting's attitude came through clearly when a white paper he commissioned on the role of the press concluded that American interests in Saigon were being hurt by "sensational" reporting. Halberstam also contended that Nolting "did his best to keep us from finding out anything which reflected on the [Diem] Government."[24] *New York Times* correspondent Homer Bigart observed ruefully in 1962, "Too often correspondents seem to be regarded by the American mission as tools of our foreign policy."[25] At least Bigart was aware of the problem, which is more than one could say for his colleagues during most of the Cold War.

The willingness of the U.S. embassy to support the Saigon government's censorship agenda decreased briefly when Henry Cabot Lodge replaced Nolting as ambassador in August 1963. Lodge preferred co-option to confrontation. Military historian William Hammond describes Lodge's method of operation. "Although officialdom's concern for putting the best possible face on the war grew as optimism faded in Washington, Lodge knew that repeated attempts to restrict the press could only cause more friction. He therefore took personal responsibility for the U.S. mission's dealings with the press, making the leak a prerogative of the ambassador and providing newsmen with the stories he wanted to see in print."[26] That more conciliatory strategy—eventually dubbed "Maximum Candor" by Lyndon Johnson's administration—was reinforced when Barry Zorthian replaced Mecklin as mission public affairs officer in January 1964. Nevertheless, such changes were merely a shift in the strategic mix. The overall goal of containing and deceiving the press did not change, nor did the use of stonewalling and censorship entirely abate. In fact, it surged again later in the decade when Washington gave its full support to the repressive regime of Nguyen Van Thieu.

Washington continued to pursue a two-pronged strategy for dealing with the "press problem" in Vietnam. Administration officials exerted pressure on newspaper and magazine editors to reassign troublesome correspondents, and that effort gradually paid off. By 1965–66 the Saigon press corps had become (temporarily) more acceptable to U.S. military officials. "Today there is no Halberstam

140

group," *Time* quoted one "relieved" Pentagon spokesman as say-ing.[27] Similarly, Adm. Ulysses G. Sharp, commander in chief, Pacific, informed the Joint Chiefs of Staff that although news reporting from South Vietnam remained "troublesome," it was hardly as unfavor-able as it had been in the past.[28] The government did not, however, entirely abandon efforts to appeal to the patriotism of correspon-dents. "When you speak to the American people," Vice President Hubert Humphrey urged reporters during a visit to Vietnam in 1967, "give the benefit of the doubt to our side. . . . We're in this together."[29]

Such appeals had only limited effectiveness, especially as the war dragged on with no victory in sight. Even less useful was the ongoing propaganda campaign of the military command and the Johnson administration. The State Department's celebrated white paper, released in late February 1965, purporting to prove that most of the communist fighters in South Vietnam were North Vietnamese infiltrators actually generated more skepticism in the media about the government's veracity, both in Saigon and back in the States.[30] The strategy of providing detailed briefings for reporters on the government's assessment of the war's progress, which would work so effectively in the 1990–91 Persian Gulf War, failed miserably in Vietnam. Journalists increasingly derided the daily briefings, which concentrated on the "body count" of enemy soldiers to measure how well the war was going, as the "Five O'Clock Follies." By the end of the 1960s the credibility of military spokesmen at those ses-sions approached absolute zero. Military officials never seemed to understand, then or later, why they lost credibility during the Viet-nam conflict. A long-time Pentagon press officer subsequently stated, apparently in all sincerity, "The major problem was not that military spokesmen consistently or deliberately falsified information, but, rather, that they sometimes withheld specific information that might be detrimental to a continuing belief in the eventual success of U.S. policy."[31] Aside from the point that sins of omission can be just as grievous as sins of commission, such attitudes ignored the fact that the Saigon press corps was no longer taken in by the military's deceptions.

A Growing Estrangement

Despite the Saigon command's best efforts to woo the press, the propaganda campaign repeatedly ran aground as actual develop-ments in Vietnam failed to match the government's optimistic por-trayals. As press criticism of the war effort mounted and became

more biting—especially following the Tet offensive in early 1968—
U.S. officials reacted with increasing petulance. Anger at the unprecedented lack of cooperation on the part of journalists began to reach
the boiling point.

Although government officials' animosity became especially
prominent after the Tet offensive, some manifestations of hostility
appeared long before. Adm. Harry D. Felt, commander of Pacific
forces, typified officials' long-standing intolerance of any sign of
criticism when he bristled at a probing question from Malcolm
Browne at a Saigon news conference in the early 1960s. "So you're
Browne," the admiral fumed. "Why don't you get on the team?"[32]
Felt's attitude echoed the comment of the Army's chief public relations officer in Korea reacting to an attempt by *New York Herald
Tribune* correspondent David McConnell to report that a B-26 had
bombed the truce-talks zone at Kaesong. "Don't you forget," the
officer warned, "which side you're on."[33]

Allegations of "disloyalty" also became more frequent as the
decade progressed. At a background briefing in November 1965,
Gen. William Westmoreland gave a blistering indictment of the
press coverage of the bloody battle in the Ia Drang Valley. Various
reporters, including Neil Sheehan, had filed reports stating that U.S.
casualties were higher than the military command had indicated and
that American troops as well as communist forces had committed
atrocities. Westmoreland affirmed that he had no intention of letting
the press jeopardize the U.S. effort in South Vietnam. It was revealing
that Westmoreland did not allege that the media reports had in any
way endangered the security of the Ia Drang operation or the lives
of U.S. soldiers. Instead, he accused correspondents of revealing
American mistakes and vulnerabilities, of discrediting the United
States in front of its allies, and of lowering the morale of both troops
in the field and their families back home.[34] In other words, anything
other than press accounts favorable to the U.S. war effort was a
manifestation of disloyalty and helping the enemy cause.

Westmoreland's tongue-lashing of critical reporters in South Vietnam was mild compared with the Pentagon's reaction to press
accounts from Western correspondents in North Vietnam. When
New York Times correspondent Harrison E. Salisbury went to Hanoi
to report in December 1966, Pentagon spokesmen began referring
to him as "Ho Chi Salisbury" and his employer as the *New Hanoi*

Times.[35] (A quarter century later CNN correspondent Peter Arnett—
an alumnus of the "disloyal" Vietnam press corps—received similar
opprobrium for reporting from Baghdad during the gulf war.) Some
criticism of Salisbury's performance was justified. He too readily
repeated Hanoi's contention that the U.S. B-52 bombing campaign
(Operation Rolling Thunder), begun earlier that year, deliberately
targeted civilian centers. Not only were some of his specific facts in
error, but some of his dispatches either repeated allegations from
North Vietnamese propaganda pamphlets without attribution or
failed to mention that the dispatches were subject to censorship.[36]

Nevertheless, even with the strictures of North Vietnam's suffocating censorship system, Salisbury's accounts had some validity.
Among other things, his reports revealed extensive damage to civilian neighborhoods and forced U.S. officials to admit that U.S. bombs
had struck civilian targets in North Vietnam, however inadvertently,
something Washington had vehemently denied before that time.[37]
Hammond notes that "the Johnson administration continually gave
ground on the reporter's allegations. While early in the controversy
official spokesmen would concede only grudgingly that American
bombs might have injured a relatively small number of civilians, by
its end they were admitting, for example, that during one strike on
the Yen Vien railroad yard three bombs had fallen on the target and
forty outside."[38] Although Salisbury's record did not fit perfectly
the anti-war movement's picture of him as an intrepid debunker of
American lies or the Pentagon's stereotype of him as a communist
dupe (or worse), it seemed much closer to the former. Furthermore,
one must ask whether a government that only grudgingly acknowledged embarrassing facts after they had emerged would ever have
released such information on its own.

Salisbury was not the only journalist subjected to allegations of
disloyalty. After the Tet offensive, Secretary of State Dean Rusk was
barraged by questions about the failure of U.S. intelligence agencies
to anticipate the ferocious communist attacks. Reporters also scoffed
at the contention of General Westmoreland and other military leaders that Tet was a great victory for U.S. and South Vietnamese forces
and a veritable catastrophe for the communists. Rusk lashed out at
his critics, especially ABC newsman John Scali, who had disputed
such sanguine conclusions. "There gets to be a point," Rusk stated,
"when the question is, whose side are you on?"[39]

Scali later recalled his reaction to the accusation. "I got angry. I got out of my chair. I was going to hit him in the nose. But two reporters restrained me."[40] An episode in which the secretary of state implied that a prominent mainstream journalist was a traitor and the journalist had to be kept from slugging the secretary was a perfect symbol of the deteriorating relationship between the press and the government.

The incident also illustrated the conflicting institutional perspectives of members of the national security bureaucracy and news professionals—if the latter are doing their jobs. More than two decades later, Rusk was asked if his question of Scali had been fair and would it be appropriate to ask a similar question of journalists in connection with the Persian Gulf War. Rusk replied, "I think it's a question news people should ask themselves occasionally. . . . There's not going to be a television network if there's not a United States of America." Bill Monroe observed, "Here in its nakedness was the thinking that sprang the blunt question. Rusk saw himself as the nation incarnate struggling against Communist aggression. He saw Scali as loyal only to his network."[41] Monroe's assessment was correct—as far as it went. But it missed the more significant point that national security officials tend to see every perceived foreign policy "crisis" as threatening the nation's existence. It was nonsense to suppose that if the United States did not prevail in Vietnam, the Republic would be in danger of extinction, but that was how Rusk and many other policymakers exaggerated the stakes. Given that attitude, it was not surprising that they viewed journalistic criticism of Washington's policy as verging on treason.

The Tet offensive, which began on January 30, 1968, was a watershed event not only in overall U.S. policy in Vietnam but for the growing estrangement between the government and the news media.[42] Criticism of Washington's conduct of the war by American journalists in both South Vietnam and the United States soared. The reaction of civilian and military officials was a combination of defensiveness and animosity. Indicative of the military command's attitude toward the press was a comment by Gen. Creighton Abrams, who had served as Westmoreland's deputy and then replaced him in July 1968. "Gentlemen, we had a very sad thing happen this week," Abrams told his commanders and staff officers at a meeting.

> The finest division commander that we've ever had in Viet-
> nam made a mistake. That fine division commander had a

friend and that friend was a member of the press. . . . He confided in that friend, and the next day he found himself in the headlines. That commander has been embarrassed and this command has been embarrassed, and gentlemen, with regard to the press, that magnificent commander forgot just one thing: THEY'RE ALL A BUNCH OF SHITS.[43]

Unabashed supporters of the Vietnam intervention still emphasize that Tet was a military failure for communist forces, since all of the territory they seized during the early phases was later retaken by U.S. or South Vietnamese troops and Hanoi's Vietcong cadres were virtually destroyed as a viable military force. The left-leaning news media supposedly brainwashed the American public into believing that an allied victory was in fact a serious defeat. That myth is tenacious. Writing in 1992, syndicated columnist Harry Summers still berated the press coverage. "One would never know from the reporting on the Tet Offensive, for example, that the Viet Cong were so decisively defeated that for the remaining seven years of the war they played almost no part whatsoever. That's the kind of black-is-white 'Vietnam syndrome' [war opponents] would like to perpetuate." Media treatment of the Tet offensive, Summers fumed, was a case in which "'journalists' succeeded not only in turning a battle-field victory into a defeat but in overthrowing the government as well."[44]

The tone for the "stab-in-the-back" historical revisionism was set early on by Lyndon Johnson in his memoirs.

There was a great deal of emotional and exaggerated report-ing of the Tet offensive in our press and on television. The media seemed to be in competition as to who could provide the most lurid and depressing accounts. Columnists unsym-pathetic to American involvement in Southeast Asia jumped on the bandwagon. . . . The American people and even a number of officials in government, subjected to this daily barrage of bleakness and near panic, began to think that we must have suffered a defeat.[45]

Blaming the media for the subsequent decline in public support for the war effort may offer some comfort to those who persist in believing that the Vietnam intervention was a wise policy, but the "media guilt" theme is an illusion. Tet was indeed a military defeat

145

so hedged with official optimism that even the Johnson administration was unprepared for the broad extent and violence of the attack that developed."[51]

Much of the mainstream press responded favorably to the government's propaganda barrage in the final months of 1967. An article by Orr Kelly of the *Washington Star* with the headline "In a Military Sense, the War Is Just About Won," captured the extent of expectations. Similarly, the *Philadelphia Inquirer*'s Bob Considine told critics of administration policy to "stop griping. We're winning this lousy war. It is not, repeat not, a stalemate."[52] Having conducted a vigorous public relations offensive to sell the view that the war effort was going well, the administration could not justifiably complain about the subsequent press and public disillusionment when it became clear that such optimism was, at the very least, excessive.

The massive, well-coordinated nature of the Tet offensive—with communist forces striking simultaneously at dozens of objectives throughout South Vietnam—completely discredited the administration's rosy scenario. Communist units attacked 36 of South Vietnam's 44 provincial capitals, 5 of the 6 largest cities, and approximately one-fourth of the 242 district capitals. The television footage of communist forces overrunning much of the city of Hue and of Vietcong sappers penetrating the U.S. embassy compound in downtown Saigon was a dose of sobering reality.

It was apparent to all except the most obtuse that victory was not just beyond the horizon. The unavoidable implication of the Tet offensive was that America was entangled in a conflict that was proving far more bloody and prolonged than anyone had anticipated.[53] Doubts about the wisdom of Washington's Vietnam strategy, to this point held only by an ineffectual minority of Americans, began to spread. For the first time rumbles of criticism in Congress were heard beyond the small circle of doves. Six years had passed since the first U.S. military advisers had been sent to Vietnam, and three and a half years had passed since the Gulf of Tonkin episode marked the sharp escalation of Washington's military effort, yet the United States seemed no closer to victory. It was not surprising that frustration and war weariness were setting in.

The news media reflected more than shaped that change in sentiment. Indeed, Tet represented a rude awakening for a journalistic community that had generally supported the war effort, however much it might criticize specific aspects of the strategy. CBS anchor Walter Cronkite's reaction when he saw the first bulletins—"What the hell is going on? I thought we were winning the war"—captured the response of the domestic press corps to Tet.[54] Similarly, a *New York Times* editorial contended that "these were not the deeds of an enemy whose fighting efficiency has 'progressively declined' and whose morale 'is sinking fast,' as United States military officials put it in November."[55] The *New Republic* concluded bitterly, "A year before, President Johnson had said that the enemy was losing his grip on South Vietnam. With Tet, that prophecy seemed as broken as the policy it served."[56] A growing number of reporters and editors began to reassess their own assumptions about the Vietnam intervention, and that process was accompanied by a mounting suspicion that U.S. policymakers were either incompetent or deceitful. As Peter Braestrup noted in his exhaustive treatment of the media's response to the Tet offensive, the response of many journalists—especially those in Washington—was "to indulge in retribution for prior manipulation by the administration."[57]

The new confrontational posture became even more pronounced during the Nixon years, as press coverage of U.S. actions in Vietnam and the rest of Southeast Asia became openly hostile. In addition to presenting Washington's conduct in a less than flattering light, reporters routinely disclosed details of top-secret operations, such as the bombing of Cambodia that commenced in the spring of 1969. Such investigative journalism would have been unthinkable earlier in the Cold War. The Nixon administration railed against the revelation of such secrets, contending that irresponsible journalists were aiding the enemy cause and jeopardizing the lives of American military personnel.[58]

But the bombing of Cambodia illustrated the fallacy of such arguments. Who exactly did not know that U.S. planes were bombing communist positions inside Cambodia? The North Vietnamese undoubtedly knew, since their forces were the targets. And if Hanoi knew, it was a certainty that the information was passed along to Beijing and Moscow. The Cambodian government was aware—a point that even administration spokesmen subsequently conceded. The only parties who had been kept blissfully ignorant of the U.S. operation were Congress and the American people.[59] Nixon candidly admitted his motive for keeping the attacks secret: "We wanted to avoid the domestic uproar that might result from a publicized air strike."[60] According to Nixon's national security adviser, Henry Kissinger, Secretary of Defense Melvin Laird had opposed the bombing mission for fear that it could not be kept secret. "The press would be difficult to handle, and public support could not be guaranteed," he had warned. Laird's caution drew a snide rebuke from Kissinger: "It was symptomatic of the prevalent mood of hesitation, the fear to wake the dormant beast of public protest."[61]

The arrogant elitism expressed by Nixon and Kissinger was disturbing, albeit all too typical. If one takes democratic accountability seriously, the American people had every right to know about the administration's actions in Cambodia, and the press performed a public service by enlightening them.

Nevertheless, Nixon and his advisers bitterly resented such revelations since they interfered with the administration's ability to pursue the war in Southeast Asia free from the monitoring of an increasingly hostile Congress and public. Administration leaders came to regard the press as an avowed adversary on foreign policy matters, and that perception was not incorrect. As the government's effort to co-opt the press rapidly lost effectiveness, officials placed greater emphasis on more confrontational techniques. In Vietnam during 1970 and 1971, Operation Maximum Candor was moribund as the U.S. military command became increasingly surly. Official American sources virtually shut their doors to reporters, and even field sources became less cooperative. Correspondents reported cases in which officers refused to let their troops speak to reporters or even to provide them accommodations.[62] At home, the changing attitude led to a proliferation of attacks on the patriotism of critics and to intensified surveillance of government employees who might be leaking embarrassing information and of journalists who received and published such disclosures.

Why the Absence of Formal Censorship?

The one puzzling aspect of the press policies pursued by the Kennedy, Johnson, and Nixon administrations in Vietnam was their failure to impose a rigorous censorship system. It may have been simply a miscalculation—a belief that the government's propaganda apparatus was so effective that it would drown out contrary information and analyses and would even win over skeptical war correspondents. Col. David R. Kiernan, a Pentagon public affairs officer, later speculated, "Perhaps it was realized too late that wars are not only fought on the battlefield, but also psychologically in the published articles that influenced the morale of the nation involved in the conflict."[63]

Officials did consider censorship. In February 1965, at the start of the introduction of large numbers of U.S. ground troops, General Westmoreland recommended that formal censorship be instituted to protect military security. The U.S. military command also restricted the access of reporters to certain installations, most notably the air base at Da Nang, and required that the reporters given access be accompanied by military escorts at all times. Associated Press managing editor Wes Gallagher denounced the latter measure. "Providing an 'escort' for every correspondent," he said, "is clearly aimed not at security matters but at controlling what American fighting men might say."[64] The contrast between the resistance of Gallagher and his colleagues to such government restrictions and the acquiescence of much of the news media to identical Pentagon requirements during the Persian Gulf War is revealing and depressing.

A three-day conference was convened in March in Honolulu by representatives of the State and Defense Departments to evaluate Westmoreland's censorship proposal and to determine whether more stringent procedures for managing press coverage of the war were warranted. The conference concluded that such a system would probably be unworkable, and the representatives recommended against making the attempt.

Their reasoning was quite interesting as well as naive. They concluded that in the absence of a congressional declaration of war, military commanders in Vietnam would lack the legal authority to impose censorship. They also argued that the military lacked the control over transportation and communications necessary to enforce a censorship system. Finally, they feared that controlling the flow of news would reawaken suspicions, kindled during the U-2 spy plane incident and the early phase of Washington's Vietnam intervention, that the government was trying to conceal information from the public.[65]

That was clearly a more innocent age than its successor. Executive branch leaders did not let constitutional technicalities about a declaration of war deter them from censoring and otherwise suppressing the news media in Grenada, Panama, or the Persian Gulf. They also discovered that it was relatively easy for the military command to control transportation and communications, thus placing reporters at the Pentagon's mercy for logistics. And they did not worry unduly about public suspicions of a cover-up. Instead, they replaced independent news coverage with a blizzard of government-generated propaganda, confident that a majority of the public would accept official accounts as accurate. Policymakers also calculated (correctly as it turned out) that in the name of patriotism and national security the public would support censorship or even outright exclusion of the media from military operations. In retrospect, the great surprise is that executive branch leaders during the Vietnam era did not realize their potential power to control information.

Washington flirted with imposing formal censorship on at least two other occasions. President Johnson was clearly not pleased with the conclusions of the Honolulu conference. Two months later he directed Defense Department officials to reevaluate the censorship option. The new report, however, largely restated the objections that the conferees at Honolulu had mentioned. Later in 1965 the Department of Defense, at the direction of Arthur Sylvester, commissioned several reports on the subject. The last one was completed in August 1966 by Gen. Winant Sidle, who would later head the commission that came up with the press pool concept after the exclusion of all news personnel from covering the invasion of Grenada (see chapter 7). Sidle's report included a censorship plan so cumbersome that it was virtually certain never to be adopted. That was apparently the last time a formal censorship system for the Vietnam War was seriously considered.[66]

Whatever the underlying reason for inaction, the government continued to give reporters unprecedented (and largely unsupervised) access to combat zones. The military even supplied much of the transportation. The only major exception occurred during the invasion of Cambodia in the spring of 1970, when Washington insisted that South Vietnam was in charge of the operation, and reporters had to ask Saigon for logistical help. Not surprisingly, the Thieu government was not about to assist American reporters, many of whom the regime regarded as little more than communist propagandists. That obstructionism did not prove terribly effective. Correspondents simply got whatever vehicles they could—from jeeps to motorcycles—and rode to the front.[67]

Granting liberal access to combat zones and failing to impose censorship was a foolish policy from the standpoint of the government's interests. "The [Johnson] administration's policy proved self-defeating," concludes Phillip Knightley. "By making every facet of the war unusually accessible to any correspondent who turned up in Saigon, it lost control of the situation. When there were eventually nearly 700 war correspondents in South Vietnam, it became inevitable that some of them would refuse to accept the official line at face value and would get out into the field to see things for themselves."[68] All any correspondent needed was a letter from a newspaper requesting accreditation (freelance journalists needed two letters) and to sign an agreement to abide by 15 "ground rules," virtually all dealing with narrow aspects of military security.[69]

Although the lack of restrictions on the press in the Vietnam War may have been galling to military officials, there is no evidence that the system compromised the security of military operations. Admiral Sharp, Admiral Felt's successor, conceded at the height of the war that "sensationalized reporting" and "premature revelations" that so worried Lyndon Johnson had done nothing to affect the security of U.S. forces in South Vietnam.[70]

Letting the government decide what should be published about Washington's Vietnam intervention would almost assuredly have created a worse situation for the American public. Certainly on those occasions when the Pentagon did have control over the release of information, the results were disturbing. For example, the initial story of the My Lai massacre, put out by the Pentagon, had hailed it as a great military victory. A front-page *New York Times* story on March 17, 1968, proclaimed that U.S. forces in a successful "pincer movement" against communist forces had killed 128 enemy soldiers. The information was attributed to the "American headquarters in Saigon."[71] Although the true story of the My Lai massacre was not broken by reporters in Vietnam—it was revealed after diligent digging by freelance journalist Seymour Hersh and others in the United States—there is little doubt that the Pentagon's news managers would have suppressed the story had they been able to.[72] The kind of stifling information control system in place during the U.S. invasions of Grenada and Panama, and the even more comprehensive version in the Persian Gulf War, would have made it less likely that the media could ever have uncovered the truth.

Perhaps more important, the press overall gave a more accurate depiction of the situation in Vietnam than did the U.S. government. The military command in Saigon and officials in Washington repeatedly insisted that journalists conveyed an excessively defeatist image of the war, but such allegations had little validity. The communist forces proved to be far more resilient than U.S. leaders anticipated; the ARVN frequently failed to fight in a dedicated or competent manner; the Saigon government was—despite U.S. propaganda about its democratic credentials—both corrupt and authoritarian; and most significant, the prospect of a definitive American victory was remote at best. Journalists did not invent those facts; they merely reported them. Even the U.S. Army's official history of media coverage in Vietnam concluded that it was "undeniable" that press reports were "often more accurate than the public statements of the administration in portraying the situation in Vietnam."[73] When American officials criticized the press for undermining the war effort, they were blaming the messenger for the message.

The Myth That the Media Lost the War

The Johnson and Nixon administrations—as well as their successors—were convinced that graphic television coverage had strengthened anti-war sentiment. Military leaders shared that view. A survey of 100 senior officers who served in Vietnam found that only 4 percent believed that the public had benefited from such coverage; 91 percent believed that television coverage of the war was "not a good thing," primarily because it was too sensationalistic or presented events "out of context."[74]

The notion that viewers had been saturated with "graphic" television coverage was exaggerated. William Hammond points out that the American public "although treated nightly" to scenes of men in battle "rarely, if ever, before 1968 and the Tet offensive saw the war in all its bloody detail."[75] Even then the combat footage was usually less graphic than the fare that television audiences had come to expect in their favorite fictional dramas. According to media critic Michael Arlen, the version of the war telecast into American living rooms was "a generally distanced view" of a disjointed conflict "composed mainly of scenes of helicopters landing, tall grasses blowing in the helicopter wind, American soldiers fanning out across a hillside on foot, rifles at the ready, with now and then (on the sound track) a far-off ping or two, and now and then (as the visual grand finale) a column of dark, billowing smoke a half mile away, invariably described as a burning Viet Cong ammo dump."[76] Indeed, from August 1965 to August 1970—the period of the most ferocious fighting—only 76 of more than 2,300 television news reports from Vietnam clearly depicted the terror and horrors of combat—especially scenes of dead and wounded on the battlefield.[77] Even then the scenes were usually of enemy, not American, dead. The belief that television brought a massive quantity of bloody combat footage into American living rooms and thereby undermined Washington's war effort is one of the most tenacious but inaccurate aspects of the stab-in-the-back myth.

Moreover, the military hierarchy's anger at criticism of U.S. policy extended to print journalists as well. Air Force Gen. Milton B. Adams declared in an official debriefing that the policy that required official tolerance of news personnel was the only significant source of frustration that he had encountered during his tour of duty in Vietnam.[78] Such hostility toward journalists was not confined to a few high-ranking officers. Georgetown University professor Loren B. Thompson describes the impact of the Vietnam experience on the attitude of the junior officer corps, as well as that of the military hierarchy, toward the media.

> Vietnam was a severe trauma for the U.S. military, one from which it would not recover for many years. In the search for explanations, many military officers concluded that the frequently critical coverage of the war effort had been an important factor in bringing about the U.S. defeat. By questioning government policies in Vietnam and highlighting the worst aspects of American involvement, it was argued, the media made it impossible to maintain public support for the war.[79]

The most revealing aspect of the officer corps' reaction is that the objection to press coverage had nothing to do with protecting the security of military operations—the principal official justification for all the censorship schemes that would be implemented in the 1980s and early 1990s. Instead, the worry was that independent media scrutiny of military operations had jeopardized the government's *policy* objectives.

More than any other factor, the perception that the media had undermined the war effort made military and civilian leaders determined to never again allow the kind of unrestricted press coverage that characterized the Vietnam War. Ironically, there is reason to doubt the conventional view that the media played a decisive role in reducing public support for the war. A 1967 *Newsweek* survey found that graphic coverage—such as it was—actually tended to make viewers *more* supportive of the war effort.[80] A more detailed study of public opinion trends by University of Rochester professor John E. Mueller suggested that casualty rates had a much greater impact on negative attitudes toward the war than did any aspect of media coverage, including explicit television scenes. Mueller noted that rising casualties in the stalemated Korean conflict had produced similar responses in public opinion despite the absence of such footage.

> [The] amount of *vocal* opposition to the war in Vietnam was vastly greater than that for the war in Korea. Yet it has now been found that support for the wars among the general public followed a pattern of decline that was remarkably similar. Although support for the war in Vietnam did finally drop below those levels found during Korea, it did so only after the war had gone on considerably longer and only after American casualties had far surpassed those of the earlier war.[81]

But most journalists and government officials (both at home and abroad) accepted the view that negative media images of the Vietnam conflict had contributed to public pressure for withdrawal. William Small, director of CBS television in Washington, wrote, "When television covered its 'first war' in Vietnam it showed a terrible truth of war in a manner new to mass audiences. A case can be made, and it certainly should be examined, that this was cardinal to the disillusionment of Americans with this war, the cynicism of many young people towards America, and the destruction of Lyndon Johnson's tenure of office."[82] BBC commentator Robin Day concluded that the coverage had made Americans substantially more anti-militarist and anti-war: "One wonders if in future a democracy which had uninhibited television coverage in every home will ever be able to fight a war, however just."[83] The director of defence operations at the British Ministry of Defence, Brig. Gen.

F. G. Caldwell, mused that in light of the Vietnam experience, if Britain went to war again, "we would have to start saying to ourselves, are we going to let the television cameras loose on the battlefield?"[84] The British government's answer to that question came in 1982 during the Falklands War, and the U.S. government's response came a year later during the invasion of Grenada.

7. The Bureaucracy's Revenge: Learning from the Vietnam Experience

The myth that hostile and unfair media coverage had been a major cause of the U.S. defeat in Vietnam festered throughout the 1970s and early 1980s. Members of the military hierarchy, as well as conservative political figures, were determined that journalists would never again undermine a U.S. war effort. Government officials had little opportunity to exact revenge in the immediate post–Vietnam War period, however. The abuses of power associated with the Watergate scandal caused the reputation and influence of the national security bureaucracy to fall to their nadir, and the policies pursued by President Jimmy Carter's administration were not generally conducive to bold new moves against the media. That situation changed dramatically after Carter's 1980 defeat in the growing atmosphere of tension between the United States and the Soviet Union. The opportunity for revenge had arrived at last.

During the presidency of Ronald Reagan, attempts to intimidate the press or deny coverage of controversial foreign policy actions increased. Indicative of the administration's aggressiveness was its treatment of the news media during the October 1983 invasion of Grenada. When U.S. troops, along with token paramilitary units from the Organization of Eastern Caribbean States, went ashore on the morning of October 25, there was no press coverage whatsoever.

Setting the Precedent: The Grenada News Blackout

A 1985 Twentieth Century Fund report on the military and the media noted that the "government's failure, at the outset, to allow an independent flow of information to the public about a major military operation was unprecedented in modern American history."[1] Not only did Washington exclude reporters from covering the initial stages of the invasion, it prevented news representatives from coming to the island for more than 48 hours. Television camera crews were excluded for an additional two days, apparently a reflection of the government's post–Vietnam War hypersensitivity to the consequences of having combat footage televised into American living rooms. Indeed, the Pentagon resorted to unprecedented measures to prevent eyewitness coverage. Enterprising journalists who chartered private boats from nearby Caribbean countries found themselves turned away by U.S. naval patrols. In at least one such incident, military personnel made it quite evident that they would use force to maintain the exclusion zone. A radio and television crew from ABC was intercepted at sea in a vessel they had chartered in Barbados to take them to Grenada. A U.S. jet dropped a buoy with a message warning them to go back to Barbados. When they failed to respond, the jet proceeded to make mock strafing runs with its bomb doors open.[2]

On another occasion, a group of journalists who succeeded in chartering a plane and landing it at Pearls airport on Grenada were taken into custody by U.S. military police and ordered to return to Barbados. *Washington Post* correspondent Edward Cody and three other reporters, who had successfully chartered a fishing boat in Barbados and landed in Grenada, had a similar experience. Military personnel took them to the USS *Guam* when they attempted to file their stories and proceeded to hold them there; they were under constant surveillance for several hours and not allowed to contact their home offices.[3] Rear Adm. Joseph Metcalf, commander of the U.S. naval task force, warned reporters against any independent action even as late as October 30—some five days after the start of the invasion.

> Any of you guys coming in on press boats? Well, I know how to stop those press boats. We've been shooting at them. We haven't sunk any yet, but who are we to know who's on them.[4]

When reporters were finally admitted to Grenada, they were restricted to carefully conducted military tours. And the military was quick to retaliate for any violation of the ground rules it had established. For example, when a *Newsweek* photographer left his tour group, military authorities promptly barred any further press trips to the island by the magazine's personnel.[5]

The Reagan administration's rationale for banning press coverage of Operation Urgent Fury was transparently disingenuous. Secretary of Defense Caspar Weinberger, Deputy Secretary of State Kenneth W. Dam, and other spokesmen insisted that the action was taken to ensure the secrecy of the operation and to "protect" journalists. Given the certainty of combat on Grenada, they stated, it would have been impossible to guarantee the safety of reporters.[6] Media representatives scoffed at both justifications. They noted that Soviet spy satellites had certainly tracked the invasion force for more than 24 hours, and unless Moscow was uncharacteristically negligent, that information had been forwarded to officials in Cuba and Grenada. Moreover, once troops started going ashore, the issue of secrecy was obviously moot. Yet reporters were excluded long after the fighting had commenced.

On the second point, members of the media retorted that no one had ever asked the government to guarantee the safety of news personnel operating in war zones and that the government had never before contended that it had that responsibility. They also reminded the administration that reporters had covered combat operations in both world wars, Korea, and Vietnam, as well as more recent hot spots such as Lebanon.[7] There was, of course, a certain measure of danger, and journalists occasionally perished; it was a risk that went with the job, and one that news professionals accepted. It was patently absurd to contend that the invasion of Grenada was more dangerous than previous, much larger, wars or that the latest generation of reporters was incapable of assuming the attendant risks. The "safety" justification also failed to explain why the military command prevented journalists who were already on the island from filing stories.[8]

A more credible reason for the exclusion was the administration's fear that there would be critical, even hostile, press accounts of the invasion. High-ranking military leaders still fumed about the conduct of the media during the Vietnam conflict, believing that many of the stories had been slanted and unfair to the U.S. war effort. Several Pentagon spokesmen even implied that certain reporters had been disloyal and had given aid and comfort to the North Vietnamese.

Top civilian leaders, including Secretary of State George Shultz, Weinberger, and Reagan shared that perception. Shultz observed on one occasion that reporters went along with the troops in World War II because in those days the media were on "our side." The apparent implication was that in subsequent conflicts they were on the enemy's side, or were at least agnostic about the U.S. cause. President Reagan employed the same innuendo when challenged by ABC News's Sam Donaldson at a December 20, 1983, press conference to clarify the statement made by his secretary of state. Reagan replied that, beginning with the Korean conflict and "certainly" in Vietnam, the media were no longer on "our side, militarily."[9] Journalist I. F. Stone observed of that statement,

> No one can shoot poisoned arrows more amiably than Mr. Reagan. He has a genius for the subliminal slur. . . . This was in effect saying that if the media are not "on our side, militarily" why should they go along with the troops? The phrasing implies treason.[10]

Many of the president's political allies shared his hostility toward the press and entertained similar suspicions about its loyalty. Reed Irvine, the head of Accuracy in Media, strongly endorsed the decision to exclude journalists from covering the Grenada invasion. His reasoning was most revealing. Anti-Reagan elements in the press, he insisted, were upset only because they had been prevented from filing stories that would have portrayed the "liberation" of Grenada in an unfavorable way. The administration, Irvine concluded, had been right to prevent the spread of such false accounts. Accuracy in Media even began distributing bumper stickers with the message "GRENADA: MEDIA DEFEAT."[11]

Gen. Norman Schwarzkopf, deputy commander of the invasion force, recalled in his autobiography that the command agreed to let the press onto the island at five o'clock on the second day of the invasion, "because by then Grenada would be ours."[12] In other words, it would then be a moot point if journalists wanted to undermine public support for the operation.

The government's mistrust of journalists was evident in other actions taken during the Grenada operation. For example, when ABC News reporters on Barbados spotted a massive influx of U.S. Navy planes and helicopters on October 24, in what was obviously a staging operation for an invasion of Grenada, and relayed that information to network headquarters, Pentagon, State Department, and White House officials "waved off" ABC from the story. The way in which the administration did that was revealing. There were good military reasons for trying to discourage the network from announcing that the invasion was under way; premature disclosure could have increased the number of U.S. casualties (although, in truth, Grenadian leaders would have had to have been utterly obtuse to not have known an invasion was imminent). Even the reporter in Barbados, Mark Potter, conceded that he could have accepted a network decision that said, "We're not going to run [the report] because we're afraid someone will get hurt if we broadcast this information."[13] But instead of asking ABC correspondents in Washington to delay the story for a few hours to protect the safety of the military operation—as the Kennedy administration had asked the *New York Times* to do shortly before the Bay of Pigs invasion, for example—the Reagan administration pursued a strategy of denial and outright disinformation. (It pursued similar tactics with other journalists who confronted it about rumors of impending military action.)

Interestingly, despite the Pentagon's perception that the journalistic community was filled with radical members of a "blame America first" crowd, ABC accepted the government's lies and rejected the assessment of its own people on Barbados. Commenting on the incident, investigative journalist Mark Hertsgaard concluded, "For all its world-weary cynicism about politics, the U.S. press displayed more often than it cared to admit a remarkable tendency to accept the basic truth of what its government told it."[14] With the exception of the final years of the Vietnam War, that was, in fact, the norm throughout the Cold War era. Nevertheless, the Vietnam aberration had left political scars, and the government's attitude was now clearly that the press was an enemy that had to be deceived and neutralized.

In its treatment of the press during the Grenada invasion, the Reagan administration translated into policy the preferences that key Pentagon elements had harbored since Vietnam. The nature of those preferences and prejudices emerged clearly in early 1984 during an interview with one of the architects of America's Vietnam policy, Gen. Maxwell Taylor. Years earlier Taylor had implied that the Vietnam War could have been won if only the media had been kept away.[15] Taylor had not altered his views, affirming that he "did not regret" the press exclusion from Grenada. Although he stated that the American people have a right to know what the nation's armed forces are doing, he stressed that information about military operations should be given "not today, not tomorrow, but at the appropriate time." When asked who decides the right time for the press to inform the nation about a military intervention, Taylor unhesitatingly replied, "It should be the President of the United States."[16]

The general's bitterness about media coverage was still evident. "In World War II, the press was admirable because they felt they were American citizens and that their country was sacred. In Vietnam there was the feeling on the part of some of the press that their task was to destroy the American command and to work against what was being done." He added ominously, "That kind of thing should not be tolerated."[17]

Taylor's comments also implied something more than fear that the media might be hostile. Military leaders believed that the sheer magnitude of coverage during the Vietnam conflict—especially the television images of combat that brought its horrors into American living rooms—had eroded public support for the U.S. war effort. Again, Taylor reflected the attitude of his fellow officers when he stated that information given to the American people about a military enterprise must be packaged properly. "If they get the information in a block," he stated, "they might well know what to do with it, but when they get it piecemeal, there's just confusion."[18] In other words, Taylor wanted the president and his subordinates to determine not only when information would be released but also what form it would take. The most charitable assessment one can make of his formulation is that it would severely weaken the First Amendment as it applies to press coverage of military interventions by the United States.

The administration achieved Taylor's first goal with respect to the Grenada invasion, and it took the first steps toward attaining the second goal. In Grenada the interventionists applied one important lesson they had learned in Vietnam. As Stone observed, "The most luscious dream of the Joint Chiefs must be an antiseptic surgical strike with no television cameras or reporters snooping around until the triumphal march up Pennsylvania Avenue."[19]

Learning from the Mother Country: The Falklands War

U.S. leaders also noted the successful British restraints on media coverage of the Falkland Islands campaign in 1982 when the government of Prime Minister Margaret Thatcher severely restricted press access. A mere 29 correspondents, photographers, and technicians were placed in media pools and distributed among several British warships. Officials cited the remoteness of the Falklands as a reason for the arrangement, noting that it was not feasible for reporters to reach the islands on their own and that the British navy could scarcely transport every correspondent who might want to cover the action. It was clear, however, that London also had other motives. The pool arrangement made it possible for the government to exclude excessively critical or inquisitive journalists, and the confinement of reporters to warships made it easy to control their movements. Indeed, the media pools managed to cover little of combat operations. Limiting access in such a drastic fashion did not fully satisfy the Thatcher government, however. The pool correspondents were also subjected to strict military censorship of the meager dispatches they were able to file.

As noted in chapter 4, such pertinent information as the actual circumstances of the sinking of the Argentine cruiser *General Belgrano* was concealed from the public. Other reports of suppressed information—including evidence that British forces may have summarily executed Argentine soldiers who had surrendered—have begun to surface a decade later.[20] Military leaders repeatedly fed reporters false information as part of a campaign of "strategic deception" directed against the Argentine government. The obvious problem, of course, was that Argentine officials were not the only ones deceived; the British public was gulled as well. Such consequences inevitably flow from government censorship and manipulation of the media.

There is little doubt that U.S. civilian and military leaders watched the British performance with avid interest and drew important lessons. A press aide to President Reagan later admitted that there "were a lot of discussions by White House people about what the British had done in the Falklands."[21] Indeed, U.S. officials seemed to regard the Falklands operation as a possible model for controlling the press in wartime. One of the first individuals to reach that conclusion—albeit with some criticism of specific British actions—was

Arthur A. Humphries, a public affairs specialist for the U.S. Navy. Writing in the May–June 1983 issue of *Naval War College Review*, Humphries argued that "in spite of the perception of choice in a democratic society, the Falklands War shows us how to make certain that government policy is not undermined by the way a war is reported."[22]

He noted that, given the capabilities of modern communications, "there was the potential in the South Atlantic to show the folks back home a vivid, real-life, real-time picture of men from two opposing nations on two ordinary and theretofore unimportant islands doing some very permanent, ugly things to each other."[23] But the British did not allow that to happen. Their strategy and the eventual results contrasted sharply and favorably with the more permissive U.S. policy in Vietnam. Humphries clearly subscribed to the theory that graphic (even when not overtly hostile) media coverage of Vietnam combat eventually weakened public support for the commitment to South Vietnam. "When relatives of servicemen see their boy, or someone who could be their boy, wounded or maimed, in living color, through imagery right in front of them, that tends to erode their support for the government's war aims. That happened during the Vietnam war."[24]

Humphries then asked, "What can a government do about that sort of problem, given the factors of high-tech communications capabilities and worldwide public attuned to freedom of information?" The answer was a multipronged strategy: "control access to the fighting, invoke censorship, and rally aid in the form of patriotism at home and in the battle zone."[25] Although Humphries acknowledged, "It is vital that no government seeks, in its urgent need to prosecute a war successfully, to insulate itself from the process of public accountability," other portions of his analysis ran counter to that pious objective. Using rhetoric reminiscent of George Orwell's *1984*, Humphries stated that the government's goal should be to assure "favorable objectivity." He was blunt and cynical about how to achieve that result, insisting that "you must be able to exclude certain correspondents from the battle zone." He also favorably quoted a British correspondent from World War II: "Objectivity can come back into fashion when the shooting is over."[26]

Although he admired much of the British media strategy in the Falklands conflict, Humphries was critical of some aspects. In particular, he regarded British censorship methods as "heavy-handed" and criticized military authorities for not supplying reporters with enough information. "Few people at the Ministry of Defence seemed to appreciate that news management is more than just information security censorship. It also means providing pictures."[27] He specifically chided the ministry for failing to hold background briefings during crucial phases of the operation and urged U.S. officials not to make that mistake. "It is essential that a government and its military branch give regular briefings to representatives of all news organizations, as practicable, in order to sustain a relationship of trust, to foster the flow of correct information, and to halt faulty speculation." In other words, if government spokesmen do not give the media reasonably credible propaganda to disseminate, reporters will become restless and be tempted to ferret out information on their own. That, of course, can lead to accounts at variance with the version of events the government would like circulated. Conversely, if the media can be supplied with enough government-generated information, the political dividends can be handsome. Pentagon officials must never be "neglectful of the needs of the news correspondents," Humphries admonished. "The news media can be a useful tool, or even a weapon, in prosecuting a war psychologically, so that the operators don't have to use their more severe weapons."[28]

Humphries's article was a blueprint for controlling media access to war zones and for managing the news that eventually emerges. It apparently received considerable attention from higher level military and civilian officials, and many of its suggestions were put into effect when the United States invaded Grenada. Not all of the elements were implemented, however, until the Persian Gulf War. (The U.S. commander in that conflict was none other than the deputy commander of the Grenada operation, Norman Schwarzkopf.) Compared with the sophisticated and comprehensive manipulation of the media during the gulf war—which one writer aptly described as "Operation Desert Cloud"—the methods employed in Grenada were crude.[29] Indeed, Reagan administration official Henry Catto, a former Pentagon press officer, complained that the restrictions on the media were excessive and needlessly confrontational, adding, "Unhappily, the average joint chiefs of staff member has all the public relations sense of Attila the Hun."[30] Nevertheless, in the most basic sense, the exclusionary policy worked. Reagan aide Michael Deaver concluded that the American public supported the Grenada operation because "they didn't have to watch American guys getting shot and killed."[31]

Exclusion of the press from Grenada may have been a trial balloon to gauge public reaction and to prepare for even more onerous restrictions in the event of a larger intervention in Central America or the Persian Gulf. If the techniques used in Grenada were a trial balloon, the public response gave considerable impetus to the campaign to restrict media coverage. Most conservative groups blindly supported the administration's position, and the public also endorsed the exclusion, at least initially. A *Los Angeles Times* poll conducted three weeks after the invasion, for example, showed that the public approved the policy of "denying unrestricted press access" by a margin of 52 percent to 41 percent.[32] Other surveys indicated even wider margins of support for the administration's actions.

The reasons for such a distressing response were complex, reflecting latent hostility toward the liberal-dominated press that the Reagan administration assiduously fanned, national euphoria over the easy and relatively bloodless Grenada victory, and a conditioned response to more than three decades of Cold War rationales for limiting constitutional freedoms in the name of national security. Public acquiescence helped to ratify another dangerous precedent that eroded First Amendment freedoms. A *Washington Post* editorial cited the underlying danger: "If the American news media can be excluded by their own government from direct coverage of events of great importance to the American people, the whole character of the relationship between governors and governed is affected."[33] Unfortunately, much of the public seemed oblivious to the implications of the precedent being set by the Reagan administration.

Consequences of a Government News Monopoly

The Grenada operation demonstrated the perils of allowing the government to restrict the flow of information about a military enterprise. To Americans who took the First Amendment seriously, there should have been more than a slightly unsettling aspect to a *New York Times* story, published more than 24 hours after the U.S. invasion had begun, noting that since no reporters had been allowed to accompany American forces, "the major stories were written by reporters in Washington *based on information given to them by State Department and other Government sources.*"[34] When "news" about an important issue consists entirely of information spoon-fed to the press by the national security bureaucracy, the public's ability to gain an accurate view of events is fatally impaired. Caspar Weinberger clearly assumed that the media should be happy with such coverage by briefing and seemed a bit miffed that some journalists did not seem happy with the arrangement. "The press was regularly briefed by General Vessey and by me," he stated, "but that did not appease them, and they continued to rankle over the fact that they had not been allowed to go in the first day, even though by Herculean efforts, we did manage to get various groups of the press in beginning on day two, and more every day thereafter."[35]

Not surprisingly, there were significant episodes of misinformation during the period that the government excluded the press from Grenada. For example, Defense Department figures on the number of Cuban soldiers on the island ballooned to more than 1,000. It later became evident that there had been barely half that number, and many of them were construction workers at the Port Salines Airport project, not professional soldiers.[36] But first impressions are everything in the propaganda game, as *Los Angeles Times* bureau chief Jack Nelson admitted several years later. "Grenada is the perfect example. There are still people who think that the place was crawling with Cubans. It doesn't matter how many times you go back and say that the fact was there were only five or six hundred Cubans."[37]

Government claims about the quantity of Soviet weapons found on the island were also exaggerated. Pentagon spokesmen contended that a large warehouse full of arms and ammunition had been captured, and they released and showed an Army videotape that seemingly verified that account. Reporters who later viewed the cache, however, noted that it was not nearly as large as the Pentagon had claimed.[38] Years later Walter Cronkite pointed out the inherent credibility problems that arise when the government can prevent independent scrutiny of its claims. "I don't know whether we really found a warehouse full of AK-47s there or not. Maybe we planted them there. I'm not saying we did, but we had three days to do it if we wanted to because we had no reporters there at the beginning."[39]

The Pentagon also reported a raging battle for Fort Rupert, a fortress atop Richmond Hill, where Cuban and Grenadian troops were entrenched. *Newsweek* subsequently published a vivid account of the alleged battle, based on information supplied by the U.S. military command.

> From behind the limestone walls of the French-built, 18th-century fortress, Cuban and Grenadian defenders showered small-arms fire on the U.S. attack squads. Grenadian soldiers fired their AK-47s straight up at dive-bombing U.S. jets and helicopters. . . . Eventually the American air attack reduced Fort Rupert to a smoldering shell, with only one full wall left standing.[40]

There was one problem with that story: such a battle never took place. At most there had been a minor skirmish, and most of the evidence uncovered subsequently by enterprising reporters indicated that Fort Rupert had surrendered with scarcely a shot being fired on the morning of October 27.[41] In any case, the fort still had its full complement of walls and had not been reduced "to a smoldering shell." But such are the hazards when the media must rely on official accounts of military operations for stories. Military leaders, like other bureaucrats, have an institutional incentive to magnify the difficulties faced in accomplishing their mission, the diligence and competence of the personnel they direct, and the overall success of their efforts.

In addition to such sins of commission, there were at least two significant sins of omission. One was the Army's botched assault on the west side of the island during the initial stage of the invasion. Coordination of the forces was appallingly bad, and most of the initial U.S. fatalities (18) were suffered there. At one point Marine units had to be brought around from the east side of the island to prevent the attack from stalling entirely. Communications were so muddled that one artillery spotter reportedly went to a pay phone and used his credit card to call the Pentagon and ask that offshore fire power be called in to support the U.S. position. Richard Gabriel and Paul Savage, both former Army intelligence officers, later concluded, "What really happened in Grenada was a case study in military incompetence and poor execution."[42] The Pentagon did not report those problems at the time and only grudgingly revealed them later when there were no possible concerns about maintaining the security of the operation.

The second sin of omission was even more blatant. During the course of the fighting, American aircraft inadvertently bombed the island's mental hospital, killing at least 18 and perhaps as many as 30 individuals. Yet the story of that tragedy did not emerge until the press ban was lifted. The numerous dispatches military officials sent to Washington failed to disclose that error. The omission raises several questions: Was the information blackout deliberate? When, if ever, would the story of the attack have emerged without the presence of an independent press? In future military operations, would the Pentagon use a more prolonged denial of media access to conceal incidents that might reflect badly on the conduct of American forces? There are no certain answers to those questions, but the government's conduct during the period that it exercised monopoly power over information in Grenada suggests that the potential for abuse is substantial. As British journalist Hugh O'Shaughnessy observed, "The restriction on press access to Grenada during the invasion had an immediate impact not just on the interpretation given to events but on the recounting of what in fact happened."[43]

Government exclusion of independent press coverage should have rendered suspect the accuracy of all information on the Grenada operation, but the media tended to accept and repeat the administration's propaganda even as they complained about the censorship policy. "Most of the inaccurate stuff came out of the press conferences [given by Weinberger and other senior administration officials]. But we took it hook, line, and sinker," ABC correspondent John McWethy conceded later. "When you are in a situation where your primary source of information is the United States government—and for three days basically your only source of information, except Radio Havana—you are totally at their mercy. *And you have to make an assumption that the U.S. government is telling the truth.*"[44]

McWethy was correct that reporters were dependent on administration officials for information about what was occurring in Grenada. But why would any journalist conversant with the systematic campaigns of lies about the CIA-orchestrated coups in the 1950s, the U-2 spying incident, the Vietnam War, and Watergate—to mention only the most egregious examples—assume that the government was telling the truth about Grenada? The very existence of the exclusion policy should have led to the opposite conclusion. News stories should, therefore, have routinely included such qualifiers as "administration officials allege," "there is no independent confirmation of administration claims," or "because of the government's barring of the press from Grenada, there is no way to evaluate the accuracy of Secretary Weinberger's statement." Such disclaimers would at least have alerted readers and viewers that they were receiving self-serving government accounts, not independent news stories, and might have embarrassed officials enough to make them ease off on the Grenada news blackout. Except for a few comments during the later phases of the Grenada invasion that stories had been cleared by U.S. military censors, however, the media did not make such badly needed disclaimers.

Snaring the Media: The "Pool" System

Having succeeded in conducting the conquest of Grenada free from the prying eyes of skeptical journalists, the administration built on that precedent by offering a compromise to the defeated news media. The government convened a joint commission of military leaders and retired journalists to formulate new arrangements for press coverage of future combat operations. That commission, the Media-Military Relations Panel, chaired by Gen. Winant Sidle, issued its report in August 1984. The report affirmed that "the U.S. media should cover U.S. military operations to the maximum degree possible consistent with mission security and the safety of U.S. forces."[45] Although that sounded promising, some journalists recalled that the blanket exclusion of the press from Grenada had been justified by the alleged need to protect "mission security."

The centerpiece of the Sidle panel's recommendations was the creation of a national press pool for the coverage of future military operations, whenever other arrangements were inappropriate. That concept was a revival of an arrangement that had been used on several occasions in both world wars, although now it was designed to be the *sole* form of coverage of many military operations during their early, most critical phases.[46] While the press pool proposal seemed to be a concession by the administration, it was merely a more subtle form of restriction. Which side was dictating the terms became all too apparent in the comments section of the report. "Media representatives appearing before the panel were unanimous in being opposed to pools in general. However, they all also agreed that they would cooperate in pooling arrangements if that were necessary for them to obtain early access to an operation."[47] In other words, the Pentagon made it clear that the alternative to media pools was exclusion, and the news media reluctantly agreed to the government's terms.

It was also revealing that the original proposal would have allowed the government to dictate the composition of the pools.[48] Although the media members on the panel put up some resistance to such a power grab, they were something less than pit-bull defenders of an independent press. "The media representatives generally felt that DoD should select the organizations to participate in the pools, and the organizations should select the individual reporters."[49] The version that became operational creates the pools from a rotating list of news organizations, but that list is heavily biased in favor of "major" organizations—principally the television networks, large metropolitan daily newspapers, and mass circulation news magazines. The press pool covering the U.S. naval build-up in the Persian Gulf during the summer of 1987, for example, consisted of reporters from the Associated Press, United Press International, Knight-Ridder Newspapers, the *Washington Times, Time,* ABC Radio, and CNN.[50]

Although the pool arrangement theoretically guaranteed at least some press access to military operations, the clear implication was that nonpool reporters could be barred indefinitely from a war zone. The practical effect was to ensure a news monopoly to members of the mainstream media, who were unlikely to be vehement opponents of America's interventionist foreign policy. That arrangement greatly benefited the interests of the national security bureaucracy. Although critical stories have certainly surfaced on occasion from mainstream media outlets, truly hard-hitting pieces are a rarity in the likes of *Time.* By largely excluding journalists from smaller, frequently more radical, publications, the government may be able to neutralize its most probable—and potentially most tenacious—critics. One suspects that that aspect of the press pool concept was not accidental.

Unfortunately, large news organizations also frequently find it in their interest to support that governmental bias. In the aftermath of the Persian Gulf War, for example, *Washington Post* "ombudsman" Richard Harwood stated that the media ought to do what the military learned to do after Vietnam—send only well-trained professionals to war. The 1,400 "reporters" who went to the gulf were unnecessary,

Harwood argued, because "the war could have been reported with great skill and thoroughness, and the public interest could have been properly served, if the task had been given to the 20 or so major news organizations that normally provide 99 percent of the international news."[51]

Harwood's assumption that the best reporters and analysts are invariably employed by the largest news organizations is fallacious elitism. Throughout the 19th and 20th centuries some of the most searing and insightful accounts of a range of public policy issues have come from independent analysts or writers affiliated with mid-sized or small publications. For example, it was freelance journalist Seymour Hersh, not a regular reporter for a major media outlet, who broke the story of the My Lai massacre in Vietnam. According to Harwood's standards, such journalistic giants as William Allen White and H. L. Mencken would have been considered unworthy of membership in the elite ranks, given their respective affiliations with the tiny *Emporia Gazette* and the midsized *Baltimore Sun*. The quality of coverage of the gulf crisis also fails to support Harwood's equation of size with quality. Many of the worst, most shallow, and most jingoistic accounts appeared on the television networks and in the major metropolitan newspapers and mass circulation news magazines.

The Reagan administration's press pool concept had an impact on even the establishment press. Agreeing to the proposal for a media pool tacitly ratified the administration's position that press coverage of a military intervention was not a First Amendment right but a privilege that the government could restrict or revoke. The press pool arrangement strongly implied that the reporting of such enterprises would be done according to terms dictated by the government. And there were even indications in the Sidle panel's discussions that the terms might not be all that favorable. Pentagon representatives wanted to delay even notifying pool members until after the first U.S. troops had landed in a combat theater.[52] That provision would mean that reporters would get to the scene, as they did in Grenada, long after the action was under way. Although the press members of the commission opposed the Pentagon's preferred standard, no agreement was reached and no promises were made.

The Sidle panel report should have been a warning flag to the entire journalistic community. Instead, most members viewed it as an attempt by the Pentagon to make amends for its "overreaction" in Grenada, and they sought ways to cooperate with the government's plans to restrict their First Amendment rights. Nearly a decade later, *Washington Post* columnist Stephen S. Rosenfeld offered a sobering retrospective view of the significance of the Sidle panel's report.

> This is how a new, unlovely, and largely unremarked phe-
> nomenon came to American journalism: a willingness by the
> media to register, to be "responsible" in their coverage, and
> to countenance sanctions (loss of accreditation) for breaking
> the rules. Indeed, they accepted the very requirements that,
> when presented in a foreign country, journalists properly
> denounce as the abridgments of a totalitarian or Third World
> order. The principal flaw that journalists identified among
> the new procedures was that they might not always be guar-
> anteed a place in the pool.[53]

The *World Policy Journal*'s Marie Gottschalk was more caustic in her assessment of the Sidle panel episode: "Basically, the elite media made a pact with the devil, agreeing to accept more military control of the press in return for access to the war zone in future conflicts."[54]

Lies and Cover-Ups: The First Gulf War

Coverage of naval operations in the Persian Gulf in 1987 and 1988 justified many of the fears of those who were apprehensive that the pool arrangements would restrict rather than assist the press. Military officials delayed the release of several reports for up to 24 hours. And the Pentagon entirely deleted one dispatch reporting that American naval officers and the skipper of the reflagged USS *Bridgeton* sipped beers on the tanker after it had been damaged by a mine. Such interference had little to do with bona fide national security issues and suggested how determined military operatives were to control every aspect of the information flow. Yet even that "tethered" coverage was unacceptable to some military leaders. "It was like pulling teeth" to get the press pool concept in operation, according to one Pentagon official. "There was constant opposition. . . . There were those who thought we would be better off if the press didn't cover anything."[55]

Petty attempts to conceal such public relations embarrassments as the well-known propensity of naval personnel to imbibe occasionally

175

were not nearly as troubling as the military's determination to conceal more damaging information. The most egregious example of the latter was the concerted propaganda blitz in response to the downing of an Iranian civilian airliner by the USS *Vincennes* on July 3, 1988, in which 290 passengers were killed. Applying Arthur Humphries's admonition that it was essential for a government to get its version of events out quickly to preempt competing accounts, the Pentagon provided a detailed scenario of the tragic accident. Chairman of the Joint Chiefs of Staff Adm. William Crowe, Vice President George Bush, and other officials made strong statements defending the Navy's actions and suggesting that the Iranian government had deliberately provoked an incident. "One thing is clear," Bush affirmed, "and that is that the USS *Vincennes* acted in self-defense."[56]

Crowe offered the Navy's official version at a press conference some 11 hours after the incident. He stated flatly that "the suspect aircraft was outside the prescribed commercial air corridor." Given the extremely tense situation in the gulf at the time—including ongoing skirmishes between U.S. vessels and Iranian patrol boats—being outside the corridor would have been negligent, if not provocative. Moreover, according to the Navy, instead of climbing in its flight as it should have, the airliner was descending toward the *Vincennes*—an inherently threatening action. In Crowe's words, "The aircraft headed directly for *Vincennes*, on a constant bearing, at high speed, approximately 450 knots. [It was] decreasing in altitude as it neared the ship." Finally, and perhaps most damning, the airliner's transponder supposedly put forth a signal that resembled the signal emitted by combat planes, which led the *Vincennes* "to believe that the aircraft was an [Iranian] F-14."[57] The consequence of such provocative moves, the Navy contended, was a terrible but understandable error by the *Vincennes*'s skipper, Capt. Will Rogers III, and his crew, who concluded that the ship was under attack. Most of the initial news accounts accepted the Pentagon's explanation with few, if any, expressions of doubt.[58]

It was a compelling case, except for one small problem: all three of the major points that the Navy cited to support its case were erroneous. Subsequent investigations revealed that the airliner was well inside the commercial flight corridor, was ascending and moving away from the U.S. ship, and was emitting a transponder signal identifying it as a commercial aircraft. Although the Navy ultimately conceded those facts in a report issued nearly four weeks later, such admissions received far less attention than did the original allegations.[59] Again, as all skilled propagandists know, first impressions are crucial, and the American public's initial impression of the incident (generously provided by Admiral Crowe) was of a tragic accident caused by recklessly provocative actions of the fanatical Iranian government.

Nearly four years later, a joint investigation by *Newsweek* and ABC News's *Nightline* indicated that Crowe's "misstatements" on July 3, 1988, were not the only inaccuracies in the Navy's account. The admiral and his subordinates had maintained that the *Vincennes* was in international waters throughout the incident. Maps and graphics supplied by the Navy at Crowe's media briefing and a UN Security Council session two weeks later showed the same thing. In reality, the *Vincennes* was in Iranian territorial waters, apparently attempting to "bait" patrol boats into attacking. *Newsweek* correspondents John Barry and Roger Charles charged that the "top Pentagon brass understood from the beginning that if the whole truth about the *Vincennes* came out, it would mean months of humiliating headlines. So the U.S. Navy did what all navies do after terrible blunders at sea: it told lies and handed out medals."[60]

Admiral Crowe vehemently denied that any cover-up had occurred. "I just reject and am offended by the idea that this was an orchestrated coverup," Crowe said in an interview. "Granted, we were feeling our way. Granted, we made some mistakes. But to leap from that to an orchestrated coverup to deceive the American people—it simply isn't true."[61]

Despite Crowe's denials, it is difficult to escape the conclusion that the Navy engaged in a campaign of distortions. At the very least, it is curious that all of the "mistakes" conveniently served to exonerate the Navy. Although it is conceivable that the officers of the *Vincennes* supplied incorrect information to their superiors in Washington to conceal their blunders, that would have been an extraordinarily dangerous course; anyone filing a false report would have risked a court martial and possible imprisonment. The most plausible thesis is that the Navy hierarchy did in fact fear damaging publicity if the truth about the episode came out immediately and in one dose, rather than in informational droplets over the course of weeks or—in the case of the position of the *Vincennes* in Iranian waters—years.

The episode should remind the American people that the national security bureaucracy will engage in deception whenever it has the opportunity and that course serves its institutional interests. In this case, a diligent press managed to gradually uncover the truth; it certainly was not volunteered by the Navy. The *Vincennes* incident demonstrates why the public cannot rely on the national security bureaucracy for accurate information but must insist on the scrutiny of governmental actions by an independent press.

The pattern of Pentagon deception also should make journalists cautious about the accuracy of *any* information supplied by the military. CBS defense correspondent David Martin's assertion that television could confidently use DoD film footage because "the Pentagon would never be so crass and devious as to edit footage in order to give a misleading picture of what really happened," seems more than a little naive.[62] If military leaders were willing and able to supply inaccurate maps and graphics to conceal material facts about the location of the *Vincennes*, why is distorted editing of film footage so difficult to imagine? Furthermore, the Pentagon's propaganda offensive in the 1990–91 Persian Gulf War demonstrated that such crass tactics are not always necessary to create a profoundly misleading impression; sufficient selectivity about which footage is given to the press can accomplish that objective. Pentagon tapes invariably showed U.S. high-tech weaponry working perfectly and, to all appearances, bloodlessly. Television viewers did not see American bombs or missiles missing their targets or inflicting massive casualties, although such footage existed.

Grenada Tactics Revisited: The Invasion of Panama

Anyone who believed that the news blackouts and flagrant exclusion of the press that characterized the Grenada operation were an aberration learned otherwise when the Bush administration ordered the invasion of Panama (Operation Just Cause) in December 1989. Pentagon spokesman Pete Williams would later insist that the government had taken every reasonable step to accommodate the media.

> The President personally made the decision to deploy a pool
> of reporters to cover Just Cause with the agreement of the
> Secretary of Defense and the Chairman of the Joint Chiefs

of Staff. Their decision should dispel the fear that the media pool would never be used in actual combat. Every decision that we made during Just Cause was intended to facilitate open, timely media coverage of the operation.[63]

Williams's statement was disingenuous. Members of the pool were sent to Panama, but Pentagon officials delayed their departure from the United States until barely two hours before the fighting began. Matters did not improve much when the reporters arrived in Panama. *Time* correspondent Stanley W. Cloud noted, "The Pentagon-sanctioned pool of reporters did not arrive on the scene until four hours after the fighting began, and they were unable to file their first dispatches until six hours after that." Indeed, "during their first crucial day in Panama, the reporters were kept for several hours in a windowless room at Fort Clayton [a U.S. base outside Panama City] and treated to a tedious, history-laden briefing."[64]

During that period, the only "information" they were able to transmit to the people in the United States was what they received from military sources. Not surprisingly, "the initial pool report shed almost no light on the confused military situation, leading off with the hardly titanic news that the U.S. chargé d'affaires in Panama, John Bushnell, was worried about the 'mischief' that deposed dictator Manuel Noriega could cause."[65] The situation improved only marginally after the initial blackout—which coincidentally caused pool members to miss the most significant phases of the military operation. Instead of being taken to battle sites, the pool was taken on guided tours of Noriega's pornography collection.[66]

Frustrated reporters began to describe themselves as hostages and complained that they were being treated like mushrooms—kept in the dark and fed manure. Jon Bascom of ABC radio sketched a T-shirt design with the sarcastic protest message, "If it's news today, it's news to us."[67] Other members quipped that the pool's motto ought to be *semper tardis* (always late).[68]

The Pentagon's insistence on using the pool arrangement for covering the Panama operation should have caused suspicion. Even the Hoffman report—the DoD postmortem on media coverage—observed that "the Pentagon pool was established to enable U.S. news personnel to report the earliest possible action in a U.S. military operation *in remote areas where there was no other American press presence*. Panama did not fit that description."[69] Washington's insistence on a pool in such a situation, therefore, reeked of ulterior motives. Pool member Steven Komarow of the Associated Press noted that some Southern Command officers "used the pool's existence as an excuse to detain at the airport 300 news people who had flown in from the States."[70]

As had been the case in Grenada, by the time reporters were able to have meaningful access and conduct independent inquiries, the action was largely over. They were only able to see the aftermath and speculate about what might have occurred. Komarow conceded, "To the extent that we got any news at all, it was pretty much by accident." As an example, he noted that he and his colleagues did witness looting in Panama City, but only because their military driver lost his way.[71]

That lack of meaningful coverage appeared to be precisely what the military wanted. As one CBS producer noted later, "In watching U.S. television coverage of Operation Just Cause, we noticed constant updating of U.S. casualty figures without mention of Panamanian dead or injured; the playing of stock scenes of heroic American soldiers in helicopter gunships or parachuting onto the beaches but no scenes of hospitals with civilian casualties; the upbeat news conference by President Bush; . . . the constant descriptions of Manuel Noriega as a voodoo-practicing pervert and drug runner, never as a longtime U.S. ally."[72] In short, the military was able to put the proper "spin" on the Panamanian operation and ensure that only a positive, sanitized version of events reached the American people.

Some of the reporters seemed to have never suspected that the Pentagon might have harbored such motives. Instead, they attributed the problems to bureaucratic foul-ups and mundane military incompetence. For example, Kevin Merida of the *Dallas Morning News* described the situation as "a Keystone Kops operation." He complained that the military "seemed to have no concept of what our role was. The whole first day was devoted to taking us to places where the action was already over."[73] On another occasion he stated, "If the pool is to operate effectively in the future, better coordination is needed between the Pentagon and the military command center."[74] Merida should have more seriously considered the possibility that the military knew exactly what it was doing and that its concept of the role of the press was quite different from that of reporters.

It is puzzling that journalists were not more suspicious about the military's motives. Retired Marine Corps Lt. Gen. Bernard E. Trainor, who also served as *New York Times* defense correspondent in the mid and late 1980s, provided a vivid description of the hostility toward the media that permeates the military. "It is clear," Trainor concluded, "that today's officer corps carries as part of its cultural baggage a loathing for the press." The credo of the military "seems to be 'duty, honor, country, and hate the media.'" Although the blatant hostility toward journalists during the decade following the end of the Vietnam War—and which was so evident in the Grenada episode—was no longer the norm, Trainor believed it had merely assumed different, somewhat more subtle forms.

> Although most officers no longer say that the media stabbed them in the back in Vietnam, the military still smarts over the nation's humiliation in Indochina and subconsciously still blames television and the press for loss of public support for the war. Today, the hostility manifests itself in complaints that the press will not keep a secret and that it endangers lives by revealing details of sensitive operations. The myth of the media as an unpatriotic, left-wing antimilitary establishment is thus perpetuated.[75]

One of the most unfortunate consequences of the Pentagon's tight control of news coverage of the Panama invasion was that there was no independent verification of the extent of civilian casualties. U.S. military and civilian officials insisted that Panamanian casualties were relatively light, but that assurance must be viewed with skepticism since governments have always sought to squelch accounts of civilian deaths and injuries inflicted by their armed forces. In World War II, for example, censors frequently banned stories that revealed such suffering. Phillip Knightley describes two such incidents.

> W. W. Chaplin of NBC wrote a bitter but illuminating description of General Charles de Gaulle making a political speech in a little village in Normandy before an audience that included a peasant woman with a wheelbarrow holding the body of her child, killed by allied bombardment. The censor would not pass it. He wrote about a French town showered from the air with leaflets warning the inhabitants to leave because the Allies would have to shell and bomb the town. The wind carried the leaflets miles away, the people received no warning, and they died in the rubble of their houses. The censor killed the story.[76]

Washington also responded to critical accounts with brazen disinformation campaigns. When British war correspondent Wilfred Burchett published stories stating that survivors of the U.S. bombing of Hiroshima were dying "mysteriously and horribly" from what he termed an "atomic plague," U.S. officials reacted by accusing him of "falling victim to Japanese propaganda." Gen. Leslie R. Groves, the head of the Manhattan Project that had developed the bomb, condemned Burchett and stated flatly, "This talk of radioactivity is so much nonsense."[77] For his pains to tell the truth about what the atom bomb had done to thousands of innocent civilians in Hiroshima, Burchett was rewarded with an expulsion order by U.S. military officials in Japan.

The government has frequently sought to cover up the extent of civilian casualties. Even the My Lai massacre was first reported by the Pentagon as a military victory, and the Vietnamese casualties were described as Vietcong and North Vietnamese "soldiers." And the military did not rush to report the accidental bombing of the mental hospital in Grenada. It would have been entirely in character for the Pentagon to have concealed the extent of civilian casualties in the Panama invasion, and there were obvious institutional incentives to do so.

Without independent press coverage of that invasion, however, it is extremely difficult to refute the Pentagon's version of events. There are evocative after-the-fact accounts by Panamanian witnesses that certainly cast doubt on the "official" figure of 202 civilian fatalities. In particular, it appears that the assault on the slum neighborhood of El Chorillo (where Noriega had his headquarters) was considerably more ferocious and destructive than one would have gathered from the reports issued by the U.S. military command. Freelance journalist Barbara Jamison, reporting from Panama in December 1992, noted, "The last time I saw the once-bustling neighborhood of El Chorillo, it was a desolate rock-and-rubble landscape that reflected the violence of the U.S. attack: The University of Panama's seismological center registered 414 detonations greater than 5.6 on the Richter scale within the first 15 minutes of the invasion."[78] Several mass graves—one containing 120 bodies—have already been unearthed, and some residents claim that there are at least 10 additional graves of that type yet to be opened. Even the most conservative independent estimates place the number of civilian deaths at more than 300, and some estimates run as high as 4,000. The best estimate, from an Army source who provided the information on a "not for attribution" basis, appears to be approximately 1,000.[79] Christina Jacqueline Johns and P. Ward Johnson, who investigated the invasion and its aftermath, offer a pessimistic but probably realistic conclusion: "We will never know how many civilians died in the invasion of Panama. . . . The government does not want us to know, and the press does not care to find out."[80]

There are, therefore, ample reasons to doubt the Pentagon's sanguine conclusions about civilian casualties, but the only cameras rolling when U.S. forces shelled El Chorillo were the Pentagon's own, and the Army has steadfastly refused to release copies of the film. Even when Rep. Charles Rangel (D-N.Y.) asked for a copy, the Army refused on the grounds of—you guessed it—"national security."[81] The result was a government monopoly of crucial news about the invasion, resulting in a portrayal that was incomplete at best and fraudulent at worst.

As on other occasions, Washington's suppression of independent coverage had little to do with protecting the security of military operations and everything to do with guarding the institutional reputation of the U.S. military. What else is one to make, for example, of the Southern Command's prohibiting media pool members from interviewing Panamanian prisoners of war? Steven Komarow admitted that photographers also "had to break the rules to get pictures of blindfolded Panamanians getting off a helicopter."[82] The most likely explanation of that restriction is that Pentagon leaders knew such a scene would have been reminiscent of the infamous pictures of U.S. hostages being led blindfolded from the embassy in Tehran, an action that produced widespread international condemnation.

The national security bureaucracy learned its own lessons from the Vietnam War, and the most important one was to keep reporters on a short leash. Grenada represented the initial test of the new strategy of sharply limiting media access, and although it was conducted in a crude fashion, the strategy proved to be effective. U.S. officials used the next few years to soften their techniques and gain media acceptance of "kinder and gentler" (but equally confining) guidelines. The Panama invasion enabled the Bush administration to test the refined version of media control, and administration leaders had reason to be pleased with the results. The public remained as comatose about the implications of such restrictions on First Amendment freedoms as it had in the case of Grenada.

Although some reporters complained bitterly about the government's exclusionary tactics, even their outcry was noticeably less shrill than their response to the Grenada news blackout. *Washington Post* correspondent Carl Leubsdorf expressed the sense of resignation. "Bad as the pool operation was in Panama," he stated, "it was better than what we had in Grenada."[83] There was at least an illusion of meaningful news coverage of Operation Just Cause, and the Pentagon concluded that the pool system had worked well—as indeed it had from the standpoint of advancing the administration's interests. Not surprisingly, the Pentagon's cover memorandum accompanying the Hoffman report stressed, "The Department of Defense is committed to the National Media Pool."

Harper's publisher John R. MacArthur aptly summarized the real import of the Grenada and Panama experiences. "The Pentagon had experienced spectacular success in Grenada, first by creating a pool and then by sending it to the island too late, and in Panama by virtually imprisoning the pool on an army base. In both cases, reporters missed the fighting entirely, and the American public was treated to antiseptic military victories minus any scenes of killing, destruction, or incompetence."[84]

The national security bureaucracy had learned its lessons well, although the Panama experience suggested that it still needed to polish its public relations skills. When the Persian Gulf crisis erupted in August 1990, the techniques of media manipulation and control were applied with unprecedented sophistication and effectiveness, enabling the Bush administration to score a propaganda triumph.

8. The Press as Government Lapdog: The Gulf War Model

The various techniques the national security bureaucracy employs to manipulate and control the press reached a climax in the Persian Gulf War. All elements came together in that episode: the successful appeals to the patriotism (if not jingoism) of news personnel, the use of the media before the onset of fighting to transmit government propaganda and condition an uneasy public for war, the exclusion of reporters from covering military operations independently, and a sophisticated campaign to supply the media with videotape and news stories that conveyed precisely the image of the war that the military and political hierarchy wanted the American public to receive. The Bush administration not only carried off a spectacular military success in the gulf war (the long-term political consequences in the gulf region may be another matter entirely), but it achieved an equally spectacular success in taming and managing the news media. When Assistant Secretary of Defense for Public Affairs Pete Williams declared that the gulf war coverage was the "best war coverage we've ever had," his statement was true if by "we" he meant the national security bureaucracy.[1]

One reason for the ease with which the administration manipulated the media is that it had a willing subject. The result was what columnist Colman McCarthy accurately termed "a media nationalism that joined press and state."[2] Marie Gottschalk, associate editor of *World Policy Journal*, was equally perceptive when she concluded, "The problem was not simply that the Pentagon and the president misled the media, but that the media generally swallowed without question whatever the military and the administration dished out."[3]

The Press as Administration Echo Chamber

That problem was evident from the beginning of the crisis. When Saddam Hussein sent his forces into Kuwait on August 2, 1990, most journalists and editorial writers reacted with a mindset conditioned by four decades of Cold War. With rare exceptions, they reflexively accepted the administration's policy assumptions. Those assumptions included (1) the invasion was a dangerous precedent that jeopardized the stability of the entire post–Cold War international system; (2) Saddam's takeover of Kuwait was probably the prelude to aggression against Saudi Arabia and the gulf emirates, a step that would make Iraq the dominant power in the region; (3) Saddam was in a position to control the world's oil supply and, therefore, have a "stranglehold" on the economies of the United States and the rest of the industrialized world; (4) it was a "vital interest" of the United States not only to protect Saudi Arabia but to expel Iraqi forces from Kuwait and restore the political status quo in that country; (5) if the United States did not lead an international effort to counter Iraq's aggression, no other nation or combination of nations was willing to do or capable of doing so; and (6) because Saddam was "the new Hitler," failure to stop Baghdad's aggression would lead to a repetition of the 1930s, eventually culminating in a global war.

All of those assumptions were open to serious question. The administration's contention that the takeover set an intolerable precedent failed to explain why it was more serious than such episodes as Indonesia's annexation of East Timor, India's amputation of Pakistan's eastern provinces to form the new nation of Bangladesh, Vietnam's takeover of Cambodia, or Turkey's invasion (and ongoing occupation) of nearly 40 percent of Cyprus—none of which impelled the United States and the international community to launch a major war to restore the status quo ante.

The allegation that Baghdad contemplated aggression against Saudi Arabia—the principal justification for the initial deployment of U.S. forces in Operation Desert Shield—was also dubious. Most of Iraq's "elite" Republican Guard units had been withdrawn from Kuwait and other portions of the Iraqi-Saudi border even before U.S. troops arrived, an action that was hardly consistent with further expansionist objectives. Intelligence analysts apparently informed the administration in August that the size of the remaining force on the Kuwait-Saudi border indicated that Baghdad did not intend to invade Saudi Arabia.[4] Not surprisingly, the administration failed to disclose that detail since it would have undermined the official rationale for the U.S. troop deployment.

The most pervasive and potent justification for U.S. action was the administration's contention that if Saddam conquered Saudi Arabia and the emirates, he would control at least half of the world's proven oil reserves and have his hand on the lifeline of the American economy. That argument contained several flaws. Merely controlling a large percentage of oil reserves would not have translated into an economic stranglehold. "Proven reserves" is simply a term used to describe oil deposits that it would be economically feasible to develop under current conditions. Such reserves are not a static quantity; changes in various factors (the emergence of new extraction technologies, the discovery of new deposits, even changes in the market price of oil) can cause major shifts in the amount of proven reserves. For example, reserves soared from 700 billion barrels to nearly 1 trillion barrels between 1985 and 1990. Furthermore, oil reserves include a great deal of oil that no one would contemplate pumping for decades—long after Saddam would have ceased to be a political factor.

The pertinent issue (and the one that the administration continuously evaded) was how much control Iraq could have gained over current oil *production*. Even a worst-case scenario never supported the administration's alarmist "stranglehold" thesis. Domination of Saudi Arabia and the gulf emirates would have given Iraq control of 22 percent of global oil production. David R. Henderson, senior economist for energy on President Reagan's Council of Economic Advisers, estimated that such control would have been sufficient only to boost prices to $30 a barrel from the preinvasion price of $20 a barrel. The total cost to the American economy, Henderson concluded, would have been merely one-half of 1 percent of the nation's gross national product—an annoying development but far short of economic strangulation.[5]

Another questionable administration assumption was that only the United States was capable of containing Iraqi expansionism. Other states in the region appeared to have more than enough military capabilities to do so. For example, just Iraq's immediate neighbors—Iran, Syria, Jordan, Saudi Arabia, and Turkey—had more than 1.8 million active duty military personnel, outnumbering Baghdad's forces nearly two to one. They had 9,900 tanks to Iraq's 5,500 and 1,300 combat aircraft to Iraq's 513. Those personnel and military hardware figures did not include the forces that more distant regional powers, such as Egypt, that also had a clear interest in preventing Iraqi regional hegemony could have brought to bear. Any move by Saddam against Saudi Arabia would have stretched Iraqi forces along a lengthy southern front and left Iraq exceedingly vulnerable to Syrian, Iranian, or Turkish attacks. Moreover, it is pertinent to recall that Iraq had been unable to prevail in its one-on-one war against Iran during the 1980s.

The unwillingness to let powers in the region deal with Iraq dovetailed with the administration's argument that Iraq was a new Nazi Germany bent on massive expansion and that failure to reverse the takeover of Kuwait would repeat the tragic errors of the 1930s. That analogy was fundamentally flawed. When Hitler began his expansionist binge with the annexation of Austria in 1938, Nazi Germany was Europe's leading economic power, its second most populous nation, and had a world-class military force. Iraq was a small (population 17 million to 18 million) Third World country with an economy that had already been devastated by more than eight years of war with Iran. Contrary to the administration's propaganda, Iraq's military—although numerically impressive—was largely a collection of ill-trained, ill-fed, and ill-equipped conscripts. Tom Marks, a political analyst who had studied the Iraqi military for U.S. intelligence agencies, accurately described Saddam's force as "a giant with feet of clay." Baghdad, he observed, "fields a competent but limited extension of its mechanisms of internal repression."[6] University of Chicago professor John J. Mearsheimer, a leading expert on military strategy, reached a similar conclusion. Even by Third World standards, Mearsheimer argued, "the Iraqi army is a below-average fighting force. It is certainly not in the same league as the North Vietnamese army, and it does not even measure up well to the Egyptian and Syrian armies."[7]

Unfortunately, such insightful assessments of Iraq's military capabilities were rare among media accounts during the months leading up to Operation Desert Storm. Far more typical were the sentiments expressed in the August 13 issue of *U.S. News & World Report* that Iraq's huge tank army, operating in open desert ideally suited to tank warfare, was "more than a match" for U.S. forces.[8] News articles routinely spoke of a "battle-hardened" army of a million troops capable of regional domination—but usually neglected to explain why that vaunted force had been unable to prevail against an internationally isolated Iran convulsed by revolutionary turmoil.

Such an inadequate treatment of the military issues was symptomatic of a larger failure. Instead of carefully examining and dissecting the various rationales for intervention, the media for the most part tamely accepted the administration's interpretation of events and gave the public a steady diet of simplistic images and analyses of developments in the gulf. The way the media framed the issues played perfectly into the administration's hands. As Marie Gottschalk observed, "Two questions dominated the coverage: will the United States go to war, and will it win? Other important questions, including whether the United States *should* go to war and whether war could be avoided, received little attention."[9]

There was also a surprising uniformity of views among the major media outlets. One survey of the nation's 25 largest newspapers from August to mid-November 1990, for example, found that only one, the *Rocky Mountain News*, consistently argued against military action to expel Iraqi forces from Kuwait. Vincent Carroll, editorial page editor of the *Rocky Mountain News*, considered it remarkable and disturbing that a potential conflict of such a serious nature did not provoke more editorial debate.[10] Other experts also noted the pervasive jingoism. "The healthy, feisty skepticism of government hoopla that is supposed to characterize a free press never came into play," concluded veteran journalist Gene Ruffini.[11] That was especially true during the crucial weeks immediately following the Iraqi invasion of Kuwait, when the basic elements of U.S. policy were put into place. As *Harper's* publisher John R. MacArthur observed, "In August 1990, the Bush Administration's task was to sell two images—an ugly one of Hussein and a handsome one of Kuwait—to the American media. Then, God willing, the media would help sell it to the American people."[12]

The administration need not have fretted about the prospects for success. The media cooperated in both the demonization of Saddam and the whitewash of Kuwait with unseemly enthusiasm.[13] Mark Hertsgaard justifiably described the initial coverage of the crisis as bellicose. "President Bush had no sooner drawn his line in the sand than the nation's leading news organizations snapped to attention like a line of buck privates."[14] Indeed, the overall impression created by the bulk of the news stories, op-eds, and house editorials that appeared in the weeks following the invasion was of a veritable international melodrama: innocent, freedom-loving Kuwait being set upon by a brutal modern-day Hitler, and the United States and other "free-world" countries prepared to ride to the rescue. Johns Hopkins University professor Mark Crispin Miller accused *Time* and most other media outlets of recycling "the same trite plot that had played so well the year before, when Manuel Noriega stood in as the tropical menace of the month."[15] That was basically true, but Saddam made a much larger and scarier villain.

The media were especially derelict in providing readers and viewers with any historical context for the gulf crisis. There was a noticeable shortage of stories about how the British had arbitrarily drawn the boundaries of Iraq, Kuwait, and Saudi Arabia in 1922 or about the other techniques that London had employed in its divide-and-rule strategy for preserving its imperial sway throughout the region.[16] Americans were also unlikely to learn that in 1938 the advisory council to the Kuwaiti emir passed resolutions endorsing a union with Iraq, only to be prevented by the British from carrying out that objective.

It was difficult to find stories that mentioned that Iraq had vehemently protested Britain's decision to grant independence to Kuwait in 1961 and had reiterated its claim that Kuwait was rightfully Iraqi territory. Indeed, British troops were dispatched to discourage Baghdad from pressing its claims through military action. The historical record, in short, suggested that the August 1990 invasion was not merely a case of shocking aggression by Saddam; there had been complex and vexing issues in the Iraqi-Kuwaiti relationship for decades. But the media's analyses of the gulf crisis too often became a melodrama with Saddam as the mustachioed villain. Although he was certainly villainous, his brutality and aggressive behavior were hardly the whole story.

The media's depiction of more recent developments was scarcely better than the treatment of historical factors. Accounts of Kuwait's corrupt, repressive regime and its systematic violations of human rights—documented by Amnesty International, Middle East Watch, and other human rights organizations—were in surprisingly short supply. There were not many inquiries into the U.S.-Iraqi relationship before August 1990, despite ample evidence of close cooperation between the two countries.

Washington had openly tilted toward Iraq in its long war with Iran during the 1980s, culminating in the decision to send U.S. naval units to protect shipping in the Persian Gulf—an action that resulted in a number of skirmishes with Iranian forces. In addition, U.S. officials at the very least ignored, and perhaps abetted, the transfer of sophisticated weapons and military technology to Saddam's regime, as well as the diversion of U.S. agricultural credits to military purposes.[17] A large quantity of information about the de facto U.S.-Iraqi alliance has emerged since the end of the gulf war. Some of that information was known at the time, and more could almost certainly have been uncovered by determined digging by investigative reporters. Very little digging was done, however. In assessing the media's treatment of the U.S.-Iraqi connection before August 1990, William A. Dorman, a professor of journalism at California State University, Sacramento, concludes, "During the first weeks after the invasion of Kuwait, there would have been little reason for a newspaper reader to think that President Bush (not to mention Secretary of State Baker and others in the present administration) had ever held a post under the previous administration, or was in any way connected to past policy toward Iraq."[18]

The nature of the U.S.-Iraqi relationship was an important matter for several reasons, not the least of which was the doubt it cast on the administration's portrayal of Saddam as Hitler and Iraq as the new Nazi Germany on the march. If Saddam was really such an odious character bent on achieving regional hegemony, the obvious questions were, why had the Bush administration been oblivious to that danger before August 1990, and why had it instead—along with its predecessor—pursued a consistent policy of building up Iraqi military power? As the American people weighed the risks and benefits of possible war against Iraq, they needed a complete picture of the background to the gulf crisis. Yet during the months leading up to Operation Desert Storm, the media displayed a noticeable lack of curiosity or initiative when it came to such issues.

Disseminating War Propaganda

Perhaps even worse was the media's credulity about the crudest elements of the propaganda campaign orchestrated by the Bush administration and the Kuwaiti government (through its front organization, the Committee for a Free Kuwait). The tendency of journalists to parrot the administration's argument that Iraq was a military powerhouse poised for regional domination was only one example. A more egregious example was the media's complicity in publicizing atrocity stories involving the Iraqi occupation of Kuwait. The primary atrocity charge was that Iraqi soldiers had forced nurses to remove babies from their incubators in the maternity ward of Kuwait City's al-Addan hospital and two other hospitals, resulting in the deaths of 312 infants. That story, attributed to anonymous sources, began to circulate in Britain and the United States in early September, but it was not until October 10, when the congressional Human Rights Caucus held a session featuring alleged eyewitnesses, that the "baby killers" story became prominent.

The featured witness to the alleged incident was a tearful 15-year-old girl brought forth by the high-powered Washington public relations firm of Hill and Knowlton, which was being paid more than $5.6 million by the Committee for a Free Kuwait (which in turn was being funded to the tune of more than $11 million by the Kuwaiti government in exile). Caucus chairman Rep. Tom Lantos (D-Calif.) identified the witness as "Nayirah." A more detailed identification, Lantos contended, would endanger her friends and relatives in Kuwait. Nayirah described herself as a volunteer at the al-Addan hospital who personally saw Iraqi soldiers commit the brutal murders.

Nayirah's accusations created a media sensation. Soon the charges were being repeated by President Bush and other administration officials, and U.S. ambassador to the United Nations Thomas Pickering arranged for the Committee for a Free Kuwait (i.e., Hill and Knowlton) to present an expanded version of the atrocity story— complete with additional "witnesses" and a slick audiovisual presentation—before the UN Security Council in November. The baby incubator incident played a central role in the propaganda offensive of the gulf war and assuredly hardened the attitude of the American people toward Iraq. Indeed, it was reminiscent of British allegations that German forces had bayoneted babies and raped nuns during the invasion of Belgium in 1914. Both reports were designed to convince the American public that it confronted an enemy so brutal as to be inhuman—a monstrous aggressor that must be stopped at all costs. As John MacArthur notes, "The significance of the baby incubator story in the larger propaganda campaign against Saddam Hussein and for the war option cannot be underestimated. Without it, the comparison of Hussein with Hitler loses its luster; to make the case effectively, one had to prove Hussein's utter depravity."[19]

There was another important similarity between the two atrocity accounts: the bulk of the evidence indicates that they were false.

Subsequent investigations by MacArthur and others revealed several interesting facts about the baby incubator story. The most spectacular revelation was that "Nayirah" was the daughter of Kuwait's ambassador to the United States—a fact that caucus chairman Lantos knew but concealed from the press.[20] (Lantos later justified his action with the astonishing statement, "The notion that any of the witnesses brought to the caucus through the Kuwaiti embassy would not be credible did not cross my mind.")[21] The credibility of the other Hill and Knowlton "witnesses" presented to the United Nations was scarcely better. Virtually all of them turned out to be Kuwaiti government operatives.

What was so striking about the press coverage of the baby killer allegations was the marked lack of skepticism and the pervasive failure to ask hard follow-up questions. Not only did journalists fail to make a serious effort to evaluate the credibility of Nayirah and the other accusers by uncovering their identities and backgrounds—which was a bad enough lapse—but they misstated obvious facts. For example, news stories and op-eds repeatedly referred to the allegations as "testimony," a term that implied that the witnesses were under oath. That was not the case, however. The session conducted by the Human Rights Caucus was not a formal congressional hearing, and those giving statements were not placed under oath (and were, therefore, not risking perjury charges). The same was true of the "witnesses" in the multimedia event Ambassador Pickering produced at the United Nations.

A little probing by reporters at the time would have uncovered some other interesting facts, including the extremely cozy association between Tom Lantos (as well the Republican cochairman of the caucus, Illinois representative John Porter) and Hill and Knowlton. Had they bothered to make inquiries, journalists might also have discovered that several of the Kuwaiti spokesmen at the United Nations had used false identities without indicating that they were doing so and had concealed their affiliations with the Kuwaiti government.[22]

The credulity with which the press accepted the baby incubator story was troubling. Granted, Saddam's regime was among the most brutal in the Third World, and there were well-documented cases of previous human rights violations published by various human rights organizations. The most notorious case involved the apparent use of poison gas against Kurdish civilians whom Saddam suspected of being Iranian sympathizers during the Iran-Iraq war. In one incident, more than 5,000 people in the town of Halabja were slaughtered. Given Saddam's previous thuggish behavior, the notion that his troops had murdered helpless infants in Kuwait City undoubtedly seemed plausible. Moreover, there was credible evidence that the invading Iraqi forces had committed other, albeit less spectacular, atrocities against Kuwaiti civilians.

Nevertheless, even in that context, one must wonder at journalists' willingness to blithely accept the baby incubator story without adequate verification, especially since false reports of atrocities had been staples of propaganda campaigns in World War I and other conflicts. Even the most basic adherence to professional standards should have caused journalists to demand independent confirmation before treating the accusations as gospel. Instead, they were pliant accomplices in the propaganda offensive orchestrated by the Bush administration and the Kuwaiti regime. It was not as though no counterevidence existed. A Palestinian doctor and an Icelandic doctor who were in the Kuwait City hospitals at the time of the alleged incidents disputed the incubator story, but their statements were either ignored by the mainstream press or buried on inside pages.[23]

True, MacArthur's diligent digging (as well as belated investigations by Amnesty International and other human rights organizations) ultimately raised serious questions about the baby incubator allegations.[24] But their achievements, however useful in helping to correct the historical record, came far too late to affect the political debate that preceded Operation Desert Storm. As Phillip Knightley observed of the British use of similar propaganda in World War I, "By the time the atrocity story was discredited, it had served its role."[25] By the time the "babies pulled from incubators" story had been scrutinized and undermined, the United States had bombed Iraq back into a preindustrial state and liberated Kuwait—or more accurately, restored the emir's autocratic regime to power. Although one might hope that journalists were chastened by that experience, the lack of skepticism with which the press has repeated the State Department's flamboyant accounts (and the even more dubious stories put out by the Croatian and Bosnian regimes) of atrocities committed by Serbian forces in the former Yugoslavia does not inspire confidence.

Bush administration officials had reason to be pleased with their success in using the press to intensify pro-war sentiment in the

United States. Media dissemination of the government's propaganda line almost assuredly helped condition the public for war and helped secure the congressional resolution in January 1991 authorizing the president to use force against Iraq if it did not withdraw its forces from Kuwait before the January 15 deadline specified by the UN Security Council.[26]

The administration's attitude toward the press in the months before Operation Desert Storm was probably similar to that of Leninist governments throughout the communist era toward noncommunist "progressives" in the West who were easily manipulated into echoing communist policy views. Such unwitting allies the Leninists cynically derided as "useful idiots." Even as the administration courted pro-war journalists and fed them helpful information, Pentagon officials were busy with plans to restrict, and if necessary exclude, media coverage of the Persian Gulf theater once combat operations began. In formulating those plans, Pete Williams and other officials were able to draw on the media management techniques the government had used so successfully in the Grenada and Panama operations. MacArthur's assessment that "from the moment Bush committed troops to Saudi Arabia on August 7, the Administration never intended the press to cover a war in the Persian Gulf in any real sense, and it intended to tightly manage what coverage it would permit" is harsh but accurate.[27]

Keeping the Media on a Short Leash

Although there were plenty of warning signs of what the government had in mind, most members of the media failed to heed those signals. One of the earliest administration ploys was to collaborate with the Saudi government in restricting the number of reporters who would receive visas. That placed administration officials in an ideal position. They were able to let the authoritarian and xenophobic Saudi regime implement a policy that dovetailed perfectly with the U.S. national security bureaucracy's long-standing objective of keeping inquisitive reporters away from theaters of potential or active military operations. At the same time, the administration did not have to bear the onus of undermining First Amendment freedoms.

Officials responded to complaints by pointing out that Saudi authorities had the legal right to control access to their country.

Indeed, American news organizations were reduced to begging Washington for assistance in persuading Riyadh to relent, a "favor" that enhanced the bureaucracy's leverage on other issues related to press coverage of the gulf crisis.[28] Only a handful of suspicious news personnel wondered aloud why America had to play the role of supplicant, given that the supposed purpose of Operation Desert Shield was to protect Saudi Arabia from imminent invasion and subjugation.

While the visa issue was being sorted out, the Pentagon was busy drafting guidelines of its own to govern press coverage of U.S. military operations in Saudi Arabia. Within days of Bush's announcement that the United States was deploying troops to shield Iraq's neighbors from further aggression, the U.S. Central Command drafted a 10-page secret memo, "Annex Foxtrot," that constituted a detailed blueprint for the Pentagon's information policy in the gulf theater. According to *New York Times* writer Jason De Parle, the policy outlined in that memo "began with a decision by the Administration's most senior officials, including President Bush, to manage the information flow in a way that supported the operation's political goals and avoided the perceived mistakes of Vietnam."[29] The primary objective was most revealing: it was not to protect the security of military operations but to ensure favorable press treatment of *political* objectives.

Two basic principles were evident in the Pentagon's plan. One was to be as "helpful" as possible in satisfying the media's thirst for information. Long before fighting broke out, the military hierarchy formulated strategies for briefing reporters, supplying visually appealing videotapes for television, providing detailed information sheets, and making carefully selected military personnel available for interviews. That part of the strategy addressed the criticism expressed by Arthur Humphries in his 1983 article about the deficiencies in British information management techniques during the Falklands War. The underlying premise was that if reporters were kept sated with "information" provided by the military itself, they would be less restless and less inclined to try to ferret out stories on their own.

The corrupting influence of the Central Command's actions was acknowledged even by the *Wall Street Journal*'s John Fialka, one of the more pro-war reporters. Comparing the misinformation passed out in the gulf war briefings to the fallacious "body count" figures presented in Vietnam War briefing sessions—the infamous "Five O'Clock Follies"—Fialka stressed one important difference.

> In Vietnam, the print press, in particular the ones who had been in the field and knew what was going on, could filter that stuff out by the time it reached the United States. But in the gulf, it was like the Five O'Clock Follies were live on TV. Every press briefing was on CNN. And no reporters were let out in the field to get independent information during the air war.
>
> The Pentagon's control of that briefing room was Orwellian. They even got these avuncular, folksy types to handle the briefings, which made reporters asking tough questions look ridiculous. Once the Pentagon put their spin on it, it was very difficult to un-spin it.[30]

The incessant briefings were the central feature of the "good cop" component of the military's "good cop, bad cop" strategy. In the role of good cop, military officials were to be ever so helpful to reporters in the Saudi theater. They were also determined to be friendly, in contrast to the animosity and media bashing of the Grenada and Panama operations. Of course, the "information" fed to the press would be carefully screened to ensure the most favorable impression of the military and its mission. That was press relations and propaganda at their most sophisticated.

Nevertheless, the Pentagon was not about to rely solely on its ability to entice and dazzle the media. The other principle embodied in "Annex Foxtrot" was to closely monitor and supervise all press coverage of military operations. There would be no repetition of the system in Vietnam under which reporters made their own arrangements with combat units and proceeded to conduct unsupervised interviews with U.S. troops and shoot graphic footage of the war and its consequences. Instead, the Pentagon intended not only to return to the more restrictive practices of the two world wars and the Korean conflict but to apply in a more rigorous fashion the practice followed in Grenada and Panama (once the military deigned to allow the press into the area at all) of insisting that reporters be accompanied by military escorts at all times and that most of the coverage be by members of authorized media pools. The controls were so tight that veteran correspondent Malcolm Browne complained, "The only war I have covered where the access to the front was as limited as it has been in Saudi Arabia was the 1971 war between Pakistan and India."[31]

Jason De Parle noted that the gulf war "marked this century's first major conflict where the policy was to confine reporters to escorted pools that sharply curtailed when and how they could talk to the troops."[32] That conclusion was basically true, but the operative phrase was "major conflict," for the Pentagon's policy clearly built on the precedents established in the "minor" skirmishes in Grenada and Panama. *Newsday* columnist Sydney Schanberg was on the mark when he contended that the invasions of Grenada and Panama "were the dress rehearsals for the press muzzling in the Gulf—test runs, so to speak, to see if either the public or major news organizations would raise much of an outcry (they didn't)."[33] The inability of the news media to arouse public wrath at the government's exclusionary policies during those earlier incidents made it possible (indeed, surprisingly easy) for the Pentagon to invoke similar measures during the gulf crisis. Even worse than the ineffectual media response to the mugging they received at the hands of U.S. officials running the Grenada and Panama invasions (which was due in part to the public's myopic enthusiasm for the government's restrictions) was the collaboration of news organizations in the pool system. Their cooperation in such a brazen arrangement to manage the news signaled to the Pentagon that only the most feeble opposition to the military's censorship blueprint could be anticipated. That assessment proved to be accurate.

Time's Washington bureau chief Stanley Cloud ruefully conceded as much in the aftermath of the gulf conflict.

> The DOD National Pool is the mother of all pools. . . . The rules agreed to [after the Grenada invasion] are the basic rules we lived under in the Gulf War. They were amplified and they grew from little seedlings into jungles in the Gulf War, but . . . it is membership in that pool that gave the Pentagon the opening to allow them to control everything we did in the Gulf War.[34]

Unfortunately, neither Cloud nor most other journalists seemed to understand the problem during the months leading up to Desert

Storm, when such understanding really mattered and when concerted opposition might have caused serious difficulties for the national security bureaucracy. As MacArthur notes, "Back in August, not a single newshound even growled. They made polite inquiries, held informal meetings, and sent respectful letters, but they voiced no strong objection."[35] Their passive acceptance of a tightening array of government restrictions on coverage did not decrease substantially in the following months.

Reporters continued to labor under the illusion that the Pentagon would let them pursue independent coverage of the military build-up and any subsequent combat operations. Yet early on there were clear indications that officials had no such intention. Before being granted access to the staging areas in Saudi Arabia, reporters had to sign the Pentagon's "ground rules" document, which contained the ominous phrase (inspired by the policy goals in "Annex Foxtrot") "You MUST remain with your military escort at all times until released, and follow their instructions regarding your activities." The ground rules document offered the comforting assurance that the instructions "are not intended to hinder your reporting. They are only to facilitate troop movement, ensure safety, and protect operational security."

That assurance was pure bureaucratic bilge. The military escort requirement effectively guaranteed that there would be no off-the-record interviews with military personnel who might dissent even mildly from the administration's portrayal of its noble intervention to restore the Kuwaiti ruling family to power. Military leaders had learned important lessons about the value of military escorts from the Vietnam experience. A sizable number of the negative news stories that appeared in the United States, Gen. William Westmoreland stated in an October 1967 memo to all major commanders, were the fault of unthinking soldiers who made disparaging remarks about the war effort or Washington's South Vietnamese ally. That problem would never occur, he concluded, in the presence of a qualified military observer.[36] Although the military command in Saigon was never to implement that policy, commanders in the gulf did so with a vengeance.

Incredibly, most reporters covering Operation Desert Shield seemed willing to ignore the inevitable chilling effect that the escort provision had on potential interviewees. Watched by military escorts, virtually all the troops expressed enthusiasm for the campaign against Iraq, and credulous news personnel sent such "news" back to the United States. Granted, a majority of the troops probably did support the decision to intervene, since a military career tends to attract more hawkish than dovish individuals. But did it never occur to members of the media that having a uniformed guard at their elbow might inhibit candid comments from those who held dissenting views, since they knew that "disloyal" comments would undoubtedly get back to their superiors and might incur retaliation? Was it really credible that all of the interview subjects had nothing critical to say about the wisdom of the intervention, the president's authority to send them into harm's way without congressional consent, the autocratic policies of their Saudi hosts, or the corrupt authoritarianism of the Kuwaiti regime they were pledged to restore even at the risk of their lives? To assume that none of the military personnel deployed in Saudi Arabia questioned the administration is to assume that they were unaware of the debate in which their fellow citizens back home were engaged.

Reporters who believed that they always received honest responses from interview subjects who were under the watchful gaze of military escorts were as gullible as Western visitors who thought that the expressions of enthusiastic support for the Soviet government by residents of Moscow and Leningrad during the pre-Gorbachev years were genuine. It rarely seemed to dawn on such Western dupes that the "tour guides" who served as translators for encounters with Soviet citizens were assumed to be KGB agents by any reasonably sophisticated Russian. The "man on the street" realized that candid comments about the regime would result in a prompt trip to the gulag and, not surprisingly, told Western visitors only what the government wanted them to hear. Interview subjects in Operation Desert Shield were in a similar, albeit less horrific, position, given the ubiquitous military escorts.

Some of the escorts seemed to go out of their way to emphasize their mission of intimidation. NBC correspondent Gary Matsumoto described the actions of one especially zealous public affairs officer.

> Whenever I began interviewing a soldier, this PAO would stand right behind me, stare right into the eyes of the soldier, stretch out a hand holding a cassette recorder and click it on in the soldier's face. This was patent intimidation ... which was clear from the soldiers' reactions.[37]

In a letter delivered to Secretary of Defense Richard Cheney in June 1991—long after the war was over—media executives charged that escorts frequently interrupted questions they deemed "inappropriate." And they did not take kindly to protests about such arbitrary field censorship. When Stephanie Glass of the *San Antonio Light* complained about the military's interference, she was told that she would be "put back on the bus" for "being a smart ass." (Glass later contended that her complaints were fully justified because escorts "frequently finished sentences for those being interviewed, or answered for them entirely.")[38] On another occasion, ABC reporter Linda Patillo was blocked by her military escort from covering a group of Marines listening to "Onward Christian Soldiers" because it might "offend Saudi sensitivities."[39]

Although the press operated in a carefully controlled environment throughout the military build-up, conditions became even more oppressive once combat operations commenced on January 16, 1991. The Pentagon used three techniques to ensure that its version of events would rarely be disputed. First, military authorities continued, indeed intensified, their requirements that reporters be accompanied by escorts at all times and that only members of authorized media pools cover combat operations in the field. (Since the initial weeks of the gulf war were dominated by air strikes against Iraqi targets, that requirement had less impact than if there had been large numbers of ground battles, but it still produced largely sterile accounts.) Second, as a substitute for independent coverage, the military supplied a large quantity of its own information—both videotape and print handouts—and conducted a seemingly endless series of briefings by U.S., British, and Saudi officers.[40] Those in charge of the briefing sessions were unfailingly patient and polite, even when confronted by naive, incomprehensible, or inappropriate questions (e.g., queries about troop movements or invasion strategies) from reporters. Finally, military authorities tightened their system of censorship at the source—by requiring a "security review" that delayed and altered stories before they were released.

The result was a most peculiar news product. Americans received an unprecedented quantity of coverage—much of it visually impressive. The problem, however, was that the version of the gulf war sent back to the United States by the press corps bore about as much resemblance to the real situation as a Disneyland exhibit does to the outside world. With rare exceptions, the news stories were highly sanitized accounts of the conflict—a fantasyland image of the war that the Pentagon wanted the public to see. Wittingly or unwittingly, the news media became little more than conduits for the administration's propaganda.

MacArthur correctly observes that "the obstacles to producing good journalism during the Gulf War were considerable. At the top of the list was military censorship—the twelve hundred U.S. journalists covering the mostly American side in Saudi Arabia (the media had little choice but to cooperate with the Administration's evocation of World War II in calling it the 'allied' or 'coalition' side despite the hugely disproportionate share of U.S. troops) simply weren't permitted to file much that was worth either reading or watching." For the most part, he concludes, "the journalists in the Gulf were reduced to the level of stenographers."[41]

Stanley Cloud reached a similar conclusion, and he conceded that the government's strategy of strangling independent news coverage—especially officialdom's insistence on the pool arrangement—did not suddenly materialize with the gulf conflict. He faulted his colleagues for failing to respond to a problem that had been building since the invasion of Grenada. "Although there was some grumbling from journalists about the system before the gulf war, the participating news organizations generally sat passively by and allowed themselves to be shackled. Only in the gulf did they begin to realize how much they had given away."[42]

MacArthur and Cloud were rightly indignant about the stifling environment in which the news media had to operate, but they were too easy on their colleagues. Why, for example, did the media have "little choice" but to describe the overwhelmingly American force arrayed against Iraq as an "allied" force? That would have been precisely the kind of passive defiance of Bush administration propaganda that the military authorities in Saudi Arabia would have found difficult to suppress. (Not to mention that journalists who believed in accuracy should have insisted on using a more honest label.) Instead, most correspondents echoed the administration's preferred terminology. Why did virtually no reporters (especially television correspondents) either refuse to conduct interviews under the military escort requirement or at least file stories that denounced the Pentagon's motives for having public affairs officers hovering over interview subjects and intimidating them? Such timidity revealed an unpleasant truth about the press coverage of the gulf crisis: the media were seduced at least as much as they were coerced.

Although the military hierarchy concentrated most of its attention on plying the media with favorable accounts of the prowess of "coalition" forces, it never relaxed its constraints on independent coverage. News personnel who attempted to evade the military escort requirement or defy the media pool arrangements soon found out how rough the Pentagon was willing to play. Malcolm Browne charged that "nearly all the reporters who have tried to reach American front-line units have been arrested at one time or another, and sometimes held for up to 12 hours in field jails, facing the threat that their press credentials would be permanently confiscated and their Saudi visas canceled."[43] Such cancelation was not an empty threat. A senior Pentagon official, Col. William Mulvey, reportedly sent Saudi officials a list of reporters who had been seen in "restricted areas" or who were otherwise uncooperative. Showing himself to be less than an ardent defender of the First Amendment, the colonel urged Saudi authorities to "pull a few visas to make a point."[44] A French film crew that attempted to cover the skirmish at the Saudi border town of Khafji (which was also being filmed by pool members under the watchful eyes of their military handlers) had their videotape confiscated by authorities. *New York Times* reporter Chris Hedges was detained by U.S. military officials for six hours, then stripped of his credentials and forcibly returned to Dhahran for having tried to acquire a story without an escort. What top-secret military operation was he jeopardizing by his actions? He sought to report on alleged price gouging of American GIs by Saudi merchants.[45]

The treatment of other journalistic mavericks was even worse. One photographer, for example, was blindfolded and held for 30 hours by military authorities. All in all, the military detained or otherwise disciplined at least 24 reporters during the Persian Gulf operation.[46] *Newsweek* columnist David H. Hackworth, a much decorated Vietnam veteran, recalled,

> Those few pool members who were out with the troops became part of a military machine that imposed total control over what the public would see, hear and read. I tried to short-circuit the system by talking to the grunts the way

> Walter Cronkite, Ernie Pyle and Ward Just had done. On
> sprints through the desert, I had more weapons pointed at
> me by "friendlies" trying to block my story than by anyone
> from Saddam Hussein's side.[47]

Quisling Journalists

Perhaps more depressing than the military command's high-handed conduct was the collaboration of news personnel in efforts to coerce independent-minded colleagues. For example, NBC correspondent Brad Willis, a member of the authorized media pool covering the battle of Khafji, reportedly berated Robert Fisk, a reporter for the London *Independent*, for attempting to report on the engagement independently. Willis apparently not only went into a tirade at Fisk for violating the pool guidelines but reported him to the Marines, who promptly escorted the interloper out of the area.[48]

Collaboration was evident in other ways. The U.S. command in Dhahran established a system under which "pool coordinators" (reporters selected by the military) would determine which of their colleagues were assigned to which pools—or if they received any pool assignments at all. MacArthur aptly describes the arrangement as "a situation akin to a prison system of inmates guarding inmates."[49] *San Francisco Chronicle* reporter Carl Nolte, who evaded the pool restrictions and sought to report unilaterally, made even more caustic comments about the arrangement and reporters, such as John Fialka, who seemed eager to serve as pool coordinators.

> They administered the system by favoritism, innuendo, by
> whispering in your ear like a grand vizier in the court of the
> Ottoman Empire . . . by taking care of their pals and phasing
> out the ones they didn't like, and particularly the ones who
> showed any enterprise. . . . You went out on your own, they
> fixed you. You didn't have to wait for the military to fix you,
> the media fixed themselves.[50]

Malcolm Browne exaggerated only slightly when he stated that in effect, "each pool member is an unpaid employee of the Department of Defense, on whose behalf he or she prepared the news of the war for the outer world."[51]

Instead of resisting such an insidious system, too many news organizations went along with it, hoping to strengthen their own positions vis-à-vis the competition. *Time*, *Newsweek*, and *U.S. News*

& World Report, for example, reportedly made a deal with the Defense Department that guaranteed them places in the various pools and excluded reporters from all other magazines.[52] In testimony before a Senate committee investigating the restrictions, Frank A. Aukofer, Washington bureau chief for the *Milwaukee Journal,* excoriated the mainstream media for their collaboration. "Instead of battling for access for all in the name of press freedom, they eagerly traded their journalistic principles for a few crumbs for themselves and starvation for many of their colleagues."[53]

The quisling mentality exhibited by pool enthusiasts in the journalistic community persisted into the final days of the war. Even after Kuwait City had been recaptured, initiative seemed scarce. Tony Horowitz of the *Wall Street Journal,* who had abandoned the pool arrangement and "gone unilateral," described an encounter with pool reporters. According to Horowitz, when he and a few independent colleagues arrived at the outskirts of the city, the pool members immediately asked, "Who are you? Where's your pool? Where's your escort?"[54] One is reminded of the World War II era reporters who, even after the conflict had ceased, wondered where they should go to get their stories cleared by military censors.

The Pentagon's Double Cross

The military's last line of defense against uncontrolled news reports was the power to censor—the requirement for "security review" that reverted to, and in some cases exceeded, World War II and Korean conflict standards in its severity. Throughout Operation Desert Storm, the pettiness of the military censors knew no bounds. Pool stories that quoted the sometimes graphic language of Navy pilots were sanitized by the censors. Journalists on the USS *Kennedy* who noted that pilots sometimes watched sexually explicit videotapes had that information stricken from their dispatches. When Frank Bruni, a reporter for the Detroit *Free Press,* had the temerity to describe the mood of returning pilots as "giddy," his military censor changed the word to "proud." Perhaps even more curious was the censor's insistence on changing Malcolm Browne's description of the F-117 "Stealth" aircraft from "fighter-bomber" to "fighter." The reason, Browne suspected, was that the Air Force was waging a vigorous campaign to save the beleaguered (and extremely expensive) B-2 Stealth bomber and feared that describing the F-117 as a fighter-bomber would give more ammunition to congressional critics who contended that the B-2 was unnecessary.[55] In any case, such petty actions made a mockery of the notion that the sole purpose of censorship was to protect the security of military operations.

If those who collaborated in the pool arrangements and other aspects of the government's news management system thought that their reward would be access to worthwhile stories once the ground combat phase of Operation Desert Storm began, they were disappointed. In earlier meetings with media representatives, Pete Williams had offered assurances that the journalists would ultimately be able to cover combat operations on their own. He outlined a "three-phase" system of coverage. Although in the first stage—the immediate prelude to and the initial phases of the fighting—there would be a virtual blackout of coverage, those restrictions were to ease substantially as soon as possible. In the second stage, the media would have more opportunities for coverage but would still have to operate within the confines of the pool system and censorship at the source. The third stage was the carrot the Pentagon held out to media representatives. ."Phase III would begin when open coverage is possible and would provide for unilateral coverage of all activities. The pools would be disbanded and all media would operate independently, although under U.S. Central Command escort."[56]

There were several aspects of Williams's assurances that should have made journalists suspicious of the Pentagon's intentions. The most obvious was the qualifier that even when "unilateral" coverage was authorized, reporters would still have to operate with their military escorts in tow. That is not exactly what most journalists think of as truly independent news sleuthing. A more subtle deficiency in the guidelines was the failure to specify time frames. It was not clear whether phase III would begin days, weeks, or months after the commencement of military operations—or whether it would begin when the Pentagon concluded that it had so controlled the way the conflict was portrayed that it could finally risk the appearance of a few uncontrolled stories. Moreover, even during phase III, the Pentagon retained the power to censor at the source.

As it turned out, the promise to allow unilateral coverage was virtually meaningless. During the initial stages of the ground offensive, even the pool reporters were kept far away from most significant action. As soon as the ground offensive began, Secretary of

Defense Cheney imposed a comprehensive news blackout, contending that the release of any information could jeopardize the safety of American troops. That blackout was lifted less than 12 hours later, once it became evident to the Pentagon that the war was quickly becoming a rout. Suddenly, the safety of U.S. military personnel did not seem so crucial. Lifting of the blackout, however, meant primarily that military briefers in Saudi Arabia were once again willing to be loquacious in presenting the military's version of events; it did not mean the onset of meaningful, independent press coverage. Howell Raines, Washington bureau chief of the *New York Times*, excoriated military officials for their hypocrisy, charging that they were using the operational security justification "as a means of imposing the blanket management of information of a sort we've never seen in this country. If they've loosened it today, it was because they had good news to report and it was in their interest to report it. What they've put in place is a mechanism to block out bad news and to keep good news in the forefront."[57] The *Washington Post*'s Michael Getler admitted later, "The ground war ... was described primarily by military briefers in the Pentagon and Saudi Arabia, which is what the Pentagon wanted all along; for them, not the pools or the press, to control the flow of information."[58]

The television networks were undoubtedly the most disappointed at the result. Instead of spectacular footage of a war in progress, viewers saw file films of military units training for the invasion of Iraq and occasional live shots of endless vistas of sand in which "coalition" forces appeared as clouds of dust on the horizon. In its first issue following the war, *Newsweek* lamented that "except for some archival footage shot by the military, historians will have no record of most of the actual fighting in the war."[59] That was television's reward for having cooperated with the military hierarchy. The print medium fared little better. Indeed, by the time reporters were authorized to work outside the pool system, most of the ground combat operations were already winding down. Furthermore, military authorities used a variety of techniques—including the tried and true methods of bureaucratic delay—to keep them as far away from ongoing combat as possible. Journalists in the theater of operations often did not know much more about the supposedly fierce tank battles between U.S. forces and units of Iraq's Republican Guard, for example, than did Americans back home, 8,000 miles away. When journalists were able to get access, the Pentagon's security review requirement typically meant that dispatches and film were delayed so long that they were useless. Marie Gottschalk noted sarcastically,

> During the Civil War, accounts of the Battle of Bull Run reached New York in 24 hours. During the Gulf War, it often took three to four days and in one case two weeks for reports filed from the battlefield to make the eight-hour drive to headquarters in Dhahran. Such delays allowed U.S. military officials to break and thereby shape major news stories.[60]

The Pentagon's explanation of the limited independent press coverage was that the collapse of Iraq's military resistance occurred so quickly that by the time phase III was implemented, the war was virtually over. There may be some truth to that defense, but military obstructionism never truly abated. Moreover, the way the coverage of the ground combat stage of Operation Desert Storm was handled must be viewed in the context of the government's conduct toward the media throughout the gulf crisis. From the beginning, U.S. officials viewed independent press coverage as a threat to be neutralized, and phase III was merely a more subtle continuation of that overall strategy. Unfortunately, the government succeeded all too well in achieving its objectives.

After the conflict, Stanley Cloud ruefully concluded that he and his colleagues had been both outmaneuvered and abused by U.S. officials.

> They figured out a way to control every facet of our coverage. They restricted our access to a point where we couldn't do any of our own reporting. They fed us a steady diet of press conferences in which they decided what the news would be. And if somehow, after all that, we managed to report on something they didn't like, they could censor it out. . . . It amounted to recruiting the press into the military.[61]

Sanitizing the War

The Pentagon's control of the news coming out of the Persian Gulf resulted in a version of events that was, at best, a distortion of reality. The pattern of "sanitized news" that characterized the invasions of Grenada and Panama was repeated in the gulf war. One notable piece of disinformation concerned the size and capabilities of the Iraqi army of occupation in Kuwait. The Bush administration's attempt to exaggerate Iraq's military strength, which began with the earliest phases of Operation Desert Shield, continued throughout the war—and the media swallowed it like carp gobbling larvae. According to the Pentagon, there were more than half a million battle-hardened Iraqi troops in and around Kuwait when the war commenced in January. The surprisingly anemic opposition to the ground war phase of Operation Desert Storm was attributed to the effects of the massive and sustained air campaign.

In reality, the Iraqi army confronting the U.S.-led forces was almost certainly no larger than 300,000 men when the war began and, given the epidemic of desertions, was probably under 200,000 at the time of the ground offensive.[62] Moreover, the bulk of those troops were ill-trained, half-starved conscripts whose morale was virtually nil. Even the Republican Guard units, which the press invariably called "elite," echoing the Pentagon's description, were only marginally better. One Pentagon official later conceded that the Republican Guard tanks "never fought the way you thought a division would fight. We just kind of chased them across the plains shooting at them."[63] The quality of Iraq's military in the gulf war can be gauged from the incidents in which troops waved white flags at low-flying drone aircraft and, in at least one case, tried to surrender to a television news crew. The equivalent of Germany's *Wehrmacht* in World War II, Saddam Hussein's forces were not.

Although in the immediate postwar period the Pentagon stuck to its claim that there had been more than 540,000 Iraqi troops in the Kuwaiti theater of operations, there were indications that officials had known otherwise all along. Even General Schwarzkopf conceded that U.S. military leaders overestimated the size and capabilities of Iraq's forces. An unnamed senior military commander was even more candid, admitting that official assessments of Iraqi defenses had been highly exaggerated. "There was a great disinformation campaign surrounding this war," he stated with apparent satisfaction.[64]

Why would the Pentagon deliberately inflate the capabilities of enemy forces, thereby increasing concerns about the possibility of thousands of American casualties? On the surface, that strategy would appear to run counter to the best interests of those who favored war against Iraq, since the fears generated would predictably strengthen public aversion to the military option. That conclusion, however, assumes that President Bush might have let public or congressional opposition dissuade him from resorting to force. In reality, he never entertained that possibility. Given the likelihood of war, the military hierarchy had two important motives for exaggerating Iraq's military power. First, by so doing the Pentagon increased pressure on civilian policymakers to authorize the deployment of overwhelming force to ensure victory. There would be no half-hearted incremental commitments as there had been in Vietnam; the military brass consciously opted for a strategy of overkill. Second, the inevitable military triumph over Iraq would be magnified if it appeared that the United States had defeated a powerful adversary. Defeating a rag-tag, Third World military opponent would not have the same impact.

One is reminded of the Spanish-American War, when most Americans were led to believe that the conflict would be long and bloody. That brief, comic-opera war actually produced few American combat deaths (about the same number as did Desert Storm), which proved to be a great relief to an anxious public. That the vaunted "Spanish Empire" was a military paper tiger did not prevent Theodore Roosevelt and other militarists from hyping the great U.S. victory. Likewise, the gulf war victors engaged in an orgy of triumphalism, conducting victory parades that went far beyond welcoming the troops home and expressing relief at the gratifyingly low number of U.S. casualties. Welcoming festivities were completely appropriate, but many of the celebrations were so ostentatious that one would have thought that the United States had defeated Nazi Germany, Imperial Japan, and Stalinist Russia combined.

It is relatively easy to understand why the Bush administration exaggerated Iraq's military prowess, but it is mystifying why the media passively transmitted such disinformation. Granted, reporters did not have ready access to intelligence data that would have debunked the Pentagon's claims. But they showed an appalling lack of curiosity and skepticism even when there was evidence in the public domain that should have raised serious doubts. A January 6, 1991, story in the *St. Petersburg Times*, in which an expert on satellite imagery concluded that commercial Soviet photos contradicted U.S. estimates of the number of Iraqi troops in Kuwait at the start of the gulf crisis, was ignored by other media outlets.[65] So too was the assessment of Iraq's military deficiencies by Tom Marks in the *Wall Street Journal*.

The gullibility of the media was equally evident in their helping the Pentagon to portray the gulf war as a "clean" war waged for the most part with surgical precision using the most sophisticated weaponry. The implication was that Washington was carefully pursuing a humane strategy to minimize civilian Iraqi casualties. Television viewers were treated to hours of videotape depicting the wonders of laser-guided "smart bombs" that could take out bridges or hit Baghdad's military command-and-control centers while leaving nearby civilians largely untouched. Indeed, there was almost a video game quality to the imagery—as though only electronic "targets" were being destroyed, not human beings. Investigative journalist Martin Yant conceded that "military officials magnificently stage-managed the war through briefings that featured gamelike videos and desensitizing descriptions of civilian casualties as 'collateral damage,' U.S. casualties as 'KIAs,' and killing as 'attriting.' "[66]

It is true that the U.S. strategy in the gulf war compared favorably with the saturation bombing campaigns of World War II (or in selected areas in Vietnam) that terrorized civilians. Given the massive application of air power, the number of Iraqi civilian casualties was surprisingly low (credible independent estimates range from 2,000 to 10,000 fatalities).[67] Nevertheless, the notion that the gulf conflict was waged primarily with precision-guided weapons is misleading. Weeks after the war, the Air Force conceded that such bombs and missiles constituted only 7 percent of the explosives dropped on Iraq. The rest were conventional bombs, many dropped from B-52s flying at high altitude. As the Vietnam experience demonstrated, the likelihood of "collateral" (i.e., civilian) damage from such weapons was high. And 10 percent of the "smart" bombs missed their targets, the Pentagon admitted, while the estimate for conventional bombs was 75 percent.[68]

The administration's propaganda that it had no quarrel with the people of Iraq—merely with Saddam Hussein—and that U.S. air strikes were directed only at military targets was equally misleading. Central Command leaders, it turned out, had a rather broad definition of military targets. Electrical generating plants and water purification plants, for example, met their criteria. Indeed, large portions of Iraq's civilian infrastructure came under attack, resulting in massive suffering. Hardest hit were the children, who often no longer had access to uncontaminated food and water or to antibiotics to fight off the inevitable infections. A survey conducted by an independent international panel of public health experts concluded that the infant and child mortality rate (the number of deaths per 1,000 live births) had risen approximately 200 percent in the months following the war—from a prewar level in the 30s to a postwar average in the 90s. That increase would have meant an excess of nearly 47,000 deaths of Iraqi children under five years of age.[69] Those children and the other civilians who perished were casualties of war just as surely as if they had been killed directly by U.S. bombs.

The Bush administration effectively manipulated the news media so as to hide the ugly realities of the gulf war. There were virtually no battlefield photographs of American casualties. Even photos of dead Iraqis were tightly controlled by the U.S. military. Martin Yant observes that control was so tight "that a photographer who tried to take one without permission was clubbed with a rifle by a soldier."[70] Correspondent Gregg Easterbrook later remarked that the reason the most "visual" war in history was strangely bereft of uncensored combat footage was not hard to fathom.

> Military censors went crazy when one field commander let reporters watch a gun camera video from an Apache gunship that snuck up on an Iraqi squad. In the tape, terror-stricken teenagers rush wildly in all directions as cannon rounds from the helicopter, which they can't see, slice their bodies in half. This video was quickly withdrawn from circulation. When I asked a senior Pentagon official why, he replied, "If we let people see that kind of thing there would never again be any war."[71]

It is not a coincidence that the vast majority of images of the human suffering caused by the war came from the tiny contingent of Western reporters, led by CNN's Peter Arnett, who remained in Baghdad to cover the conflict from the other side. They did so despite pressure from the administration on news organizations to evacuate all of their personnel from Iraq. Although the ostensible reason for the government's "requests" was concern about the safety of reporters, it is more likely that U.S. officials realized that reports from Baghdad would break the news monopoly they had labored so hard to achieve. The ugly innuendoes about Arnett's "loyalty" expressed by anonymous officials—and even more stridently by such prominent administration allies in Congress as Sen. Alan Simpson (R-Wyo.)—increase the suspicion that the government's motive for wanting no coverage from Baghdad was not concern for the safety of journalists.[72]

Arnett's dogged determination to transmit accounts of the war and its suffering despite heavy-handed Iraqi censorship and U.S. efforts to impugn his character was a refreshing exception to the media's compliant collaboration in the Bush administration's propaganda campaign. Overall, the media failed to cover an international crisis effectively and intelligently. *Time* correspondent Richard Zoglin's comment that "many journalists had the uneasy feeling that they had been routed nearly as decisively as the Iraqis" was all too true.[73]

Some members of the media did not seem to realize that there was a problem. Jeff Gralnick, executive producer in charge of ABC's gulf war coverage, echoed Pete Williams's assessment, contending that his network's performance was "as close to perfect as we can get."[74] Similarly, *Washington Post* columnist David Broder dismissed the complaints of many of his colleagues about the Pentagon's restrictions. "If the 160 'pool' reporters with combat units were not capable of describing the look, the sound and the feel of war, the news organizations that hired them should replace them. But in fact they proved their capability." Broder added that much of the "most valuable" reporting occurred after the war, and that was as it should have been because no war "can be adequately described or analyzed as it is happening."[75]

Marie Gottschalk responded that Broder's reasoning was troubling on several counts, not the least of which was that it downplayed "the importance of having information critical to the public debate come out at a time when a public debate is still possible." She noted, for example, that "the American public's enthusiasm to immediately dispatch hundreds of thousands of troops to the Middle East to defend Saudi Arabia from imminent attack might have been dampened if it were widely known that Iraqi troops had not massed on the Saudi border and that U.S. intelligence officials were doubtful that Iraq would invade Saudi Arabia."[76]

Part of the reason for the media's ineffectual performance in the gulf crisis was that the public, much as it did during the invasion of

Grenada, backed the government's policy of controlling information about the war. Indeed, according to one survey, 57 percent favored even stronger controls by the military.[77] Nonetheless, a considerable number of the media's wounds were self-inflicted. Journalists spent more time being cheerleaders for the war effort than they did assessing the pertinent issues. Instead of strenuously resisting the Pentagon's efforts to stifle press scrutiny of U.S. policy in the gulf, news personnel frequently exhibited signs of the Stockholm Syndrome, the pattern of prisoners' currying favor with and eventually beginning to identify with their captors. Martin Yant's assessment is an appropriate epitaph for the media's coverage of the gulf crisis.

> The Persian Gulf War was undoubtedly the most watched war in history. But it also was one of the least understood. It was a war in which truth was not only the first casualty but its last concern, as media manipulation and censorship took new and sinister forms.[78]

9. Yugoslavia and Somalia: The Media as 20th-Century Bourbons

The French statesman and political cynic Charles Maurice de Talleyrand concluded that the Bourbon monarchs of 18th- and 19th-century France exhibited a most peculiar reaction to being ousted from and restored to the throne. They forgot nothing of and learned nothing from those experiences. Much the same could be said of the American news media's experiences with foreign policy crises. Smarting from the humiliations they had endured in connection with the military operations in Grenada, in Panama, and—once they realized how badly they had been gulled—in the Persian Gulf, many journalists vowed that they would never again allow themselves to be manipulated by the government into promoting Washington's self-serving policy objectives. Stanley Cloud, in an especially combative mood, even ventured that the best course might be for editors simply to tell the Pentagon, "You go in and invade some Third World country, and we don't play. We'll get there on our own and somehow we'll cover it. We don't need these [press] pools."[1]

Members of the media had made similar vows after the Vietnam War, however, with little lasting effect, and it appears that the latest display of anger will have no greater significance. Indeed, within months after Cloud's brave declaration of independence, press representatives were negotiating with military officials about the rules of coverage for future U.S. armed interventions.

Once More into the Pool

In May 1992, after eight months of negotiations, an agreement was reached by the Defense Department and an alliance of key press associations and representatives of 20 news organizations. The nine principles of wartime news coverage that emerged from those negotiations were as follows:

> 1. Open and independent reporting will be the principal means of coverage of U.S. military operations.

215

2. Pools are not to serve as the standard means of covering U.S. military operations. Pools may sometimes provide the only feasible means of early access to a military operation. Pools should be as large as possible and disbanded at the earliest opportunity—within 24 to 36 hours when possible. The arrival of early-access pools will not cancel the principle of independent coverage for journalists already in the area.

3. Even under conditions of open coverage, pools may be appropriate for specific events, such as those at extremely remote locations or where space is limited.

4. Journalists in a combat zone will be credentialed by the U.S. military and will be required to abide by a clear set of military security ground rules that protect U.S. forces and their operations. Violation of the ground rules can result in suspension of credentials and expulsion from the combat zone of the journalist involved. News organizations will make their best efforts to assign experienced journalists to combat operations and to make them familiar with U.S. military operations.

5. Journalists will be provided access to all major military units. Special operations restrictions may limit access in some cases.

6. Military public affairs officers should act as liaisons but should not interfere with the reporting process.

7. Under conditions of open coverage, field commanders should be instructed to permit journalists to ride on military vehicles and aircraft whenever feasible. The military will be responsible for the transportation of pools.

8. Consistent with its capabilities, the military will supply PAOs [public affairs officers] with facilities to enable timely, secure, compatible transmission of pool material and will make these facilities available whenever possible for filing independent coverage. In cases when government facilities are unavailable, journalists will, as always, file by any other means available. The military will not ban communications systems operated by news organizations, but electromagnetic operational security in battlefield situations may require limited restrictions on the use of such systems.

9. These principles will apply as well to the operations of the standing Department of Defense National Media Pool system.[2]

It is indicative of the supplicant mentality of the media that representatives of the news industry regarded the adoption of such principles as a substantive victory, even though the pool system remained intact and journalists' access to future battlefields was still at the sufferance of the government. Clark Hoyt, Washington bureau chief of Knight-Ridder Newspapers, described the pact as "a large step forward from where we were when the Persian Gulf War started." Even the oft-burned Stanley Cloud stated that, although it required "an act of faith" on the part of the news media to believe that Pentagon officials had negotiated in good faith, "I assume they did."[3]

In reality, the agreement was a barely disguised media surrender to the government's suffocating news management policy. The Pentagon refused to budge on one of the most crucial issues: mandatory review of all news stories from military theaters of operations. Moreover, even when the government appeared to make concessions, they were either meaningless or were so hedged by caveats, conditions, and provisos that they could easily be rendered meaningless. Such phrases as "whenever possible" or "whenever feasible" pervaded the guidelines—leaving the government unrestricted power to make the final decision in any given case. Similarly, the Defense Department's commitment to facilitate news coverage was typically couched in terms of "should" not "will"—providing an easy escape clause. As if the government's promises were not meaningless enough, even the principles officially agreed to were acknowledged to be "nonbinding."

Marie Gottschalk, associate editor of *World Policy Journal*, provides a devastatingly accurate indictment of the document.

> With this agreement, the media have once again rolled over and played dead, allowing great constitutional questions to be bargained away in a series of negotiations with military officials who have a history of trampling on previous agreements. The gaps in the latest agreement are wide enough to drive an M-1 tank through, and it includes no mechanism that would allow the media to compel the Pentagon to abide by its provisions.[4]

True, there was little the journalistic community could do (absent the support of an outraged public) to prevent the Pentagon from arbitrarily excluding all coverage—as the invasion of Grenada had demonstrated. The media probably concluded that getting the government's advance consent for even tethered coverage was preferable to enduring another blackout. That attitude was understandable, but in some ways the negotiations were worse than risking total

217

exclusion. Philosopher Ayn Rand aptly concluded that the most insidious repression is one that involves the "sanction of the victim." When journalists sit down with military officials to bargain about the conditions under which the government will deign to respect fundamental First Amendment rights, they sanction their own repression.

The facade of accord was razed in September 1992 when the Pentagon unilaterally proposed revisions to the agreement, effectively rescinding most of the concessions that news organizations thought they had obtained in May. In some respects, the September guidelines are worse than previous arrangements. For example, Pentagon officials took the position that only U.S.-owned and U.S.-operated media organizations with large Washington bureaus and a military affairs reporter should be eligible to participate in pools. As would have the government's earlier unsuccessful attempt, spearheaded by Gen. Winant Sidle in 1984, to pick the news organizations that would be members of the pool, that requirement would effectively exclude smaller, more iconoclastic publications. The new military guidelines specify that once a pool is activated, "representatives of member organizations must remain with their media escort at all times."[5] In other words, reporters in future combat operations would again be unable to conduct interviews without their military handlers looking over their shoulders. In addition, the guidelines would give Department of Defense officials and even local military commanders the right to implement new rules of coverage at any time for "security" reasons.

An editorial in *Editor and Publisher* captured the sense of betrayal within the "go along to get along" faction of the journalistic community. "By unilaterally writing rules for the National Press Pool and publishing them in the *Federal Register* as if it were a 'done deal,' officials at the Pentagon have put a knife in the back of every news executive who negotiated in good faith last spring to produce the agreed-upon nine principles of combat coverage."[6] This time, however, media representatives reacted with somewhat greater fortitude, demanding that the Department of Defense either rewrite the rules or dissolve the pools.

The inability of the press to learn from its mistakes is mystifying. Twice before, journalists tried to be cooperative and entice the government to respect their First Amendment rights—and twice before they were double-crossed. In the immediate aftermath of the Grenada news blackout, media representatives became part of the Sidle panel that came up with the original pool concept and established other guidelines for coverage of future military operations. With the issuance of the Sidle panel report, the press thought it had a commitment from the Pentagon to allow journalists to do their jobs. The prevailing assumption was that DoD officials had negotiated in good faith. Associated Press correspondent Fred Hoffman expressed the consensus of his colleagues. "I think there is a general recognition that things should have been done differently in Grenada."[7]

The faith of journalists that the government had merely overreacted in Grenada was as touching as it was naive. How naive became apparent five years later when the Pentagon deftly excluded the press from covering the invasion of Panama. Ironically, Hoffman was the author of the Pentagon's March 1990 postmortem on that event. (In the intervening years Hoffman had become a Pentagon spokesman—yet another example of the revolving-door problem.) The Hoffman report repeated most of the assumptions of the earlier Sidle report. Although Hoffman had expressed some sharp criticism of Assistant Secretary of Defense for Public Affairs Pete Williams and even Secretary of Defense Richard Cheney, the exclusion of the press was attributed largely to excessive concern on the part of military leaders for maintaining the secrecy of the operation, to poor organization, and to inadequate communication between the military hierarchy and the media. "So far as I could determine," Hoffman stated, "there was no effort to manipulate the [media] pool in Panama. Rather, it was a matter of maladroitness, sometimes good intentions gone awry, and unanticipated obstacles."[8] The underlying premise was that the DoD had acted in good faith, merely botching the execution of a basically workable pool system. Indeed, Hoffman later went out of his way to stress how the pool arrangement had worked well in covering the Persian Gulf reflagging operation in 1987–88.[9]

Pentagon leaders accepted most of the recommendations in the Hoffman report—the common theme of which was how to make the pool system work better and to prevent misunderstandings between reporters and the military. Again, the journalistic community thought that it had a commitment from officials that would permit effective coverage of future military engagements. The restrictions placed on the media during the gulf war barely six months later demonstrated that the new promises were no better than the previous ones. One might have thought that having been burned twice by the Pentagon, journalists would have refused to participate in any further negotiations, or at least would have viewed any government commitments with more than a little skepticism. Yet most mainstream media representatives shied away from a confrontational approach, preferring a strategy of cooperation and quiet lobbying.

The media's timidity was apparent when several critics of the gulf war, including *Harper's*, the *Nation*, and *Mother Jones*, filed suit in federal court challenging the Bush administration's restrictions on coverage. The media establishment was noticeable by its absence. Various mainstream editors and publishers even condemned the court action as "counterproductive." Perhaps even more indicative of that supplicant mentality was the reaction of the television networks and many of the large metropolitan dailies to Senate committee hearings on the government's shackling of the press during the gulf conflict. Instead of seizing that opportunity to focus the glare of publicity on the Pentagon's conduct, Sydney Schanberg noted with disgust, the mainstream media, "looking more and more like an arm of the government's executive branch, chose not to send representatives to testify."[10]

The favorable reaction to the May 1992 agreement, and the expressions of disillusionment when the Pentagon reneged on some of its provisions, showed once more that the media still did not understand that the government had its own agenda—and permitting effective, independent coverage of military operations was not part of it, unless such coverage happened to serve administration goals. Like the Bourbons, the media seemed utterly incapable of learning from their mistakes.

Somalia: The Media as Pentagon Press Agent

Despite its ongoing efforts to control the press, the Pentagon did give the media far greater latitude in covering the military mission in Somalia—at least until it began to go badly in the summer of 1993. Indeed, some critics of the press contended that the Pentagon had become too lax in its restrictions. The spectacle of Navy SEALS and Marine advance units coming ashore in Mogadishu in December

1992 under the blaze of television klieg lights and being met by a phalanx of reporters bordered on the tragicomic.

Fortunately, there were no hostile forces capable of exploiting the chaos to inflict casualties on U.S. personnel, but reporters could not be positive that such danger did not exist. Their conduct violated long-standing standards of avoiding press coverage that would endanger ongoing military operations. Not only was the media's conduct irresponsible, it was the worst sort of political blunder since it gave media bashers in the Pentagon and elsewhere additional ammunition.[11]

It is equally important to note, however, that the military was not blameless for the Mogadishu landing fiasco. In marked contrast to its obsession with limiting coverage of the gulf crisis, the Pentagon leadership wanted maximum attention paid to the armed forces' "humanitarian" mission in Somalia. That enterprise was in part an advertisement for the continuing relevance of U.S. military forces in the turbulent post–Cold War world and a not-so-subtle message to the American people that no further budget or personnel cuts should be made. Media coverage of the Mogadishu landing was expected and encouraged; it just turned out to be too much of a good thing.[12]

The military command's willingness to give journalists easy access to the Somalia operation despite the plethora of armed militias and the chaotic political situation in the country also casts doubt on the official justifications for previous restrictive measures. Correspondent John Lancaster noted, "Pentagon officials are eager to advertise—both to Somalia and the rest of the world—the precedent-setting humanitarian mission. . . . As a result, they have generally avoided the tight media restrictions that prevailed during the 1991 Persian Gulf War, *freely sharing operational details that normally would remain secret.*"[13] Retired Army Col. David Hackworth, now a columnist for *Newsweek*, observed the same phenomenon. "During Desert Storm, press officers treated reporters as the enemy and kept them pinned down. This time the brass gave away every detail of Operation Restore Hope: mission, assault beach, objectives, troop strengths, even commanders' names."[14]

It was not credible to argue that the security environment in Somalia was less dangerous than that in the Persian Gulf, Panama, or Grenada. Indeed, it would have been more plausible to assert the opposite. (The outbreak of attacks on U.S. and UN forces in June 1993 and the rapid escalation of incidents—including the slaying of several journalists—in the succeeding months confirmed that point.) The reason for the national security bureaucracy's atypical encouragement of widespread coverage was that, at least initially, the military hierarchy believed that unrestricted media coverage of developments in Somalia was in the institutional interests of the Pentagon.

Predictably, when the Somalia operation changed from an ostensibly humanitarian mission to guerrilla warfare in Mogadishu against the forces of Gen. Mohammed Farah Aideed, the U.S. military command quickly became less cooperative. Reports (especially television footage) of American troops distributing food to hungry Somali children were appreciated; coverage of U.S. Cobra helicopter gunships slaughtering Somali civilians, or pictures of an angry Somali mob dragging the body of an American soldier through the streets of Mogadishu, was not. After the fighting escalated in October, *Washington Post* correspondent Howard Kurtz concluded, "The Defense Department has not gone out of its way to facilitate news coverage."[15] By October most U.S. and other Western journalists had left Mogadishu because of the danger.

The Pentagon did not even activate the combat press pool, thus seemingly ignoring the military's own stated objectives. Defense Department spokesperson Kathleen deLaski insisted that the Pentagon's guidelines for press coverage did not apply in Somalia because technically the operation was a UN humanitarian effort, not a U.S. combat mission.[16] That was yet another example of the DoD's interpreting the rules in whatever manner seemed to benefit its institutional interests, no matter how cynical or implausible the interpretation. Only after the mainstream media howled in protest did the military hierarchy relent, and even then, the White House sent its media affairs director, Jeff Eller, to "assist" the press pool (i.e., try to make certain that pool members muted their criticism of the Clinton administration's Somalia policy).[17]

The military's reaction to negative press coverage went beyond lack of cooperation. As the Somalia intervention became increasingly bloody and controversial, military officials refused to allow reporters to interview commanders or soldiers returning from missions. In the most startling incident, a U.S. helicopter deliberately fired stun grenades at Peter Northall, a British photographer for Associated Press, as he was taking pictures of the aircraft attacking crowds near a skirmish between U.S. forces and a militia unit of General Aideed.[18]

Not only were reporters at the mercy of the Pentagon on military matters; they also toed the government line on practical and political matters. In fact, most mainstream journalists, wittingly or unwittingly, fell into the habit of disseminating government propaganda and hyping the interventionist cause.

Reporters rarely questioned the allegations of the United Nations and the State Department that the various Somali militias were hijacking most of the relief supplies sent to aid starving civilians. Yet Rakiya Omaar, an expert on Somalia and—until she dared oppose the U.S.-led military intervention—the head of Africa Watch, contended that most experienced private relief organizations, such as the International Red Cross and Save the Children, were able to get 80 percent or more of their supplies to the intended recipients. Losses of that magnitude were entirely normal for relief operations in the Third World. Only the less experienced organizations, which failed to understand the need to bribe the right authorities, and the chronically inefficient UN bureaucracy found it impossible to deliver aid. Omaar argued that military intervention was unnecessary and smacked of neocolonialism.[19] All that was needed, in her view, was a more astute understanding of the political realities on the part of some of the humanitarian organizations and, possibly, a strategy of simply flooding Somalia with so much food that even the various armed factions could not siphon off enough to do major damage.

Other knowledgeable regional specialists echoed Omaar's thesis, but the mass media in the United States virtually ignored such arguments. Yet once the U.S. intervention was under way, it became apparent that the threat of starvation in Somalia—while bad—was less severe than Washington and the United Nations had alleged. Instead of the "more than one million people facing starvation" figure that appeared in numerous media accounts, the actual number at risk appeared to be about 10 percent of that number, or 100,000. Moreover, the worst of the problem appeared to be over by the time U.S. troops arrived—a detail that only a few publications mentioned long after the intervention began.[20]

Exaggerating the extent of the threat of starvation in Somalia was not the only way the media helped to promote Washington's policy agenda. Few reporters bothered to analyze the military's institutional (especially budgetary) stake in demonstrating capabilities in an environment typical of those in which problems could be anticipated in the post–Cold War world. Yet even Gen. Colin Powell offered barely concealed hints of such motives when he noted that if severe cuts in military spending were made, the military might some day be incapable of undertaking missions like the one in Somalia. After the American forces went ashore, some Pentagon officials were even more candid—at least on a "not for attribution" basis. "We're letting service politics play this out," conceded one official in late December. "Because the Marines didn't get to exercise an amphibious operation in the Persian Gulf, we let them do it in Somalia."[21] Media analyses of possible self-serving motives were in short supply, however, in the weeks leading up to the intervention. Although, given the widespread public support for the humanitarian mission, such stories might not have made much difference, they would have at least caused some Americans to view the government's justifications for future military enterprises with greater skepticism.

Perhaps even worse was the credulity with which the media accepted the government's portrayal of the political situation in Somalia. Journalists invariably described feuding Somali political leaders as "warlords" and the militias as "bandits" and "gangs." Such depictions were little more than oversimplified State Department propaganda that was used to lull the American people into accepting the government's contention that the United States could intervene militarily without being caught up in intractable political disputes. If the various factions were not motivated by ideology, or even discernible political agendas, but were merely "armed thugs," the image of the United States as a humanitarian rescuer restoring law and order was more credible.

Such a condescending evaluation of Somalia's political landscape was profoundly misleading. True, there were rarely deep ideological or political differences between the various factions; family or clan loyalties, or simply personal ambitions, frequently were more important than ideology. And many of the militia units did routinely engage in thuggish behavior. Nevertheless, it is interesting to compare Washington's depiction of Somalia's political environment with that of the equally chaotic and fragmented situation in Afghanistan a few years earlier. U.S. officials never described even the most

224

authoritarian and ruthless leaders of the *mujaheddin* as "warlords" or the often feuding factions as "gangs." Instead, Washington called them all "freedom fighters"—a term that persisted even after the Soviet Union withdrew its army of occupation and the *mujaheddin* spent as much time fighting among themselves as they did trying to oust the communist government in Kabul.[22] It is equally interesting to note that most members of the news media slavishly repeated the government's positive terminology, just as they would later echo the negative descriptions of the Somali factions.

Once Washington and the United Nations singled out Aideed as the principal villain in Somalia's political turmoil after the clash between Aideed's militia and UN forces in June, the media followed suit in their interpretations. Aideed became the personification of evil in most American news reports, while the vilification of rival Somali leaders went into eclipse. News stories might have led readers to assume that Aideed's first and middle names were Fugitive and Warlord. When U.S. policy shifted after the bloody fighting in early October, and the Clinton administration then sought a dialogue with Aideed, however, the media treatment of the onetime odious warlord underwent a remarkable transformation. Princeton University professor Richard Falk excoriates that flip-flop as another in a series of episodes that demonstrate the "docile character" of the mainstream media.

> Without even a raised eyebrow, political assessments are altered overnight at the whim of the state. The most extreme recent instance is that of the P.L.O. and Yassir Arafat, which shed their terrorist identities as soon as the political mood changed course. But the description of Aidid was equally manipulated: When the focus was upon eliminating his opposition [to U.S. policy], he was portrayed as a hated warlord, but as soon as the United States negotiated with his representatives to achieve a cease-fire, Aidid was immediately described far more benignly as a respected "clan leader." Flattering pictures of a smiling Aidid were suddenly being shown on TV and in newspapers, which described his position as that of a relevant, even if not sympathetic, political leader.[23]

The cartoonish assessments of Aideed and his role were symptomatic of a larger failing on the part of the U.S. news media. Most journalists failed to convey any understanding of the nature of the political issues in Somalia to readers or viewers. For example, they barely mentioned the secessionist movement in northern Somalia that had already established the independent republic of Somaliland.[24] Yet examining the bid for independence by the dominant Issak clan and other groups in the north should have been relevant for a number of reasons. First, the establishment of a de facto government in that region had enabled the population to avoid most of the chaos and suffering that afflicted the rest of Somalia. Given the dismal prospects for political stability and economic progress in southern Somalia for the foreseeable future, the desire for an independent political existence was understandable. Second, there was at least a plausible historical justification for secession from Somalia. During the colonial era northern Somalia had been governed by the British as the colony of Somaliland, while the southern region had been ruled by Italy. That experience, lasting several decades (including the fascist era in Italy), led to the creation of social and economic patterns that were different in subtle but significant ways. Most notably, respect for democratic values seemed measurably stronger in the north. Third, although the available evidence was admittedly fragmentary and circumstantial, it appeared that support for independence was strong among both the Issak and smaller groups.

U.S. officials seemed oblivious to such considerations. Washington signed on as the military agent of the United Nations in Somalia, even though there were indications from the very beginning that Secretary General Boutros Boutros-Ghali was firmly committed to restoring the unity of the country. In the weeks leading up to the U.S. intervention, he stressed repeatedly that the goal of the United Nations was to orchestrate a "reconciliation" of *all* Somali political factions. That policy goal did not seem to leave much room for the secession of Somaliland.[25]

Unfortunately, Boutros-Ghali's attitude was typical of the United Nations' long-standing bias in favor of preserving the status quo around the world. Throughout its history the United Nations has displayed an aversion to secessionist movements—especially in the Third World. The organization's massive effort to preserve the unity of the Congo (now Zaire) in the early 1960s, its hostility to Biafra's attempt to secede from Nigeria in the late 1960s and early 1970s, and the enthusiasm for the unity of such inherently unstable entities as Chad and Sudan are examples.

It was not at all clear why the United States should serve as the United Nations' agent for implementing such a policy in Somalia. Yet that was one of the consequences of the intervention. Once U.S. forces restored a semblance of order to southern Somalia, the United Nations moved to take over responsibility by introducing a "peacekeeping" force of approximately 20,000 personnel in the spring of 1993. As early as February, during talks with the U.S. military command, UN officials had made clear their intent to deploy peacekeeping units throughout *all* of Somalia—including Somaliland. Since the United States agreed to leave 5,000 troops behind as a contribution to that peacekeeping force, Washington implicitly signed on to the United Nations' larger policy agenda.[26]

Journalists should have been asking hard questions early on about both the morality and the practicality of the United Nations' determination to restore a united Somalia. Even more important, they should have asked whether it was possible for the United States to become involved in Somalia for humanitarian objectives without being implicated in that dubious political goal and otherwise becoming entangled in Somalia's fractious politics. Such questions were seldom asked. As they had done in the gulf crisis, the media largely failed to analyze the historical and political context of the Somalia tragedy.[27] Americans were given the most shallow, albeit emotionally evocative, accounts of the Marines on a noble quest to save the Somalis from starvation.

Not only was that not the whole story, it was not even the most important part of the story. The journalistic community's ineptitude enabled the Bush and Clinton administrations to escape serious scrutiny of a policy that was either myopic or callous. Most Americans remained blissfully unaware that the United States was helping undermine the attempt of the people of Somaliland to secure freedom and independence, thereby consigning them indefinitely to the political and economic chaos of an unwanted union with Somalia. Likewise, they did not realize that both Washington and the UN leadership were playing favorites in Somalia's volatile, factional politics—especially by trying to undercut the position of Aideed and his subclan, the Hebr Gedir. The general lack of meaningful press analysis guaranteed that the American public would be unprepared for the unraveling of the humanitarian mission and the outbreak of heavy fighting in the summer and autumn of 1993.

An American civilian official working with the United Nations in Mogadishu conceded in September that "in many ways, the American people were misled." He added that at the time of the initial intervention, "nobody recalled hearing about this nation-building thing—that kind of snuck up on the American people."[28] One important reason that it "snuck up" on most Americans is that the press had largely echoed the self-serving statements of U.S. and UN leaders and focused on peripheral rather than central issues.

Yellow Journalism Returns: Reporting the War in Yugoslavia

The media's record in covering the Yugoslavian conflict has been perhaps even worse than their performance in Somalia. As the Yugoslavian crisis deepened, Washington painted an oversimplified picture of naked Serb aggression against the innocent, freedom-loving populations of Croatia and Bosnia. U.S. officials labeled various Serbian leaders—especially Serbia's president Slobodan Milosevic—war criminals and spoke ominously about the need for the international community to convene a war crimes tribunal. The shopworn 1930s analogy was brought out once more, with Serbia becoming the 1990s version of Nazi Germany and Milosevic playing the role of the new Hitler. There was a vigorous campaign throughout 1992 and 1993 to demonize Serbia—much as Iraq had been demonized in the months leading up to Operation Desert Storm.

A distressing number of journalists not only accepted the government's statements at face value but presented an even more simplistic caricature of the struggle. The coverage of the Yugoslavian conflict highlights how members of the media have internalized global interventionist assumptions. A mundane civil war in the Balkans has been portrayed in terms of the intellectual paradigm created during World War II and the Cold War.

In a thoughtful critique of the media's coverage of the Balkan struggle, Sylvia Poggioli, a foreign correspondent for National Public Radio, cited the tenacious quality of the Cold War mindset.

> The Cold War had accustomed generations of reporters to analyze world events almost exclusively in terms of the bipolar confrontation, where good and evil were easily defined and identified. This mindset often proved unsuitable in trying to make sense of the disorder created by the collapse of

communism. And it was easy prey for the highly sophisticated propaganda machines that have characterized the conflicts in former Yugoslavia.[29]

The media's performance in examining the Yugoslavian struggle is
especially disappointing because journalists have not had to contend
with obstructionism and massive manipulation by the U.S. government as in previous crises. News personnel have had the opportunity
to provide incisive coverage free from Washington's interference,
yet they have generally failed to do so.

The media have reflexively accepted the notion that the events
in the former Yugoslavia are a replay of the 1930s and that the
international community must take action to repel Serb aggression
or the world will again risk a military conflagration. That thesis is
an even more tortured misinterpretation of history than the earlier
campaign to portray Iraq as the equivalent of Nazi Germany. In the
first place, the fighting in Croatia and Bosnia is hardly a clear case
of cross-border aggression. Most of the insurgent fighters are members of Serbian communities in those two countries, not "outside
agitators." Although Belgrade has provided some logistical support
and some Serbian nationals have joined their ethnic brethren, the
struggles in Croatia and Bosnia show far more of the characteristics
of civil wars than of international conflicts.

Indeed, the primary reason the two conflicts became "internation-
alized" was the hasty decision by the United States, prominent members of the European Community (primarily Germany), and the
United Nations to recognize the independent nations of Bosnia and
Croatia with the boundaries those two republics had had in the
disintegrating Yugoslavian federation. That action ignored the fact
that those boundaries had been arbitrarily imposed by communist
dictator Josip Broz Tito in the 1940s, had little historical basis, and
were designed to be *internal* boundaries within Yugoslavia. Large
Serb minorities who were adamantly opposed to living under the
domination of other ethnic groups existed in both countries.[30] The
predictable results were secessionist movements and bloodshed.
Although Belgrade was undoubtedly guilty of encouraging and aiding secessionist forces, its actions were hardly comparable to Nazi
Germany's flagrant and repeated aggression against other well-
established nations.

Moreover, even if one accepts the argument that Serbia is a brutal aggressor, the argument that the world confronts a new Nazi Germany is a distortion. The situation in the 1930s involved one of the world's great powers—one with the second largest economy and a large, well-trained military force—embarking on an expansionist binge. Serbia, on the other hand, has a population of 9.8 million (about the same as Belgium's) and a gross domestic product that is less than one-fifth the size of Denmark's. (Indeed, its 1991 GDP of $18.75 billion was only modestly greater than Luxembourg's.)[31] In the 1930s Germany was capable of creating a massive disruption of the international system; in the 1990s Serbia is capable only of helping to foment a nasty but parochial conflict in the perennially unstable Balkans. Portraying Serbia as a threat comparable to that posed by Nazi Germany is even more far-fetched than portraying Iraq in that role.

The argument that Serbia is like Nazi Germany in another way—the rabid nationalism and ethnic hatred exhibited by the Milosevic regime and its followers—is more plausible. Both the Belgrade government and the Serbian rebel forces in Croatia and Bosnia have practiced the most intolerant chauvinism and committed atrocities. Nevertheless, both Washington's and the media's description of Serbian policies and practices seems designed to make a bad situation appear even worse.

Unfortunately, the State Department's most inflammatory and misleading terminology has become a routine feature of news stories. "Ethnic cleansing," for example, quickly became a synonym for genocide. But as syndicated columnist Charles Krauthammer, MIT political scientist Daryl Press, and a few other skeptics have pointed out, what is going on in Yugoslavia cannot accurately be termed genocide. Instead of exterminating members of other ethnic groups, the principal Serbian objective is to expel them from certain territories. Although that is certainly a reprehensible practice—and has been accompanied by acts of murder—it does not fit the definition of genocide.[32]

Furthermore, contrary to the impression fostered by U.S. officials, ethnic cleansing is not a uniquely Serbian activity.[33] One does not need to look too far to find pertinent examples of ethnic cleansing elsewhere in the world. One such incident occurred when the British colony of India was partitioned and granted independence in 1947.

Millions of Hindus were expelled from the new Islamic nation of Pakistan while millions of Muslims had to flee predominantly Hindu India. Nearly 250,000 people perished in the accompanying blood-shed.[34] From the standpoint of U.S. culpability, an even more odious episode took place at the end of World War II when nearly 16 million ethnic Germans were expelled from Poland, Czechoslovakia, and other East European countries solely because of their ethnicity. Not only did the United States fail to take any action to prevent that forced exodus, President Harry S Truman openly endorsed the step at the Potsdam Conference, with the sole proviso that the process be "humane."[35]

More recently, Turkey drove some 200,000 Greek Cypriots from the northern portion of Cyprus when Turkish forces invaded and occupied nearly 40 percent of the island in 1974. Again, it is instructive to compare the U.S. response to Ankara's actions with Washington's vehement condemnation of Serb policy in Yugoslavia. There has never been the slightest consideration given to using military action against Turkey to restore the Greek Cypriots to their homes. The Serbs have a point when they contend that the United States and other countries employ a blatant double standard regarding ethnic cleansing. Yet most of the American news media have failed to examine those other incidents or to ask why the U.S. response was so passive in every case other than the current one in the former Yugoslavia.

It is not that negative stories about Serbian actions in the Yugoslav conflict are totally false. Much of the conduct of the government in Belgrade and of the Serb militias operating in Bosnia and Croatia is indeed reprehensible. Nevertheless, the image of the Yugoslavian conflict that has emerged in the U.S. media is oversimplified at best and utterly unfair at worst. The Serbs are hardly the only parties engaged in ethnic cleansing. Poggioli notes that "it was not until the Muslims and Croats—erstwhile allies—began massacring each other this spring [1993] that journalists were forced to deal with the 'other war' and discovered that reciprocal 'ethnic cleansing' had been going on for months in Central and Southwestern Bosnia."[36]

A January 1993 report by the UN High Commissioner for Refugees revealed some interesting data on the number of people displaced by the fighting. The largest totals were in Croatia and Bosnia (573,000 and 810,000 people, respectively). Virtually all of the former and a majority (although by no means all) of the latter were Croats and Muslims. However, some 463,000 refugees had found shelter in Serbia, 87,000 in Croatian provinces occupied by Serbian forces, and 64,000 in Montenegro, Serbia's sister republic in the rump Yugoslavian state.[37] It is a safe assumption that the overwhelming majority of those displaced persons were Serbs, not Croats or Muslims. Yet the point that between 30 and 40 percent of the people who had been driven from their homes were Serbs managed to elude most American journalists.

An interventionist bias was evident even in the differential coverage given reports of atrocities. For example, a European Community report in January 1993, alleging that Serbian forces had raped more than 20,000 Bosnian and Croatian women, became the lead story in most major metropolitan daily newspapers. A UN commission report issued a short time later—which insisted that no reliable estimates could be made of the number of rapes and that, although Serb military personnel had committed a majority of atrocities in the Yugoslavian conflict, *all* sides were guilty of such practices— was either ignored or buried in the back pages. (The *Washington Post*, for instance, printed a brief dispatch from Reuters news service on page 16.)[38]

At times Washington's version of the rape issue verged on the bizarre. In an interview on ABC's *Good Morning America*, the U.S. delegate to the UN Human Rights Commission, Geraldine Ferraro, asserted that although rape had been part of virtually every war, this was "the first time when rape is being used as a weapon of war."[39] That statement was historically unfounded. Rape has frequently been an integral part of a victorious army's strategy for demoralizing and humiliating an opponent. As Susan Brownmiller, a leading feminist historian of rape, concludes in reviewing the situation in the former Yugoslavia, "There is nothing unprecedented about mass rape in war. . . . Sexual trespass on the enemy's women is one of the satisfactions of conquest."[40] That was true as far back as the days of the Roman Republic; indeed, it was openly encouraged by some of the republic's most successful generals, including Scipio Africanus, Gaius Marius, and Lucius Cornelius Sulla. It has been equally true in modern times; Soviet military forces invading Germany at the end of World War II raped the majority of females between the ages of 8 and 80 as a deliberate "payback" for the conduct of Nazi troops in the Soviet Union earlier in the war. Typically, however, ABC's host Joan Lunden failed to challenge Ferraro's implausible allegations.

The same willingness to parrot or even expand on Washington's propaganda was evident in the extensive media coverage of Serb-run prison camps. Much of the coverage was highly inflammatory, including frequent descriptions of the facilities as "death camps." Typical of the treatment was an ABC Television news special on the conflict in the former Yugoslavia that aired in the summer of 1994. That program began with Peter Jennings's appearance in front of the Holocaust Memorial Museum in Washington, D.C., and his unsubtle allegations that a repetition of the Holocaust was under way in Bosnia.

Such attempts to equate the events in Yugoslavia with Hitler's systematic campaign to exterminate the Jews and other minorities were grotesque exaggerations; the deaths of thousands, as terrible as that may be, can hardly be compared to the deaths of millions.[41] The horrors in Croatia and Bosnia are not remotely as bad as the Holocaust, or Stalin's terror in the 1930s or Mao Zedong's "Great Leap Forward" in the 1950s—both of which each claimed at least 20 million victims. Pol Pot's extermination of approximately 1 million of his own countrymen during the three-year period the Khmer Rouge ruled Cambodia also provides some useful perspective on the magnitude of the suffering in Yugoslavia. Indeed, one can make a good case that the violence in Bosnia and Croatia does not even compare with the atrocities committed in such places as Guatemala, Afghanistan, and Mozambique in the 1980s or that continue today in such countries as Sudan, Angola, or Rwanda. Yet given the nature of the media coverage, most Americans have every reason to believe that the human rights violations in the former Yugoslavia rival those of the Holocaust. Gen. Lewis MacKenzie, the UN commander in Bosnia, accurately described the phenomenon as one of "sophisticatedly exaggerated" atrocities in the American press.[42]

Most members of the media have failed to question those distorted presentations. The few journalists who have pointed out that the existence of detention camps—even those operated in a brutal manner—and atrocities committed by Serb militia units cannot be equated with the Holocaust have been drowned out. Even when more restrained, balanced, and accurate accounts have emerged, they have tended to come out in lower profile settings long after the inflammatory stories have attracted maximum public attention. For example, buried in the middle of a *New York Times* editorial in late January 1993 was a brief comment that although a majority of detention camps were run by the Serbs, U.S. intelligence had also identified some 35 camps run by Croatian and Bosnian government forces.[43] Most readers of previous *Times* editorials, columns, and op-eds excoriating the Serbs and calling for Western military intervention would probably have concluded that the Serbian side was the only one guilty of such practices.[44]

Peter Brock, an editor with the *El Paso Herald-Post*, castigated many of his colleagues for "negligence" and "pack journalism" in their coverage of death camps and stories of other atrocities. In a scathing critique in the pages of *Foreign Policy*, Brock enumerated a few of the more egregious "mistakes."

> The August 17, 1992, *Time* cover photo . . . showed a smiling, shirtless, skeletal man who was described as being among "Muslim prisoners in a Serbian detention camp." In fact, the man was a Serb—Slobodan Konjević, who . . . had been arrested and confined on charges of looting. Konjević, more dramatically emaciated than others who wore shirts in the picture, had suffered from tuberculosis for 10 years, said his sister in Vienna.
>
> Among wounded "Muslim toddlers and infants" aboard a Sarajevo bus hit by sniper fire in August 1992 were a number of Serb children—a fact revealed much later. One of the children who died in the incident was identified at the funeral as Muslim by television reporters. But the unmistakable Serbian Orthodox funeral ritual told a different story.
>
> In its January 4, 1993, issue, *Newsweek* published a photo of several bodies with an accompanying story that began: "Is there any way to stop Serbian atrocities in Bosnia?" The photo was actually of Serb victims.
>
> CNN aired reports in March and May 1993 from the scenes of massacres of 14 Muslims and the 10 Muslims who were supposedly killed by Serbs. The victims later turned out to be Serbs. There was no correction.[45]

For daring to criticize the media's coverage of the Bosnian war, Brock was subjected to vilification that went far beyond the bounds of hard-hitting debate. *Newsday*'s Roy Gutman, for example, not

234

only sought to refute Brock's claims and argue that there were factual errors in the *Foreign Policy* article (which is a legitimate debating technique), but implied—with virtually no evidence—that Brock was on the payroll of the Serbian-American lobbying organization SerbNet.[46]

Gutman's foray into McCarthyism was tame, however, compared with the efforts of Charles Lane. Writing in the pages of the *New Republic*, Lane employed innuendo after innuendo to suggest that Brock was a front man for Serb propagandists.[47] According to the editors of *Foreign Policy* (Charles William Maynes and Thomas Omestad), Lane even tried to determine whether Brock's wife is Serbian (she is not).[48] In their reply to Lane's *New Republic* piece, Maynes and Omestad denounced such tactics.

> In Lane's construct, the ethnic, national or religious background of an author or his or her spouse could serve as a disqualifying factor in international relations reporting in the United States. African-Americans, Arab-Americans, Asian-Americans, Hispanic-Americans, and Jewish-Americans, to name a few, would be disqualified from writing on the countries or regions with which they share national, religious, or ethnic affiliations. Such an unrealistic and unnecessary standard of objectivity would disqualify many first-rate international relations specialists, including many of our authors. No American publication should be expected to meet that standard.[49]

Lane, Gutman, and other interventionist journalists appeared to be outraged that *Foreign Policy* had published the Brock piece, even though the editors stressed that the journal was a forum for a wide range of views on international affairs. And the interventionists' anger was not just because they believed that the article was sloppily researched and badly argued, although they made those allegations. They seemed to object to the willingness of Maynes and Omestad to publish the point of view expressed in the article. "This concept of even-handedness is of questionable value in dealing with the starkest moral drama in Europe since 1945," Lane stated.[50] That phrasing revealed Lane's own ideological blinders. Having convinced himself that the Bosnian conflict was the moral equivalent of Hitler's aggression and the Holocaust, he was utterly intolerant of contrary views. Unfortunately, both his bias and his intolerance are all too typical of the media coverage of the Balkan carnage.

Although Brock's article did have flaws, many of his points have held up well, and the piece has raised important questions. For example, Brock (and others) noted that the infamous "bread line massacre" in Sarajevo, which American and most Western journalists routinely blamed on a Bosnian Serb mortar attack, may not have been what it seemed. Several UN officials, including General MacKenzie, later contended that Muslims—not Serbs—had set off explosives that killed 22 civilians outside a Sarajevo bakery.[51] Subsequent investigations of the matter were inconclusive, but the bulk of Western news stories has continued to describe the incident as though it were an established fact that the Serbs were the perpetrators.

A similar pattern occurred in the coverage of an even bloodier episode on February 5, 1994, when a mortar shell exploded in the middle of a crowded market in Sarajevo, killing 68 people. Although the UN command stated that it could not determine which faction had fired the lethal round—and later investigations likewise failed to pinpoint the source—both the U.S. government and the American media responded as though there could be no doubt that the Serbs were the culprits. The official statement by Secretary of State Warren Christopher, released by the State Department on February 7, described the incident as "part of a pattern of shelling of civilian areas by Serb artillery that has continued despite NATO's repeated warnings."[52] Washington also promptly used the carnage as a justification for having NATO issue an ultimatum demanding that Serb forces withdraw their artillery from the area and, in effect, lift their siege of the city. Although the television network, newspaper, and news magazine stories sometimes included pro forma statements that responsibility for the shelling had not been determined, the tone and substance of the coverage almost universally assumed Serb guilt. There was also an evolution of certainty in the coverage despite a dearth of additional evidence. While some of the first news stories at least perfunctorily acknowledged the ambiguity surrounding the episode, within a few days most accounts began to state that the shell "presumably" came from Serb positions, and by mid-February they were stating that the Serbs were responsible and that such heinous conduct fully justified NATO's ultimatum.

Virtually no member of the mainstream press bothered to examine the issue of motive. It should have been at least relevant to ask why the Serb forces would take an action that not only would hand the Bosnian Muslim government a propaganda bonanza but would also greatly increase the probability of NATO military intervention—the last thing the Serbs should have wanted. Although it is certainly possible that some Serb commander made a colossal blunder, it is also possible that the Sarajevo government staged the incident to obtain NATO assistance. Just as the U.S. press too readily assumed that Spain, rather than the Cuban rebels who had the obvious motive, was responsible for the sinking of the battleship *Maine* in 1898, their 1990s counterparts rushed to judgment that the Serbs committed the marketplace massacre.[53]

The situation in the former Yugoslavia is a classic example of moral ambiguity. It is an oversimplification to interpret the struggle as merely a case of aggression by Serbia against neighboring countries. The conflict exhibits far more characteristics of a complex civil war involving several factions than of cross-border aggression. The central issues include how the boundaries of the new states that have emerged from the wreckage of the old Yugoslavia ought to be drawn and the distribution of power among the major ethnic groups in the region. Those disputes must be viewed against the bitter historical background—virtually all factions have actual or perceived grievances, some of which go back centuries.

It can even be misleading to view the various factions as political monoliths. Serb insurgents in Bosnia or in the Krajina region of Croatia, for example, frequently have policy agendas that are different from Belgrade's. They are noticeably less receptive to compromise solutions and tend to be more confrontational. Although the Milosevic government exerts considerable influence on Serb secessionist forces in Bosnia and Croatia, it is an exaggeration to assume that those forces take orders from Belgrade. Yet throughout the struggle that has been the explicit or implicit premise of U.S. officials and much of the American press.

Even a cursory examination of the various regimes reveals that there are few "good guys" in the three-way struggle for power. Early attempts by Washington and its media allies to portray Croatia as an innocent bastion of democracy set upon by unreconstructed Serbian Communists foundered on a number of troublesome facts. Events soon demonstrated that the regime of President Franjo Tudjman was hardly an exemplar of democratic principles. Tudjman

237

himself had been a close associate of Marshal Tito, and his communist credentials were at least as notorious as those of his arch-rival, Milosevic. Although he won the presidency in a reasonably free election, Tudjman ruled in an increasingly authoritarian fashion. He unmercifully harassed political critics and censored the press; indeed, by February 1993 there was only one independent newspaper left in Croatia—and it was under siege by government officials.

Tudjman's government hardly displayed a spirit of tolerance toward other ethnic groups. Even before independence, it enacted statutes that were blatantly discriminatory. As Howard University professor Nikolaos Stavrou notes,

> These laws applied "ethnic criteria" for government service, restricted property rights for non-Croats, and mandated blanket dismissal of Serbian nationals from research institutions, universities, and other public entities ostensibly to "democratize" them.
>
> More ominously, Article I of the 1974 Croat Constitution, which defined Croatia as a sovereign republic of "Croats, Serbs, and other nationalities," omitted the Serbs in its 1990 version. "Democratic" Croatia was to be constitutionally a monoethnic state.[54]

Those actions suggested that Tudjman's stridently anti-Serbian rhetoric was more than political posturing. By word and deed he and his followers made it apparent that Serbs would be, at best, second-class citizens in an independent Croatia. Such open hostility made an already uneasy Serb population fear the onset of persecutions.[55]

Those fears may have been exaggerated—and Serbian nationalist leaders in both Croatia and Serbia undoubtedly exploited them for their own political purposes—but they were not unfounded. Serbs recalled all too well that during World War II many Croats had enthusiastically cooperated with Nazi Germany's occupation forces against other ethnic groups in Yugoslavia. Such collaboration by the puppet Ustasha republic led to acts of genocide in which 400,000 to 700,000 Serbs perished. It certainly did not alleviate Serb apprehensions when the Zagreb government chose a variation of the Ustasha flag as the banner of an independent Croatia.[56]

Under those circumstances it was not surprising that Serbs in Croatia rebelled against living under a hostile, Croat-dominated government. Tudjman's insistence on establishing a highly centralized, unitary state exacerbated fears that the republic would be one in which Serbs would have few rights or opportunities. A willingness to adopt a more decentralized, federal structure that would have enabled predominantly Serb regions to manage their own affairs without dictation from Zagreb might have averted tragedy, but the Croat majority refused to even consider such reforms. The result was a bid by Croatian Serb leaders, supported by Belgrade, to detach those regions from Croatia—as well as expel all non-Serbs—and create the independent republic of Krajina.

American press coverage of the prelude to the conflict in Croatia and of the fighting that raged throughout the summer and fall of 1991 failed to capture the complexities of the dispute. Instead of informing Americans of the various arguments, grievances, claims, and counterclaims, most journalists seemed to accept the Bush administration's contention that the problem was simply a matter of Serb "aggression." Only gradually did even a few stories emerge about the less savory aspects of the "democratic" government of Croatia, and those were easily eclipsed by the more numerous and visible accounts of brutal Serbs wantonly attacking innocent, peace-loving Croats.

Indeed, it was not until the fighting subsided in Croatia—with the approval of a cease-fire and the introduction of UN peacekeeping forces—and the focus of the conflict switched to neighboring Bosnia-Hercegovina in the spring of 1992 that the media's favorable portrayals of the Zagreb regime began to wane. The catalyst for that change was the emergence of evidence that Croatian and Serbian leaders had held secret discussions about how to partition Bosnia. Since the Croatian community in Bosnia had officially allied itself with the Slavic Muslim faction to support Bosnia's secession from Yugoslavia, and was committed to maintaining the new republic's territorial integrity, such discussions with Belgrade struck even pro-Croatian journalists as duplicitous. Disenchantment with Croatia increased when it became apparent that Bosnian Croat military units seemed more concerned with consolidating their control of predominantly Croat regions of Bosnia than with helping the Muslim-dominated government in Sarajevo to fend off attacks by insurgent Serbs. (Among other actions, the Croats often flew the Croatian flag and routinely used the Croatian currency in regions of Bosnia they controlled.) Indeed, it sometimes was not clear which side the Croat militias were supporting. The outbreak of fierce fighting between Croat and Muslim forces in April 1993, which produced more than 400 fatalities in just a few days, destroyed any lingering illusions that the Serbs were the only ones bent on territorial aggrandizement.[57] Although it was interesting that even then most portions of the media gave the development low-key, if not minimal, coverage.

Washington Post correspondent Steve Coll epitomized the new, more critical attitude toward Tudjman and his government that finally emerged in early 1993. "In the West Tudjman is usually seen as a lesser problem than Slobodan Milosevic. . . . But lately, Tudjman's belligerent rhetoric about Croatia's unfinished war and his January offensive against Serbian militias have raised fears that the Croatian leader may be a danger to peace himself."[58]

Coll went on to portray a man whose writings attempted to minimize not only Croatian atrocities against the Serbs during World War II but the Nazi Holocaust as well. "The estimated loss of up to 6 million dead," Tudjman wrote in one book, "is founded too much on both emotional, biased testimonies and in the postwar reckonings of war crimes and squaring of accounts with the defeated perpetrators of war crimes." Coll noted that such appalling statements had led some international Jewish leaders to accuse Tudjman of "historical amnesia."

Coll's unflattering portrait of the Croatian president injected a useful dose of realistic information into the debate on the Yugoslavian turmoil. But such accounts were relatively rare, and they were extremely late in coming.

Instead of learning from their disillusionment with the Croat cause and concluding that the Yugoslavian conflict was a moral muddle with an ample quantity of villainy on all sides, most members of the media simply transferred their favoritism en bloc to the besieged Bosnian government. As late as July 1993, one prominent journalist gushed about Bosnian president Alija Izetbegovic, describing him as a man who "little more than a year ago was poised to become a George Washington to his people, to lead them out of 40-odd years of Balkan communism into an era of political freedom and free-market reforms."[59]

Most news accounts echoed the U.S. government's version of events and once again seriously distorted reality. The dominant image in the American news media of the conflict that erupted in

Bosnia in the spring of 1992 was of Serbs, acting on orders from Belgrade, wantonly waging war against the legitimate, democratically elected government of a multiethnic state. News stories often portrayed the conflict as a case of international "aggression," as though the fighting was analogous to Iraq's invasion of Kuwait. That view corresponded almost perfectly with the State Department's official position.[60]

Examination of the background to the fighting in Bosnia casts doubt on the prevailing interpretation. True, the government in Sarajevo was duly elected, but it clearly lacked legitimacy with most of the Bosnian Serb population. The root of the tragedy was the fact that Bosnia was a miniature version of the ethnic divisions and animosities that had caused the collapse of Yugoslavia. Slavic Muslims—Croats and Serbs who had converted to Islam during the centuries of rule by the Ottoman Empire—made up the largest faction, approximately 44 percent of the population. Serbs made up slightly more than 31 percent, and most of the remainder consisted of Roman Catholic Croats.

What in fact emerged during late 1991 and early 1992 was a power play by a temporary political alliance of Slavic Muslims and Croats to bring about Bosnian secession from the crumbling Yugoslavian federation. Parliamentary elections held in November 1991 gave ample warning of the stark nature of the ethnic divisions. The political parties that included members of all three groups were routed. Loyalty to religious or ethnic factions proved stronger than any competing loyalties. An overwhelming majority of Islamic voters cast ballots for the Muslim party, and the Serbs and Croats did the same for the parties identified most closely with their respective ethnic causes. Since the Muslims had the most votes, their leader, Alija Izetbegovic, became president.

Almost immediately, Izetbegovic and his followers pressed for an independent Bosnia. In that effort, they maintained a fragile alliance with the Bosnian Croats, who favored secession from an increasingly Serb-dominated Yugoslavian rump federation. The Croats, however, viewed secession as merely the first step to merging predominantly Croat portions of Bosnia with Croatia; they had little enthusiasm for an independent Bosnia, since they would be the smallest and least influential of the three groups. Their alliance with the Muslims, in other words, was purely tactical and temporary. Most Bosnian

241

Serbs strongly opposed secession, believing they would have a second-class status in an independent Bosnia—that the government in
Sarajevo would be dominated by their two ethnic adversaries. If
Bosnia did become independent, Serb leaders insisted, it would
have to have a highly decentralized political structure similar to
Switzerland's canton system. That was the only way, in their judgment, that Serbs would have meaningful control over their own
affairs even in regions of the country that were overwhelmingly Serb.

It is possible, of course, that such proposals were disingenuous—
merely a prelude to demands for an independent Bosnian Serb
republic that would ultimately become part of a Greater Serbia. But
the Muslims and their Croat allies showed little inclination to test
the sincerity of the Serb proposals or to offer a compromise. Instead,
they went ahead with plans for secession on the assumption that
the majority had the right to make that decision. A referendum was
held on March 1, 1992, on the issue of independence—a referendum
boycotted by the Serbs. Since Muslims and Croats had a majority
of the votes, they would, in any case, have overridden the objections
of the Serb minority. Even worse, the victors (primarily the Muslims)
sought to create a unitary state, with the vast majority of the power
residing with the government in Sarajevo—something the Serbs had
repeatedly warned was utterly unacceptable. It was on that basis
that Bosnia declared independence.[61]

The Bosnian Muslims badly miscalculated. Perhaps they thought
they could prevail militarily against Serb insurgents if they dared
to launch attacks. Perhaps they believed they would receive international help to restore control. The rapid recognition of Bosnia's independence by the United States and the members of the European
Community in April 1992 and, with their sponsorship, the admission
of the country to the United Nations the following month may have
fostered such calculations. Indeed, U.S. officials may have been even
more responsible for the resulting tragedy. On the eve of civil war,
on March 18, leaders of Bosnia's three ethnic factions met in Lisbon
and concluded an agreement in principle to partition the country
into three ethnically based cantons, which were to be linked in a
loose confederation. But when Izetbegovic returned to Sarajevo, he
was reportedly encouraged by U.S. and EC officials to repudiate the
agreement and instead insist on a unified state under his presidency.
That action, the American and European diplomats stated, was justified by the results of the March 1 referendum.[62] Whether because

of outside pressure, policy divisions within the Sarajevo regime, or some combination of those two factors, the Izetbegovic government reneged on the Lisbon accord.

Bosnian Serbs then formed their own republic and military forces and, backed by elements of the old Yugoslav federal army, launched a series of attacks throughout the country in early April, including shelling the capital of Sarajevo. Stage two of the Yugoslavian civil war was under way, and it would become even bloodier than the fighting that had taken place in Croatia the previous year. (Ironically, after some 15 months of carnage that claimed thousand of Muslim, Croat, and Serb lives, the Western governments reluctantly endorsed a partition plan similar to the one they had reportedly encouraged Izetbegovic to reject—although they subsequently again backed away from that position. The principal difference was that the 1993 version granted substantially less territory to the Muslims.)

Once again, most of the U.S. media managed to oversimplify the conflict that erupted in Bosnia and echo Washington's assertion that it was a product of Serb aggression. Journalists had learned little from their 1990 experience as passive conduits for the government's highly biased version of developments in the Persian Gulf. Even a basic analysis of the issues in Bosnia would have raised major questions about Washington's thesis. For example, the fragility of the Croat-Muslim alliance, the underlying incompatibility of their agendas, and the likelihood that the war in Bosnia would become a three-sided, not a two-sided, fight were rather obvious points. Yet the eruption of combat between Muslim and Croat forces in late 1992 and again in the spring of 1993 caught the majority of American journalists by surprise. Furthermore, they gave the first round of fighting between the nominal allies incredibly sparse coverage and did only marginally better on the second round. Poggioli later mused, "I cannot help but think that one reason why the media spotlight on former Yugoslavia dimmed late this spring [1993] was that the collapse of the so-called Muslim-Croat alliance in Bosnia made it abundantly clear that there were no innocents in this war."[63] Her comment concerning the behavior of her colleagues was revealing. Why was the reaction of the press corps to the surge of Muslim-Croat fighting merely to dim the media spotlight? Why was there not instead a flurry of analyses of the implications of that conflict? The most likely answer is that the development ran so counter to the press corps' assumption that Serb villainy was the dominant feature of the Bosnian war that most journalists chose to minimize coverage rather than undertake a painful reassessment of their fundamental premises.

Much of the journalistic community, in fact, exhibited signs of denial as evidence mounted that the Croats had expansionist designs at least as ambitious as those of the Serbs. The extent of that expansionist agenda became evident in July 1993 when Bosnian Croat negotiators offered a partition plan that assigned less territory to the defeated Muslims than did the competing Serb plan.[64] Such avarice on the part of the Sarajevo government's supposed allies produced surprisingly little comment in the American press. Indeed, the dominant theme in the media and among many members of the foreign policy community remained Serb aggression in Bosnia, with tepid concessions to the increasingly undeniable evidence that the Croats' hands were not entirely clean either.[65]

The few doubts that surfaced in the U.S. press about the simplistic "Serb aggression" thesis were grudging, belated, and incomplete. Many journalists clung tenaciously to the myth of "Bosnia"—by which they explicitly or implicitly meant the Muslim faction—as innocent victim. In a most revealing passage, a *Washington Post* editorial conceded that ethnic cleansing of Muslims was conducted by Serbs and Croats "and with a painful loss of moral differentiation" of Croats by Muslims.[66] The loss of moral differentiation that the editorial writers lamented was largely a fiction of their own creation. It had never existed to the extent that Western journalists believed.

In their treatment of the turmoil in the former Yugoslavia, the media once again failed to enhance public understanding of important foreign policy issues. Even cursory examinations of the Bosnian conflict should have raised doubts about the view that the Serbs were solely responsible for the tragedy, but few journalists made the effort until the disintegration of Bosnia was a virtual fait accompli. In a rare appreciation of the complexities of the Bosnian struggle, *Washington Post* columnist Richard Cohen stressed, "It is not enough to condemn what the Serbs have done in Bosnia. It is also important to understand their behavior. They are not mere adventurers but committed nationalists who feel, however wrongly, that their continued existence as a Bosnian minority was threatened when that onetime Yugoslavian republic declared its independence."[67] One might

244

dispute the notion that Serbs were wrong in their fears of persecution, but at least Cohen was paying attention to the factors that triggered the conflict.

Another refreshing aspect was that Cohen had shown a willingness to modify his views. Early in the crisis, he wrote accounts that embraced the morality play version of the Bosnian conflict and urged strong Western intervention. After an extended tour of the former Yugoslavia, including numerous discussions with members of the various factions, however, he came away with an appreciation of the deep emotions motivating all of the parties and the resulting moral ambiguities of that tragic struggle. His articles in late 1992 and early 1993 reflected a more sophisticated level of understanding.

Not only did the news media tend to echo the State Department's line on Yugoslavia, but for the first time since 1939–41, a sizable journalistic faction was actually ahead of the government in its thirst for intervention. Indeed, the militancy of some portions of the press rivaled the interventionist frenzy of the months preceding the Spanish-American War. The most interventionist newspaper was the venerable *New York Times*, which seemed determined to replicate the role played by the Hearst and Pulitzer chains in fomenting the "splendid little war." Three of the *Times's* regular columnists— Leslie Gelb, Anthony Lewis, and William Safire—repeatedly beat the drums for Western military intervention in Yugoslavia, and their efforts were matched by numerous house editorials. In addition, nearly 90 percent of the op-ed articles dealing with Bosnia advocated some form of U.S. military action.[68]

A person assessing American attitudes toward the Yugoslavian crisis solely on the basis of opinion pieces appearing in the *Times* would have concluded that there was a virtual consensus in favor of immediate U.S. entry into the conflict. But no such consensus existed. In fact, public opinion surveys taken by NBC News and the *Wall Street Journal* in late 1992 and early 1993 showed that most Americans *opposed* military involvement.[69] The stridency of the *New York Times* was so great that at times senior policymakers in the Bush and Clinton administrations seemed to have ambivalent attitudes about its campaign. Officials were happy about media efforts to strengthen public sentiment against Serbia and to condition the public for intervention if they eventually decided to take that step, but the pressure from the *Times* (as well as a few other arch-interventionist publications) threatened to be too much of a good thing.

Indeed, a major portion of the media was not so much supporting the government's official policy as backing the views of the most hard-line elements in the State Department and the NSC who favored strong action (i.e., U.S.-led military intervention against the Serbs). The interventionist press increasingly criticized pragmatic elements in the Bush and Clinton administrations, led by JCS chairman Gen. Colin Powell, and embraced the views of their opponents. When George Kenney, acting chief of Yugoslav affairs in the State Department, resigned in August 1992 to protest what he viewed as an insufficiently tough U.S. policy toward the Serbs, the *New York Times* and its ideological compatriots gave the story maximum coverage. Predictably, an op-ed by Kenney appeared in the *Times* the following week.[70] A similar pattern of high-profile coverage emerged in April 1993 when 12 diplomats at the State Department sent a letter to President Clinton advocating U.S. military action.

One of the more troubling assessments of the Western, especially U.S., press coverage of the Yugoslavian conflict came from a senior UN official in the region who insisted on anonymity. Although the official personally sympathized with the plight of the Bosnian government and was sharply critical of Serb conduct, he or she nevertheless noticed the pervasive media bias that Brock and other critics had alleged.

> The press corps [in Sarajevo] developed its own momentum and esprit. Much of it set out to invoke international military intervention against the Serb aggressors—a principal strategy of the Bosnian government. That induced in some a personal commitment—indeed crusade—that lay uneasily with the maintenance of true professional standards. . . . According to some journalists, who discussed the matter freely with us, editors became reluctant to risk "confusing" their readers with the more nuanced complexities of the developing situation; and the collective political fury of the Sarajevo press corps became legendary among all who had to deal with them.[71]

The official especially chastised journalists for their coverage of the actions and policies of the Croats.

> One of the major mysteries of the last 18 months or so is how the Croats have gotten off so lightly in the Western press. They have the most unfree press in the former Yugoslavia, if

not in Eastern Europe; their army's presence in Bosnia has been both evident and notorious for more than a year; and its members . . . have been committing atrocities in recent months both there and in Krajina. This omission has been especially bizarre and certainly requires explanation.[72]

The performance of the news media since the end of the gulf war does not inspire confidence. Journalists have failed to cast off the fetters of the Pentagon's pool requirement and other devices that exist to prevent or restrict independent coverage of future military operations. Instead they have concentrated on negotiating the terms of their continued servitude.

Even worse, the bulk of the press has again shown a willingness to be cheerleaders for Washington's military adventures. That was certainly the case in Somalia, as most portions of the media ignored numerous portents of trouble that should have been apparent long before the bloody attacks on U.S. forces took place. Similarly, reporters, correspondents, and columnists helped to transmit the government's simplistic accounts during the crucial early months of the conflict in Yugoslavia, thereby creating pressure for a potentially bloody U.S. armed intervention. More recently, major media outlets have made common cause with the most stridently interventionist elements in the government, who believe that even the intrusive policies of the Bush and Clinton administrations are insufficient. Most press accounts of the conflicts in Croatia and Bosnia not only exhibit the worst characteristics of "herd" reporting, they display the same reflexive enthusiasm for U.S. military activism that was the hallmark of the mainstream media during much of the Cold War and surfaced again during the gulf war.

10. Global Interventionism and the Erosion of First Amendment Freedoms

Nearly five decades of interventionism have had an unhealthy impact on the press freedoms guaranteed by the First Amendment and on the public's ability to assess and debate national security issues. The conventional wisdom is that First Amendment rights have expanded rather than contracted throughout the 20th century—especially since the 1930s. In certain respects that view is correct; the protection now afforded literary works and the treatment of previously taboo aspects of human sexuality is certainly much greater than it was in earlier times. That enhancement of liberty in the cultural realm, however, has tended to mask an erosion of speech and press freedoms when it comes to defense and foreign policy issues—a trend the onset of which coincided with the adoption of a more aggressive U.S. political and military role in world affairs at the beginning of the 20th century. University of North Carolina professor Robert C. Hilderbrand correctly observes,

> There has been . . . a stunning decline in the public's independence in perceiving foreign affairs. No matter how totally they distrusted the public's wisdom, nineteenth-century presidents had neither facilities nor inclination to control the popular debate over questions of foreign policy, and there often developed, at least in the press, lively if not acrimonious exchanges of ideas about international relations. This has proved less true for the twentieth century, when chief executives have consistently displayed the ability—and the desire—to manipulate increasingly complex foreign policy information to forestall, at least temporarily, the development of contradictory interpretations.[1]

During both world wars as well as the first two decades of the Cold War, most elements of the media were either co-opted or intimidated into silence. The resultant lack of press scrutiny contributed to the atrophy of public and congressional debate on substantive foreign policy issues. America's ill-advised intervention in Vietnam was the culmination of acquiescence to a foreign policy based on unexamined assumptions and Cold War shibboleths.

In the aftermath of the Vietnam tragedy, the press made some effort to resume its role as critic, and journalists subjected U.S. foreign policy to searching and frequently hostile assessments. But the media's renewed proclivity to act as watchdog rather than lapdog on national security issues collided in the 1980s with administrations that were determined to pursue global interventionist policies without interference. During the Reagan and Bush years the government attempted to repeal the legacy of the 1970s with regard to press and public scrutiny of national security issues. In a variety of ways, both administrations sought to exclude and intimidate the press, thereby reducing the prospect of embarrassing disclosures of dubious foreign policy initiatives. The Reagan administration's vigorous campaign on that front impelled even Floyd Abrams of the American Civil Liberties Union—normally a sober and restrained analyst—to ask whether the First Amendment would survive the 1980s.[2]

Abrams's fears were overstated, but the pursuit of a global interventionist policy does menace in both direct and subtle ways the health of the First Amendment's speech and press guarantees. Yale University law professor Thomas I. Emerson effectively summarizes the dangers inherent in accepting the notion that First Amendment freedoms must be curtailed whenever national security matters are involved.

> Claims of national security must always be viewed with a high degree of skepticism. Governments always resent criticism or dissent and are prone to suppress such activity in the name of national security. Governments also frequently employ appeals to national security as a method of distracting public attention from other problems with which the nation must deal. The secrecy attached to many national security issues allows the government to invoke national security claims in order to cover up embarrassment, incompetence, corruption or outright violation of law. And subsequent events almost always demonstrate that asserted dangers to national security have been grossly exaggerated.[3]

Policymakers and military leaders typically respond by emphasizing the thorniest issue: the relationship between the military and the media on the actual battlefield. They make the reasonable point that one cannot have unfettered press coverage of a war without compromising the security of military operations, thereby needlessly endangering the lives of American military personnel. Many advocates of censorship and other information control measures in the name of national security raise a subsidiary point. When the nation has committed itself to wage a war, they argue, the goal is victory over the enemy; anything, including news stories, that jeopardizes that objective must be subject to reasonable restrictions. Otherwise, a disloyal—or at least excessively stubborn—minority can undermine the policy embraced by the majority of the population and by duly elected officials.

The first argument has a certain amount of validity when applied narrowly to direct press coverage of combat operations. Clearly, military officials should have little tolerance for reporters who would publish stories based on leaked information that announced to enemy commanders in advance where an offensive would take place or disclosed specifics about troop movements. But reporters have rarely breached security in that fashion. Sydney Schanberg states bluntly that "the security issue is almost entirely a red herring. With very rare exceptions, the press has never breached any of the security rules—not in World War II, not in Korea, and not in Vietnam."[4]

The evidence strongly supports Schanberg's view—even in the case of the Vietnam conflict, which was the principal source of the current mythology about irresponsible and disloyal news media. Barry Zorthian, the official spokesman for the U.S. mission in Saigon from 1964 to 1968, conceded that although approximately 2,000 reporters were accredited to cover the war during those years, and they filed hundreds of thousands of stories, there were only five or six violations of the operational security rules. Furthermore, most of that small number of violations were apparently accidental or based on a misunderstanding of the guidelines, and—to the best of his knowledge—none subverted any military mission or endangered the lives of American troops.[5] On another occasion Zorthian added, "I have never met a reporter yet who was interested in deliberately jeopardizing our armed forces by revealing tactical military information—the timing and location of an operation, the composition of

251

units, early casualty figures and other information that would clearly be useful to an enemy field commander."[6]

Media outlets have exhibited restraint on several occasions out of concern for the safety of U.S. military personnel, even when the opportunity existed for a major scoop. For example, news personnel knew beforehand of the planned air strikes on Libya in April 1986. Yet without exception they held the information until the raids had taken place so as not to endanger the air crews.[7]

Even if military leaders are legitimately concerned about preventing breaches of security in an era of instantaneous communications, the restrictions implemented in Grenada, Panama, and the Persian Gulf went far beyond any reasonable level. Moreover, as numerous incidents in all three conflicts demonstrated, "protecting the security of military operations" frequently became an excuse for stifling news stories that cast doubt on the competence or veracity of the armed forces. Worse still, it sometimes became a pretext for suppressing information that merely disputed the policy or political agendas of the military hierarchy and the incumbent president.

Outside the narrow battlefield context, national security justifications for restrictions on information and debate have little validity. That is true even in times of overt military conflict; it is doubly so in periods, such as the Cold War, during which relations between the United States and geopolitical rivals may be tense but there are only intermittent military hostilities.

The notion that U.S. entrance into war accurately reflects the wishes of the American public may have been true throughout much of the Republic's history. Major military enterprises were preceded by extensive public and congressional debate and duly approved by a congressional declaration of war, as the Constitution requires. A case could be made, therefore, that the government not only had the rightful authority to pursue the war to a successful conclusion but had at least some legitimate latitude in preventing activities—including conduct normally protected by the First Amendment—that undermined the war effort. That was clearly the Supreme Court's logic in *Schenck v. United States.*

Even during declared wars the government was treading in dangerous territory when it constrained press and public debate. As the wave of domestic repression during World War I demonstrated, in adopting such a course America risked winning its war at the price

252

of losing the basic freedoms that made the Republic a desirable political community. But whatever the legitimacy of restrictions on the First Amendment in times of declared war, that has not been the actual political context for the past half century. Throughout the Cold War presidents acted on their own to commit the military forces of the United States to major combat operations. There was no advance debate or a declaration of war when the United States entered the Korean conflict. The same was true of the smaller, but still significant, combat enterprises in Lebanon, the Dominican Republic, and Grenada. U.S. involvement in the Vietnam War had reached the point where several thousand "advisers" were deployed and American forces had suffered dozens of fatalities before Congress was even asked to pass an authorizing resolution. The resulting Gulf of Tonkin Resolution fell far short of a formal declaration of war and was rushed through Congress in the midst of an artificial crisis orchestrated by the Johnson administration. Moreover, both that administration and its successor insisted that the resolution was superfluous—that as commander in chief the president had an "inherent" right under the Constitution to conduct large-scale combat operations in Southeast Asia or anywhere else without congressional approval.

The pattern of undeclared presidential wars has continued into the post–Cold War era. No debate—much less a declaration of war—preceded the U.S. invasion of Panama. Even the massive military operation in the Persian Gulf was conceived and executed by the president, with only pro forma congressional input at the 11th hour. Moreover, the chief executive made it clear that the United States would use military force in the gulf, if necessary, whether or not that action was approved by Congress or the American public.

The plain language of the Constitution notwithstanding, decisions to go to war in the future are likely to be made by the president and his coterie of appointed advisers, with little, if any, prior congressional or public debate. If that is the case, restrictions on First Amendment freedoms during wartime are significantly more outrageous than curtailing debate after a declaration of war. In the latter case, the argument could at least be made that the debate had already occurred; a decision had been reached; and under the rules of a democratic political system, the majority view had a right to prevail. No such argument can be made about presidential wars—especially those such as Korea, Grenada, or Panama that are presented as faits accomplis. If the people have little or no opportunity to question the wisdom of military interventions before they occur, or to have their elected representatives vote on the matter, they can do so only after the conflict is already under way. If they are then still effectively denied that opportunity by media blackouts and other elements of a government stranglehold on information, justified on the grounds of protecting military security, the concept of democratic account-ability becomes farcical.

People who argue or imply that dissent in wartime smacks of disloyalty apparently assume that Congress or the public should have no right to demand a change of policy. Even in the case of a declared war, that is a dangerous premise, but it is far more so when little or no advance debate has taken place. Political leaders do not invariably make wise choices in foreign policy any more than they do in domestic policy. Moreover, a strategy that seems reasonable at the beginning of a military enterprise may later prove to be unworkable because lethal impediments were overlooked or simply because conditions change. The Korean and Vietnam interventions were prime examples of both factors.

The view that press scrutiny and public criticism of an administra-tion's policy must cease for as long as American troops are under fire is the philosophy of political lemmings, not of citizens of a democratic republic. A meaningful exercise of First Amendment freedoms must include the right to debate the wisdom of an ongoing war, declared or undeclared. And a crucial prerequisite for such a debate is an unfettered press. It is dangerous to let government officials pass judgment on what information should be available to the public. There is an all-too-human tendency to equate policy preferences, institutional agendas, or personal reputations with "national security" imperatives.

Nobel laureate James Buchanan and other economists of the "public-choice" school have made a compelling case that members of government agencies react to incentives in much the same way that individuals operating in the private sector do. Only the nature of the incentives is different (e.g., there is no profit motive in the public sector and hence no meaningful incentive for cost control or efficiency). The dominant incentives for officials in the national security bureaucracy—as in any other bureaucracy—are to protect their turf, neutralize potential opposition, and maximize the scope of their mission. (The last goal has sometimes been described as a search for new problems or crises to be "managed.")

Not only does the incentive structure tend to bias national security practitioners toward an activist foreign policy, it also places a premium on information control. Without such control, there is always the risk that critics may be able to rally public opinion against the bureaucracy's policy agenda—an achievement that could have severe budgetary and career repercussions. Consequently, national security officials are not likely to regard a truly free press with enthusiasm—however much they may proclaim their respect for the First Amendment.

It is important to stress that the antipathy toward unfettered news media is not due to the innate malevolence of military and political leaders. On the contrary, most of them probably believe that they have the nation's best interests at heart and that it is the carping critics who may have unsavory motives. The root of the problem is the nature of the institutional incentives, not the characteristics of the personnel who control the levers of power at a particular point in time. Furthermore, the larger the national security bureaucracy— and the more activist the government's foreign policy—the more the incentives are skewed to cause bureaucrats to regard the press as either tool or enemy.

Even former National Security Agency director William Odom concedes, "The notion of 'national interest' is notoriously slippery when defined by individuals with a personal interest in defining it loosely."[8] That is especially true if a military enterprise has gone awry and an administration's stewardship of foreign policy is coming under mounting attack. It is tempting to modify Samuel Johnson's remark that false patriotism is the last refuge of scoundrels. On the surface, it would appear that in our own era false claims of national security have become their first refuge. But the problem is primarily structural and institutional, not personal.

If the vigorous exercise of First Amendment freedoms is important during times of war, it is even more crucial during periods of crisis short of war. One of the most unhealthy assumptions that emerged in the United States during the Cold War was that restrictions previously invoked only in wartime were appropriate for a period of peace, albeit one marked by great tensions between the United States and the Soviet Union. Emergency "exceptions" to First Amendment norms became ingrained habits over the course of decades. Those new attitudes gradually acquired such a powerful grip on the collective national psyche that many, perhaps most, Americans today no longer realize that extensive constraints on information in the name of national security are a relatively recent development—one that is alien to American traditions and values.

More subtle than government censorship or intimidation but equally dangerous to a free press is the tendency of much of the media to be co-opted by the national security bureaucracy. That tendency is most pronounced during wartime, but it was also evident throughout the Cold War and in most of the post–Cold War crises. It is perhaps too much to expect journalists to assess U.S. foreign policy initiatives with complete dispassion, much less objectivity. Reporters are conditioned by their upbringing and socialization into a particular society, as are members of other occupations. Jonathan Alter correctly points out, "No reporter can be expected to resolve whether he is a journalist first or an American. He (or she) is some combination of the two."[9]

Nevertheless, journalists must strive for as much detachment as possible if they are to do their jobs effectively. Alter emphasizes that "cheerleading . . . cheapens the coverage. Even the use of 'we' to describe the [U.S.] side undermines the professionalism with which a war is supposed to be reported." His definition of a balanced attitude, however, suggests the extent of the problem. "The proper approach is to neither assume the U.S. government is always lying, nor always telling the truth. Trust, but verify, as Ronald Reagan used to say."[10]

Although that attitude is certainly better than the media's naive assumption during much of the Cold War that U.S. officials were invariably truthful, it still biases reporters in favor of the government's arguments. Why should journalists give the benefit of the doubt to U.S. officials and "trust" their statements—even with the verification caveat? Verification of official statements and explanations of foreign policy initiatives is an inherently nebulous concept—unless one discovers a "smoking gun," evidence that a policymaker has lied about a crucial factual matter. The extent of the secrecy system makes it difficult to obtain such irrefutable evidence, or at least to do so in a timely manner. More often reporters are faced with nuances and interpretations; the administration's "spin" on a story may present an incomplete or even a thoroughly misleading picture without containing outright lies.

It is more realistic for journalists to assume that policymakers have an incentive to present self-serving accounts and explanations that are not entitled to any presumption of credibility. Furthermore, although one might argue that the pronouncements of a democratic government ought to be given somewhat more credibility than those of a dictatorship, there is ample evidence that democratic regimes also mislead when it suits their purposes.[11] And obviously U.S. officials are not entitled to any more benefit of the doubt than officials of other democratic systems.

It is perhaps not necessary to go as far as did the iconoclastic I. F. Stone, who once insisted that all governments consist of liars and one must never believe a word they say. Yet journalists would be well advised to at least flirt with that standard. Rather than Alter's "trust, but verify" approach, the attitude ought to be one of pervasive operational skepticism. There should be not only a diligent search for corroborating evidence but an equally vigorous effort to discover information that casts doubt on, if not falsifies, official versions and rationales.

To that end, the mainstream media need to change their habit of giving foreign and defense policymakers such a disproportionate amount of exposure during an ongoing policy debate. Too often, the pages of the major metropolitan newspapers and mass circulation news magazines and the air time of television news and public affairs programs are dominated by the statements of current or former officials. The result reminds one of writer Dorothy Parker's caustic assessment that a prominent actress's performance "ran the gamut of emotions from A to B."[12] The range of foreign policy arguments and options presented to the American public by the media is often equally narrow. During the early months of the post–Cold War era, columnist Leslie Gelb admonished his media colleagues to refresh and expand their Rolodexes to bring new participants into foreign policy discussions and thereby broaden the spectrum of debate. Although Gelb rarely followed his own advice, his point was valid. It is difficult to assess either the veracity or the wisdom of government policy if high-level officials dominate media coverage.

American journalists also need to be more cognizant of the subtle, inherent biases that may creep into their analyses of U.S. policy, simply because they are Americans. An awareness of such a national-istic predisposition should be accompanied by a determination to subject U.S. government positions to the same degree of skepticism and scrutiny that journalists would apply to the actions and state-ments of other governments. When news personnel fail to make that effort, they risk becoming propaganda conduits for the national security bureaucracy.

Similarly, they need to acknowledge that important institutional and career incentives incline journalists as well as national security officials to favor an activist foreign policy. A United States deeply engaged in a never-ending series of overseas crises makes better news copy than does a United States that remains aloof. Publisher Henry Luce's "American Century" has been a heady experience for members of the media who chronicle the activities of the world's dominant power. There is no way to negate such incentives and the activist bias they promote, but both journalists and the public ought to be aware of the problem and its potential to skew the debate on foreign policy issues. Moreover, journalists should more fully appreciate the adverse effects of an interventionist foreign policy on the overall health of their own profession. The media have every reason to be uncomfortable about their treatment at the hands of the national security bureaucracy during the interventionist era—unless they are content with a future as the pliant junior partners of political leaders.

An unfettered press is an important safeguard preventing zealots, however well intentioned, from irreparably damaging civil liberties and other components of domestic welfare in the course of pursuing foreign policy objectives. The essential relationship of freedom of expression and the viability of a democratic political system was perhaps best summarized in a committee report on government secrecy to the Australian parliament.

> The essence of democracy lies in the ability of the people to make choices: about who shall govern or about which policies they support or reject. Such choices cannot be made unless adequate information is available. It cannot be accepted that it is the government itself which has determined what level of information is to be regarded as adequate.[13]

Those sentiments echo James Madison's words: "A popular government without popular information or the means of acquiring it is but a prologue to a farce or a tragedy or perhaps both."[14] Even Secretary of Defense Caspar Weinberger once conceded that "the nature of the relationship between a free press and government in our society is constant healthy competition, an additional check and balance within the democratic process."[15] Unfortunately, the actions of Weinberger and other members of the national security bureaucracy frequently contradict such pious sentiments. Indeed, officials often act as though they believe that there ought to be a broadly defined "national security exception" to press coverage.

An unfettered press will, of course, sometimes abuse its freedom. Coverage of defense and foreign policy issues can be politically or ideologically biased, just as that of domestic issues can be. That is why a "marketplace of ideas" is so crucial. The expression of numerous points of view, and the ability of new entrants to join the fray without interference from the authorities, is the best guarantee that distorted or badly argued accounts will be challenged and discredited. Although not a perfect solution (the popularity of "tabloid" publications with their outrageous assertions and tacky sensationalism is evidence of the market's limitations in the area of quality control), it is far better than allowing the government to judge the worthiness of its critics. The comment of Pentagon press officer David Kiernan ("If the media is to enjoy continued protection under the First Amendment, it must be responsible in its role as watchdog of the government") should send chills down the spine of every supporter of the First Amendment.[16] Contrary to Kiernan's implicit assumption, the government is not an objective arbiter of "responsible" press activity. It has its own institutional interests and agendas, which are typically (perhaps inherently) at odds with the activities of a vigorous, independent press.

Although the people who contend that an unfettered press may sometimes undermine a military enterprise—perhaps prolonging the conflict and increasing the number of American casualties— make a plausible argument, they typically fail to address the opposite possibility: that unwise policies that go unexamined or unchallenged may lead to needless death and suffering. Such policies can result in the initiation of foolish military adventures or the prolongation of missions that show early signs of probable failure. Thwarting press coverage and the public debate it might generate prevents the timely reconsideration of poorly conceived policies. The price of government monopoly on information about important national security issues is sometimes exacted in blood.

Too many officials in the United States seem to regard journalists as useful agents for the transmission of propaganda, or if they will not serve that function, as annoying obstacles to be removed expeditiously from the path of governmental policy. Both views, and the actions that flow from them, are detrimental to the vitality of the First Amendment. As James Russell Wiggins concluded, "In season and out, in Democratic administrations and in Republican administrations, the normal relations between press and government have been distorted by both an excessive secrecy and a tendency of government officials to try to enlist reporters and editors as their colleagues and their collaborators."[17] Although Wiggins was writing in the midst of the Cold War and conceded that the tendencies of secrecy and press-government collusion were stimulated "by the abnormal tensions and anxieties" of that period, his observation is still valid today.

The corrosive effects on freedom of the press of the two world wars and the Cold War may still be evident long after those conflicts have become dim memories. Washington's global interventionist foreign policy made its first prominent appearance in the "war to end all wars"; accompanied by a flourish of Wilsonian rhetoric, it became the dominant long-term doctrine in World War II; and it consolidated its hold on the collective American psyche during the decades of confrontation with the Soviet Union. It would be unrealistic to expect a rapid return to pre–World War I norms with respect to First Amendment freedoms after such a lengthy and comprehensive political and ideological transformation.

Other freedoms have not been restored, either. America's economy is far more taxed, regulated, and regimented today than it was at the start of World War I. Although many of those changes came about during periods of domestic reform—primarily the New Deal and the Great Society—a surprising number were originally "temporary" wartime measures that left a residue of enhanced governmental power once the fighting ended.[18]

A similar change occurred in America's political system, especially with respect to the locus of authority to take the nation to war.

Before the interventionist era, Congress jealously guarded its war powers, and although presidents sometimes used the armed forces in minor combat operations without a formal declaration of war, it would have been unthinkable for them to have done so in large-scale enterprises. As noted earlier, that situation changed dramatically after World War II. America's new global military obligations, and especially the nature of modern warfare, in which even a seemingly minor conflict could escalate rapidly to a lethal superpower confrontation, led to tacit public and congressional acceptance of a transfer of the power to make war to the executive. That situation did not suddenly reverse with the end of the Cold War, even though there is no longer a need to have U.S. forces on hair-trigger alert, and post–Cold War era security problems are likely to be the kind that can be debated in an orderly fashion before a decision is made concerning U.S. intervention. The leisurely pace of the build-up to the Persian Gulf War is a case in point. Yet the Cold War era belief that the executive rather than Congress should decide about committing U.S. forces to combat continues. It is symptomatic of that attitude that in the Bosnian crisis scarcely anyone has even bothered to argue that Congress should play its proper (i.e., pre–World War II) constitutional role.

The decades of military activism in world affairs appear to have changed American society permanently, and many of those changes are not for the better. One of the least desirable alterations is the government's taming of a once-vociferous press on national security issues.

The result is not only that a global interventionist strategy leads to U.S. involvement in a greater number of crises and, therefore, provides more occasions for either co-opting or restricting the press. Although that is one of the effects, it is by no means the most important one. Far more corrupting is the political mindset that accompanies global interventionism. The logic of that approach to international affairs produces a garrison state mentality that equates even minor regional conflicts fomented by small expansionist powers with lethal threats to the Republic's safety. The hyperbolic rhetoric that compares Saddam Hussein or Slobodan Milosevic (or Ho Chi Minh before them) with Adolf Hitler is not entirely a cynical ploy by U.S. officials. At some level, they seem to believe their own statements. To those who embrace the doctrine that conflict

261

anywhere in the world significantly affects America's security and that "aggression" can never be tolerated because it will ultimately lead to chaos and the emergence of a would-be global conqueror—essentially a repeat of the scenario that culminated in World War II—viewing North Vietnam, Iraq, or Serbia as modern-day versions of Nazi Germany makes sense. The fact that the Cold War era threat posed by the Soviet Union did approximate the earlier fascist threat in terms of its severity strengthened the tendency to see security problems in such stark, absolutist terms.

Even though the interventionist faction's habit of viewing U.S. security requirements as part of a seamless global web is excessively rigid and increasingly detached from international realities, it still largely guides American policymakers. Given that mindset, it is hardly surprising that the "wartime" ideas of members of the national security bureaucracy about the proper role of the press persist in the post–Cold War era. If an official honestly believes that America's security is in constant danger, he is likely to view media criticism of U.S. policy as something more than an honest difference of opinion. As in wartime, dissent is considered not just poor judgment but lack of patriotism. Journalists should cooperate as "good soldiers" with the government in defending the nation's security. Not only is criticism of specific policies unacceptable; according to that view, even raising doubts about the competence, ethics, or judgment of policymakers undermines public confidence in the institutions that have the responsibility of protecting the Republic and is, therefore, undesirable.

Officials tend to see the press as merely another component of an effective national security strategy, and journalists find themselves enticed and pressured into accepting that view of their role. During both world wars and much of the Cold War, many, perhaps most, of them succumbed to the fallacy that dissent did in fact undermine national security. The passing of the Cold War has not eliminated the systemic factors that condition members of the media to see themselves as Americans first and journalists second. Press coverage of the events in the Persian Gulf, Somalia, and the former Yugoslavia suggests that that aspect of the Cold War mindset is still intact.

Although America no longer faces a serious global military rival, the habits, assumptions, and institutional behavior patterns of the half century of perpetual crisis that began with World War II and

262

continued with scarcely an interruption throughout the Cold War era remain powerful. The international phase of the Cold War may be over, but we have yet to end the Cold War at home. To a distressing extent, America is still geared economically, politically, and ideologically to wage a worldwide struggle against a powerful adversary. One area in which that garrison state mentality is most evident is the relationship between the press and government on defense and foreign policy issues.

Fortunately, the First Amendment was not killed in action during the many international crises of the 20th century. But it was seriously wounded. One of the most essential tasks of the post–Cold War era is to restore it to health.

Epilogue: Covering the Haiti Mission

In 1993 and 1994 the American news media had yet another foreign policy crisis to cover—this time in Haiti. The roots of the crisis can be traced to the military coup that toppled Haitian president Jean-Bertrand Aristide in September 1991. The United States and the Organization of American States promptly responded to the coup by imposing an embargo on the tiny Caribbean nation, and that strategy of economic coercion was subsequently endorsed and enhanced by the United Nations Security Council.

One of the most visible consequences of the economic devastation caused by the embargo was a periodic outflow of refugees bound for the United States—often in overloaded and unseaworthy craft. The Bush administration rebuffed the refugees, denying the vast majority political asylum and ordering the U.S. Coast Guard to intercept them at sea and return them to Haiti. Although Bill Clinton condemned the Bush administration's actions as cruel during the 1992 presidential campaign, as president he initially maintained the same policy. And the new administration became ever more committed to the goal of restoring Aristide to office. The crisis inexorably escalated, with the administration threatening to use force to dislodge the junta from power and eventually obtaining a UN Security Council authorization for that option. Finally in late September 1994, nearly 20,000 U.S. troops went ashore in Haiti. Only an 11th-hour agreement negotiated between junta leaders and a U.S. delegation headed by former president Jimmy Carter enabled the troops to enter the country without launching an invasion.

The media's coverage of the events and issues before the military occupation was on balance noticeably better than the treatment of the Persian Gulf War and the Somalia and Yugoslavian crises. Most correspondents at least made an effort to convey some of the complexities of Haiti's political affairs. Although news stories were generally friendly to Aristide's cause and tended to paint a negative picture of junta leader Gen. Raoul Cedras, there were relatively few attempts to portray the struggle as a stark contrast between good and evil. A surprising number of stories mentioned evidence that Aristide had sometimes behaved in a high-handed, authoritarian manner during his brief presidency. Even the more inflammatory allegations that Aristide had a history of mental problems and that he had endorsed "necklacing" (putting burning tires around the necks of) political opponents received some attention.

There was also a surprising amount of skepticism about some of Washington's cruder attempts at a propaganda offensive against the Cedras regime. When the Clinton administration leaked reports implicating several members of the junta in major drug-trafficking operations, most of the media reacted cautiously. A number of stories soon appeared suggesting that the charges were, at the very least, exaggerated. Moreover, such analyses sought to put the allegations in perspective, noting that even if some of the charges were true, similar problems were prevalent in many other Caribbean and Latin American countries—indeed, that such official corruption had existed in Haiti itself when Aristide was in power.

One important reason for the diversity of media accounts may have been the sharp divisions within America's political elite. Republican members of Congress were overwhelmingly opposed to U.S. military intervention in Haiti, and they aggressively sought access to the media to express their views. There was also an important ideological component to the debate. Conservatives loathed Aristide, viewing him as a mentally unstable anti-American, left-wing demagogue who was only marginally less odious than Fidel Castro. Most liberal and left-wing groups, on the other hand, saw Aristide as a progressive political leader deserving of U.S. sympathy and tangible support.

The debate in the press reflected that ideological split. Such conservative publications as the *Wall Street Journal*, the *Washington Times*, and the *American Spectator* were filled with anti-Aristide articles and opinion pieces, while the *Progressive*, the *Nation*, and other liberal-left publications presented the opposite view. The television networks, the mass circulation news magazines, and most of the metropolitan newspapers presented both sides—although often with a discernible pro-Aristide slant. The result was a vigorous, at times even raucous, public debate on an important issue of foreign policy.

If the media's performance before the start of the U.S. occupation was relatively good, the record once American troops landed was less impressive. True, many of the initial reports provided graphic accounts of the confused rules of engagement—U.S. soldiers stood by while Haitian police beat, and in one case killed, demonstrators—and speculated about the potential for mission creep, much to the chagrin of administration officials.[1] But after that initial foray into critical journalism, the bulk of the press showed signs of again succumbing to the cheerleader syndrome. A growing number of the stories began to be reminiscent of the early reports filed from Somalia: noble American soldiers on an idealistic mission to bring peace and democracy to a troubled land and alleviate the widespread suffering. Few pieces continued to question the arguments administration officials had made on the eve of the occupation that stopping the refugee exodus and restoring democracy in Haiti constituted vital U.S. interests, and assessments of the possible long-term consequence of Washington's high-profile role in Haiti's internal political affairs also became increasingly rare.

Even worse, journalists were extraordinarily quick to proclaim the Haiti mission a success when U.S. forces did not encounter serious armed opposition during the first few weeks. More cautious analyses were warranted. Members of the media should have recalled that the Somalia mission had not begun to unravel until some six months after the first U.S. troops had landed in Mogadishu. President Clinton had even welcomed the bulk of the U.S. military contingent home in May 1993, congratulating them on a job well done. Shortly thereafter, the militia units loyal to Mohammed Farah Aideed clashed with Pakistani troops in the UN peacekeeping force and the level of violence inexorably escalated. And the bloodiest incident involving American military personnel did not occur until October—some 10 months after the initial intervention.

Touting the Haitian occupation as a great success after two or three weeks was decidedly premature. That was especially true since the Clinton administration admitted that several thousand U.S. troops might remain in the country as part of a multilateral peacekeeping force until Aristide's successor took office in February 1996. Seventeen months is a very long time in a country with Haiti's violent history and class divisions.

The government's attitude toward press coverage of the Haiti mission also provides cause for concern. Because the U.S. invasion was transformed into an unopposed occupation at the last moment, the relationship between government and the press was not tested in a combat setting. Nevertheless, there is evidence that the views of the national security bureaucracy have not undergone a radical transformation during the Clinton years. In a meeting with representatives of the television networks on the eve of the scheduled invasion, White House and Pentagon officials demanded an eight-hour broadcast blackout. (The networks offered to agree to a blackout of one hour.) Even more alarming, the administration also wanted to restrict all reporters to their hotels until military commanders gave them permission to cover the fighting.

The latest attempt to restrict news coverage, the *Washington Post* observed, was deeply troubling.

> Since the invasion was canceled in favor of the kind of peaceful landing that the Department of Defense likes to have televised, even the networks' agreement to a one-hour delay had no practical effect. But journalists and citizens who believe in the free flow of information should take note of this effort to blindfold the press and the public. It shows that the news-management policies that took root during the Reagan-Bush years and reached their full propagandistic flower during Operation Desert Storm are still in place at the Pentagon. Those policies represent a long-term danger to American troops and to the ability of voters to judge the wisdom of elected officials who order military attacks.[2]

In sum, there is reason to be mildly encouraged by the media's record in covering the Haiti crisis. The "pack journalism" phenomenon that was so evident in the Persian Gulf crisis and Somalia, and which has reached its distressing pinnacle in the former Yugoslavia, has been largely absent in Haiti. There was a wide diversity of accounts, analyses, and interpretations in the months leading up to the invasion. And many journalists made a credible effort to grapple with the subtle, complex, but often important, cultural and political background issues. There was a sense of context in a significant percentage of the stories about Haiti that was noticeably lacking in the coverage of earlier crises. Even more gratifying, journalists showed little inclination to be duped by simplistic propaganda put out by foreign policy officials in Washington.

There are still reasons for caution and concern, however. The healthy skepticism that characterized many preinvasion accounts shows signs of giving way to uncritical boosterism. And most important, the government's attempt to restrict media coverage of the invasion of Haiti demonstrates that the national security bureaucracy's enthusiasm for censorship remains potent.

Notes

Introduction

1. Letter from James Madison to W. T. Barry, August 4, 1822, in *The Complete Madison*, ed. Saul K. Padover (New York: Harper, 1953), p. 337.

2. *Schenck v. United States*, 249 U.S. 47 (1919), p. 52.

3. Gregory F. Treverton, *Covert Action: The Limits of Intervention in the Postwar World* (New York: Basic Books, 1987), p. 188.

4. Warren T. Brookes, "The National Press and the Status Quo," *Cato Policy Report* 15, no. 5 (September–October 1993): 1.

5. Henry Kissinger, *White House Years* (Boston: Little, Brown, 1979), p. 21.

Chapter 1

1. *Documents of American History*, ed. Henry Steele Commager and Milton Cantor, vol. 1 (Englewood Cliffs, N.J.: Prentice Hall, 1988), p. 176.

2. Ibid., p. 178.

3. Quoted in Dumas Malone, *Jefferson and His Time*, vol. 3 of *Jefferson and the Ordeal of Liberty* (Boston: Little, Brown, 1962), p. 387.

4. Ibid., p. 384.

5. F. M. Anderson, "The Enforcement of the Alien and Sedition Acts," American Historical Association *Reports*, 1912; and Marshall Smelser, "The Federalist Period as an Age of Passion," *American Quarterly* 10, no. 4 (1958): 391–419. On the tensions between France and the United States in the late 1790s, see Alexander DeConde, *The Quasi-War: The Politics and Diplomacy of the Undeclared War with France* (New York: Scribners, 1966).

6. For a discussion of the Kentucky and Virginia resolutions and the general trend toward a more libertarian interpretation of the First Amendment's speech and press freedoms in reaction to the Alien and Sedition Acts, see Leonard W. Levy, *Emergence of a Free Press* (New York: Oxford University Press, 1985), pp. 294–349.

7. Theodore F. Koop, *Weapon of Silence* (Chicago: University of Chicago Press, 1946), p. 150.

8. Phillip Knightley, *The First Casualty* (New York: Harcourt Brace Jovanovich, 1975), pp. 20–21.

9. Quoted in Chuck Henry, "Military-Media Relations," *Military History Review*, January 1986, p. 2.

10. "The Media at War," Gannett Foundation Report, June 1991, p. 9.

11. Knightley, p. 27.

12. Koop, p. 153.

13. Ibid., pp. 153–54.

14. For a discussion of censorship during the Spanish-American War, see Charles H. Brown, "Press Censorship in the Spanish-American War," *Journalism Quarterly* 42 (Fall 1965): 581–90.

15. Knightley, p. 124.

16. Ibid., p. 128.

17. Ibid., p. 130.

18. Robert Hilderbrand raises the interesting point that many of the large number of newspapermen employed by the Committee on Public Information apparently had no trouble making the mental transition from being independent gatherers of news to being disseminators of "news" created by the government's propaganda apparatus. Robert C. Hilderbrand, *Power and the People: Executive Management of Public Opinion in Foreign Affairs, 1897–1921* (Chapel Hill: University of North Carolina Press, 1981), p. 147. For accounts of how the government easily co-opted historians, political scientists, and other scholars and communicators for its war propaganda apparatus, see George T. Blakey, *Historians on the Home Front: American Propagandists for War* (Lexington: University of Kentucky Press, 1970); and Carol S. Gruber, *Mars and Minerva: World War I and the Uses of Higher Learning in America* (Baton Rouge: Louisiana State University Press, 1976).

19. Frank Cobb, "The Press and Public Opinion," *New Republic*, December 31, 1919, p. 144. See also James R. Mock and Cedric Larson, *Words That Won the War: The Story of the Committee on Public Information, 1917–1919* (Princeton, N.J.: Princeton University Press, 1939).

20. For a discussion of how the Wilson administration not only tolerated but encouraged such hysteria, see Walter Karp, *The Politics of War* (New York: Harper and Row, 1979), pp. 324–31.

21. Quoted in Koop, p. 155.

22. Karp, p. 327.

23. 40 Stat. 553 (May 16, 1918).

24. Koop, pp. 158–59.

25. Karp, pp. 325–26.

26. Mock and Larson, pp. 6–7.

27. Letter and attached memorandum from Breckinridge Long to Woodrow Wilson, November 19, 1917, in *The Papers of Woodrow Wilson*, ed. Arthur S. Link, vol. 45 (Princeton, N.J.: Princeton University Press, 1984), pp. 88, 90.

28. Ibid., p. 90.

29. Letter from Woodrow Wilson to Breckinridge Long, December 19, 1917, in ibid., p. 329.

30. Letter from George Creel to Woodrow Wilson, November 28, 1917, in ibid., p. 152.

31. *Goldstein v. United States,* 258 F. 908 (9th Cir. 1919), p. 910.

32. Zachariah Chafee Jr., *Freedom of Speech in the United States* (Cambridge, Mass.: Harvard University Press, 1941), p. 51.

33. Karp, p. 327.

34. 249 U.S. 47 (1919).

35. Robert K. Murray, *Red Scare: A Study in National Hysteria, 1919–1920* (New York: McGraw-Hill, 1955), pp. 231–32, 263–73.

36. Ibid., p. 202.

37. Ibid., pp. 12, 14.

38. 55 Stat. 838 (December 18, 1941).

39. Knightley, pp. 280–83.

40. Ibid., p. 273. Even some critics of censorship curiously downplay the Roosevelt administration's restrictive practices in World War II. Juergen Arthur Heise, for example, makes the astonishing assertions that the "voluntary" censorship code under Byron Price worked well and that "under it, no significant attempts by government to

hide blunders came to light." Juergen Arthur Heise, *Minimum Disclosure: How the Pentagon Manipulates the News* (New York: W. W. Norton, 1979), pp. 56–57. The concealment for years of the extent of the damage inflicted at Pearl Harbor would certainly seem to belie that conclusion.

41. Koop, p. 148.

42. Ibid., p. 271.

43. Knightley, pp. 293–94, 323–27.

44. For the contrast between the sanitized press and propaganda accounts of the war and the reality, see Paul Fussell, *Wartime: Understanding and Behavior in the Second World War* (New York: Oxford University Press, 1989).

45. Koop, p. 178.

46. Quoted in Allan M. Winkler, *The Politics of Propaganda: The Office of War Information, 1942–1945* (New Haven, Conn.: Yale University Press, 1978), p. 27.

47. Ibid., p. 49.

48. Ibid., p. 53.

49. Quoted in ibid.

50. Ibid., p. 54; and Jerome S. Bruner, "OWI and the American Public," *Public Opinion Quarterly* 7 (1943): 129–33.

51. Quoted in J. Fred MacDonald, *Television and the Red Menace: The Video Road to Vietnam* (New York: Praeger, 1985), p. 8.

52. Clayton R. Koppes and Gregory D. Black, *Hollywood Goes to War* (New York: Free Press, 1987); "The Peoples of the U.S.S.R.: The Fighting Great Russians Brought Them All Together," *Life*, March 29, 1943, p. 23; and "Red Leaders: They Are Tough, Loyal, Capable Administrators," *Life*, March 29, 1943, p. 40. Given what we know now about the conduct of the FBI under J. Edgar Hoover, the comparison with the Soviet secret police may not have been entirely inaccurate. Many of the American war correspondents working on the Russian front were also prolific disseminators of pro-Soviet propaganda. For examples, see Knightley, pp. 264–65.

53. Quoted in Winkler, p. 56.

54. Quoted in Koop, p. 163.

55. Letter from Franklin D. Roosevelt to Attorney General Francis Biddle, May 7, 1942, Franklin Roosevelt Papers, Official File 4866, Franklin D. Roosevelt Library, Hyde Park, New York. For examples of how the Roosevelt administration attempted to harass the *Chicago Tribune* during the war—including threats of prosecution for espionage—see Lloyd Wendt, *Chicago Tribune: The Rise of a Great American Newspaper* (Chicago: Rand McNally, 1979), pp. 629–36. On one occasion, the Justice Department even convened a special grand jury to consider indicting correspondent Stanley Johnston for violating the Espionage Act of 1917. Contrary to usual practices, the grand jury revealed Johnston's name and the nature of the charges (thereby placing him under a permanent cloud), even though it ultimately failed to indict him. That tactic, along with other administration actions against foreign policy critics, bears more than a superficial similarity to McCarthyism.

56. Freda Kirchwey, "Curb the Fascist Press," *Nation*, March 28, 1942, pp. 357–58.

57. Discussions of those tactics include Richard W. Steele, "Franklin D. Roosevelt and His Foreign Policy Critics," *Political Science Quarterly* 94 (Spring 1979): 15–32; and Wayne S. Cole, *Roosevelt and the Isolationists, 1932–1945* (Lincoln: University of Nebraska Press, 1983), pp. 456–87. Unfortunately, the liberal version of McCarthyism has not disappeared with the passage of time. *Newsweek*'s Jonathan Alter, writing in late 1991, offered as one piece of evidence that Pat Buchanan might be an anti-Semite

Buchanan's alleged "isolationism." According to Alter, "His 1992 campaign slogan— 'America First'—echoes more than just pre–World War II isolationism. The America First Committee, headed by Charles Lindbergh, was also discernibly pro-German and anti-Semitic, as Buchanan (whose father was a supporter) well knows." Jonathan Alter, "Is Pat Buchanan Anti-Semitic?" *Newsweek*, December 23, 1991, p. 23. Alter's comment was either a deliberate smear of the America First Committee—and by extension of the noninterventionist tradition—or an egregious example of historical ignorance. Although some fascists and anti-Semites sought to infiltrate and manipulate the committee, the overwhelming majority of members repudiated such individuals and their values.

58. Rex Stout, *The Illustrious Dunderheads* (New York: Alfred A. Knopf, 1942); John Roy Carlson, *Under Cover: The Amazing Revelation of How Axis Agents and Our Enemies Within Are Now Plotting to Destroy the United States* (New York: E. P. Dutton, 1943); and Michael Sayers and Albert E. Kahn, *Sabotage! The Secret War against America* (New York: Harper & Brothers, 1942). All three books are especially repulsive examples of liberal McCarthyism in which honorable opponents of U.S. entry into the war are indiscriminantly lumped together with racists, fascists, and Nazi agents.

59. Stout, pp. 14–15; and Carlson, pp. 9–11, 495–500.

60. Memo from Franklin D. Roosevelt to Morris Ernst, October 6, 1942, in *FDR: His Personal Letters*, ed. Elliott Roosevelt (New York: Duell, Sloan and Pearce, 1950), vol. 4, p. 1351.

61. How the sedition prosecutions served to intimidate critics is discussed briefly in Ronald Radosh, *Prophets on the Right: Conservative Critics of American Globalism* (New York: Simon and Schuster, 1975), pp. 290–91.

62. James MacGregor Burns, *Roosevelt: The Soldier of Freedom* (New York: Harcourt Brace Jovanovich, 1970), p. 454.

63. Louis Liebovich, *The Press and the Origins of the Cold War, 1944–1947* (New York: Praeger, 1988), p. 54.

64. Ibid., p. 55.

65. "Potsdam Censorship Hit," *New York Times*, July 20, 1945, p. 5.

66. Knightley, p. 276.

67. Koop, p. 270.

68. Liebovich, p. 74.

Chapter 2

1. Theodore F. Koop, *Weapon of Silence* (Chicago: University of Chicago Press, 1946), p. 188.

2. Quoted in James Russell Wiggins, *Freedom or Secrecy*, rev. ed. (New York: Oxford University Press, 1964), p. 100.

3. Quoted in Richard M. Freeland, *The Truman Doctrine and the Origins of McCarthyism* (New York: Alfred A. Knopf, 1970), p. 138.

4. Quoted in Morley Safer, "Television Covers the War," in U.S. Senate Committee on Foreign Relations, *News Policies in Vietnam: Hearings before the Committee on Foreign Relations,* August 17 and 31, 1966, 89th Cong., 2d sess., p. 90. Sylvester later claimed that he had been joking, but the journalists present at the meeting did not share that impression. Moreover, the remark was entirely consistent with the attitude toward a free press that Sylvester exhibited on many other occasions.

5. Quoted in Clarence R. Wyatt, *Paper Soldiers: The American Press and the Vietnam War* (New York: W. W. Norton, 1993), p. 31.

6. Quoted in Wiggins, p. 239.

7. Ibid., p. 239.

8. Freeland, pp. 10–11, 62–69, 77–79.

9. Joseph Jones, *The Fifteen Weeks* (New York: Viking, 1955), pp. 142–43. Under Secretary of State Dean Acheson had used the same tactic to rouse a generally lethargic congressional delegation during the briefing on the proposed Greco-Turkish aid package. Vandenberg's response was evidence of its success. Dean Acheson, *Present at the Creation: My Years in the State Department* (New York: W. W. Norton, 1969), p. 219. There was no doubt that the use of militant anti-communist rhetoric was a deliberate ploy. Charles E. Bohlen, a high-ranking State Department official, was with Secretary of State George Marshall at a foreign ministers conference in Moscow when Truman delivered the address to Congress. Bohlen recalled, "It seemed to General Marshall and to me that there was a little too much flamboyant anti-Communism in the speech." Marshall cabled those thoughts back to Washington and "received a reply that in the considered opinion of the executive branch, including the President, the Senate would not approve the doctrine without the emphasis on the Communist danger." Charles E. Bohlen, *Witness to History, 1929–1949* (New York: W. W. Norton, 1973), p. 261.

10. See, for example, Charles L. Mee Jr., *The Marshall Plan: The Launching of the Pax Americana* (New York: Simon and Schuster, 1984).

11. Don Cook, *Forging the Alliance* (New York: Arbor House, 1989); and Ted Galen Carpenter, "Competing Agendas: America, Europe, and a Troubled NATO Partnership," in *NATO at 40: Confronting a Changing World*, ed. Ted Galen Carpenter (Washington: Cato Institute, 1992), pp. 29–34.

12. James Aronson, *The Press and the Cold War* (Indianapolis: Bobbs-Merrill, 1970), pp. 32–38, 51–64.

13. Aronson, passim; and J. Fred MacDonald, *Television and the Red Menace: The Video Road to Vietnam* (New York; Praeger, 1985), pp. 37–100. Eisenhower's admission that he had lied about the U-2 episode, though, was an important event in the creation of greater media skepticism. David Wise, *The Politics of Lying: Government Deception, Secrecy, and Power* (New York: Random House, 1973), p. 14.

14. Aronson, pp. 106–26; and MacDonald, pp. 31–35. For a discussion of Rhee's authoritarian practices, see Callum McDonald, *Korea: The War before Vietnam* (New York: Free Press, 1986), pp. 13–14, 41, 60.

15. Phillip Knightley, *The First Casualty* (New York: Harcourt Brace Jovanovich, 1975), pp. 343–47.

16. Douglas MacArthur, *Reminiscences* (New York: McGraw-Hill, 1964), p. 338.

17. Ibid., p. 339.

18. Marguerite Higgins, *The Report of a Woman Combat Correspondent* (New York: Doubleday, 1951), pp. 96–97.

19. "Korea Censorship," *Broadcasting*, December 25, 1950, pp. 28–29.

20. Knightley, pp. 345–46.

21. Ibid., p. 349.

22. Ibid., p. 346.

23. Quoted in ibid., pp. 353–54.

24. Ibid., pp. 347, 349, 355.

25. Lester Markel, "The 'Management' of News," *Saturday Review*, February 9, 1963, p. 51.

26. Dan D. Nimmo, *Newsgathering in Washington* (New York: Atherton, 1964), p. 227.

27. MacDonald, pp. 16–17.

28. Ibid., p. 86.

29. Jim Naureckas, "Two Invasions: Ours and Theirs," *Deadline* 6 (January–February 1991): 15. For a British correspondent's caustic assessment of the co-option of American reporters by the U.S. military during the gulf war, see Robert Fisk, "Out of the Pool," *Mother Jones*, May–June, 1991, pp. 56–58.

30. Walter Cronkite, "What Is There to Hide?" *Newsweek*, February 25, 1991, p. 43.

31. Harry Summers, "Testimony before the U.S. Senate Committee on Governmental Affairs," in *The Media and the Gulf War: The Press and Democracy in Wartime*, ed. Hedrick Smith (Washington: Seven Locks Press, 1992), p. 86.

32. U.S. Department of State, *Foreign Relations of the United States, 1952–1954* (Washington: Government Printing Office, 1989), vol. 10, pp. 759–60.

33. Quote in Aronson, p. 161.

34. Wyatt, p. 21.

35. "Mr K Thunders on the Left," editorial, *New York Times*, May 7, 1960, p. A22.

36. Michael R. Beschloss, *Mayday: Eisenhower, Khrushchev, and the U-2 Affair* (New York: Harper and Row, 1986), pp. 234–35.

37. Quoted in ibid., p. 235.

38. "Editorial Comment on U.S. Flight over Soviet Union," *New York Times*, May 10, 1960, p. A15.

39. "A Peculiar Moral Climate," *Nation*, May 21, 1960, pp. 433–34.

40. MacDonald, p. 91.

41. Text of Minnow's address in *Radio and Television: Readings in the Mass Media*, ed. Allen Kirschner and Linda Kirschner (New York: Bobbs-Merrill, 1971), pp. 208–9.

42. Juergen Arthur Heise, *Minimum Disclosure: How the Pentagon Manipulates the News* (New York: W. W. Norton, 1979), pp. 60–61.

43. Arthur M. Schlesinger, *A Thousand Days: John F. Kennedy in the White House* (Boston: Houghton Mifflin, 1965), p. 261.

44. Quoted in Wyatt, p. 38.

45. Office of the Federal Register, *Public Papers of the Presidents of the United States, John F. Kennedy, 1961* (Washington: Government Printing Office, 1962), p. 336.

46. Ibid., pp. 336–37.

47. Aronson, pp. 162–63.

48. Quoted in Harry Howe Ransom, *Can American Democracy Survive the Cold War?* (Garden City, N.Y.: Doubleday, 1963), pp. 242–43.

49. Heise, p. 62. For Salinger's account of the meeting, see Pierre Salinger, *With Kennedy* (Garden City, N.Y.: Doubleday, 1966), p. 158.

50. Chalmers Roberts, "Ho Tries a New Propaganda Weapon," *Washington Post*, January 2, 1967, p. A10.

51. Wyatt, pp. 154–55.

52. Ibid., p. 155.

53. MacDonald, p. 177.

54. Jonathan Kwitny, *Endless Enemies: The Making of an Unfriendly World* (New York: Congdon and Weed, 1984), pp. 160–76.

55. Quoted in ibid., pp. 175–76.

56. Ibid, p. 176. Love's may be a spectacular case of a journalist's crossing the line from reporter to participant, but it is hardly unique. Writer Stephen Crane, working as a correspondent for the *New York World* during the Spanish-American War, accepted the surrender of the Cuban village of Juana Diaz, much to the surprise of the U.S. commander who arrived with 800 troops the following day to storm the less than ardently defended village. Knightley, pp. 56–58.

57. *Intelligence Activities and the Rights of Americans, Final Report of the Select Committee to Study Governmental Operations with Respect to Intelligence Activities*, Report no. 94–755, 94th Cong., 2d sess., April 26, 1976, p. 197–98. It appears that the government may not have abandoned the practice. George Volsky, "Ex-Reporter Says Radio Marti Spies," *New York Times*, September 17, 1987.

58. Sol Stern, "A Short Account of International Student Politics and the Cold War with Particular Reference to the NSA, CIA, etc.," *Ramparts*, March 1967, pp. 29–38.

59. Stansfield Turner, *Secrecy and Democracy: The CIA in Transition* (Boston: Houghton-Mifflin, 1985), p. 100.

60. Ibid., p. 101.

61. Ibid., p. 103.

62. Ibid., p. 104.

63. Quoted in ibid., p. 102.

Chapter 3

1. Letter of May 13, 1798, in *The Complete Madison*, ed. Saul K. Padover (New York: Harper and Brothers, 1953), p. 257.

2. "Atom Control Bill Signed by Truman," *New York Times*, August 2, 1946, p. A7; and Harry S Truman, *Memoirs*, vol. 2: *Years of Trial and Hope* (Garden City, N.Y.: Doubleday, 1956), pp. 2–8, 11, 15.

3. "U.S. Aide Defends Lying to Nation," *New York Times*, December 7, 1962, p. A5.

4. James Russell Wiggins, *Freedom or Secrecy*, rev. ed. (New York: Oxford University Press, 1964), preface.

5. Juergen Arthur Heise, *Minimum Disclosure: How the Pentagon Manipulates the News* (New York: W. W. Norton, 1979), p. 57.

6. Samuel R. Gammon, letter to the editor, *Washington Post*, July 20, 1993, p. A16.

7. Quoted in "Atomic Secrets," *New York Times Magazine*, May 1, 1994, p. 25.

8. Ibid.

9. Robert Dvorchak, "America's Long Atomic Deception," *Washington Times*, April 20, 1994, p. A8. The same willingness to use the classification system to conceal information that might provoke a public outcry and lead to lawsuits was evident in a wide array of radiation experiments on humans. Philip J. Hilts, "Inquiry Links Secrecy to a Cover-Up," *New York Times*, December 15, 1994, p. A26; and Gary Lee, "New Reasons Revealed for Test Secrecy," *Washington Post*, December 15, 1994, p. A21.

10. David Lawrence, "Our Own 'Iron Curtain,' " *U.S. News & World Report*, October 5, 1951, p. 76.

11. Harry Howe Ransom, *Can American Democracy Survive the Cold War?* (Garden City, N.Y.: Doubleday, 1963), pp. 219–20.

12. Ibid., p. 220.

13. Ibid., p. 221.

14. Quoted in ibid.

15. U.S. House Committee on Government Operations, *U.S. Government Information and Practices—The Pentagon Papers (Part 1): Hearings before a Subcommittee of the Committee on Government Operations*, 92d Cong., 1st sess., 1971, p. 97.

16. Edward Teller, "The Secrecy Charade," *Reason*, November 1982, p. 43. See also Edward Teller, "State Secrecy Doesn't Help National Security," *Wall Street Journal*, June 18, 1986.

17. Useful discussions of covert operations by the CIA and other agencies include Victor Marchetti and John D. Marks, *The CIA and the Cult of Intelligence* (New York: Alfred A. Knopf, 1974); Gregory F. Treverton, *Covert Action: The Limits of Intervention in the Postwar World* (New York: Basic Books, 1987); John Prados, *Presidents' Secret Wars: CIA and Pentagon Covert Operations since World War II* (New York: Morrow, 1986); John Ranelagh, *The Agency: The Rise and Decline of the CIA* (New York; Simon and Schuster, 1986); and David Isenberg, "The Pitfalls of U.S. Covert Operations," Cato Institute Policy Analysis no. 118, April 7, 1989.

18. Treverton, p. 260.

19. Ibid., pp. 186–87.

20. Tim Weiner, "CIA Spent Millions to Support Japanese Right in 50s and 60s," *New York Times*, October 9, 1994, p. A1. Officials of Japan's Liberal Democratic party subsequently denied accepting payment. "Japanese Party Denies Report of CIA Payments," *Washington Post*, October 12, 1994, p. 29. The report's credibility is strengthened, however, by the fact that the CIA undeniably engaged in similar conduct in France, Italy, and other democratic nations after World War II.

21. Despite the evidence to the contrary, Reagan still insists that there was no intent to trade arms for hostages. Ronald Reagan, *An American Life* (New York: Simon and Schuster, 1990), pp. 528–29. For somewhat contrasting views of the Iran-Contra initiative of other key administration insiders, see Caspar Weinberger, *Fighting for Peace* (New York: Warner Books, 1991), pp. 356–80; and George P. Shultz, *Turmoil and Triumph* (New York: Scribner's, 1993), pp. 783–807. See also *The Tower Commission Report* (New York: Times Books, 1987) for the conclusions reached by the panel Reagan appointed to conduct an official investigation.

22. Bob Woodward, *Veil: The Secret Wars of the CIA* (New York: Simon and Schuster, 1987), pp. 467–68.

23. Shultz, p. 787. Emphasis in original.

24. Morton H. Halperin and Daniel Hoffman, *Top Secret: National Security and the Right to Know* (Washington: New Republic Books, 1977), p. 101. For a discussion of the corrosive effects of secrecy and deception in the name of national security on the operation of a democratic system, see Miroslav Ninic, *Democracy and Foreign Policy* (New York: Columbia University Press, 1992), pp. 124–52.

25. Once the Clinton administration decided to restore Aristide, the CIA reportedly launched an intense covert operation to bring down Haiti's military dictatorship without a U.S. invasion. Doyle McManus and Robin Wright, "U.S. Tried Covert Action to Rid Haiti of Rulers," *Los Angeles Times*, September 16, 1994, p. A1. It is possible, therefore, that for a brief time the CIA was funding both sides in Haiti's political struggle.

26. 410 U.S. 73 (1973).

27. For a concise discussion of FOIA in theory and practice, see Michael Jay Singer, "United States," in *Administrative Secrecy in Developed Countries*, ed. Donald C. Rowat (New York: Columbia University Press, 1979), pp. 312–44.

28. Sylvia Katz, "The Games Bureaucrats Play: Hide and Seek under the Freedom of Information Act," *Texas Law Review* 48 (1970): 1261.

29. Heise, pp. 128–32.

30. Ibid., pp. 64–65. On the scope of the 1974 amendments, see Halperin and Hoffman, pp. 48–52.

31. Gerald R. Ford, *A Time to Heal* (New York: Berkley, 1980), p. xxvi.

32. Singer, p. 343.

33. See, for example, Kermit Roosevelt, *Countercoup: The Struggle for Control of Iran* (New York: McGraw-Hill, 1979). For a scathing critique of the U.S. government's attempt to distort the historical record of the Iran episode, see Wilbur Edel, "Diplomatic History—State Department Style," *Political Science Quarterly* 106 (Winter 1991–92): 701–5.

34. Ibid., pp. 704–11.

35. Al Kammen, "Documents Law: 30 Years and Out," *Washington Post*, October 31, 1991, p. A19.

36. For discussions of National Security Decision Directive 84 and its implications, see Frederick W. Whatley, "Reagan, National Security, and the First Amendment: Plugging Leaks by Shutting Off the Main," Cato Institute Policy Analysis no. 37, May 8, 1984; and Edel, pp. 699–700.

37. *United States v. Marchetti* 466 F.2d 1309 (4th Cir. 1972), p. 1315. For a discussion of the significance of the *Marchetti* ruling, see Halperin and Hoffman, pp. 131–40. *Frank W. Snepp, III v. United States* 444 U.S. 507.

38. *Public Papers of the Presidents of the United States: Ronald Reagan, 1982* (Washington: Government Printing Office, 1983), pp. 412–20. For critical discussions of Reagan's executive order and his general hostility toward FOIA, see Walter Karp, "Liberty under Siege," *Harper's*, November 1985, pp. 57–58; Edel, pp. 698–99; and Diana M. T. K. Autin, "The Reagan Administration and the Freedom of Information Act," in *Freedom at Risk: Secrecy, Censorship, and Repression in the 1980s*, ed. Richard O. Curry (Philadelphia: Temple University Press, 1988), pp. 69–85.

39. James Bamford, *The Puzzle Palace: Inside the National Security Agency, America's Most Secret Intelligence Organization* (New York: Penguin Books, 1983).

40. Thomas G. Paterson, "Thought Control and the Writing of History," in *Freedom at Risk*, pp. 61–62.

41. Ibid., p. 62.

42. George Lardner Jr., "CIA Report on Openness Classified Secret," *Washington Post*, March 23, 1992, p. A1.

43. Quoted in "Well-Kept Secrets Stay That Way," *Washington Post*, October 17, 1994, p. A17.

44. "Democracy's Obsolete Secrets," *New York Times*, editorial, May 9, 1993, p. E14.

45. Halperin and Hoffman, pp. 33–34.

46. U.S. Department of Defense, *Current News*, June 10, 1993, p. 14.

47. Quoted in Tim Weiner, "President Moves to Release Classified Documents," *New York Times*, May 5, 1993, p. A18.

48. Ibid.

49. "Keeping Secrets Is Becoming a Problem for Uncle Sam," *Washington Times*, May 6, 1994, p. A7.

50. Quoted in Weiner, "President Moves," p. A18.

51. Michael Gartner, "Look Who's Hiding the News," *USA Today*, April 14, 1994, p. 11.

52. Gammon.

53. Quoted in "Well-Kept Secrets Stay That Way."
54. Philip G. Schrag, "License to Shred," *Washington Post*, August 24, 1994, p. A19.

Chapter 4

1. Quoted in Juergen Arthur Heise, *Minimum Disclosure: How the Pentagon Manipulates the News* (New York: W. W. Norton, 1979), pp. 163–64.
2. Richard M. Freeland, *The Truman Doctrine and the Origins of McCarthyism* (New York: Alfred A. Knopf, 1970), p. 221.
3. Memo from Stephen Spingarn to Clark Clifford, April 6, 1949, Clark Clifford Papers, Subject File, Box 15, Harry S Truman Library, Independence, Missouri.
4. For discussions, see Athan Theoharis, *Spying on Americans: Political Surveillance from Hoover to the Huston Plan* (Philadelphia: Temple University Press, 1978); and Richard E. Morgan, *Domestic Intelligence: Monitoring Dissent in America* (Austin: University of Texas Press, 1980).
5. F. M. Kail, *What Washington Said: Administration Rhetoric and the Vietnam War, 1949–1969* (New York: Harper and Row, 1973), pp. 217–18.
6. Quoted in ibid., p. 216.
7. Quoted in ibid., p. 217.
8. "Westmoreland Address," *New York Times*, April 25, 1967.
9. Andrew J. Glass, "Senators Blast War Widening, Dissent Curbs," *Washington Post*, April 26, 1967.
10. For examples of the contrasting views, see "Dissent Is Not Treason," editorial, *Chicago Daily News*, April 26, 1967; and "Westmoreland's Challenge to Critics," editorial, *Denver Post*, April 25, 1967.
11. Kail, p. 217.
12. For a discussion of the Army's role in the surveillance campaign, see Joan M. Jensen, *Army Surveillance in America, 1775–1980* (New Haven, Conn.: Yale University Press, 1991). On the CIA's role, see John Ranelagh, *The Agency: The Rise and Decline of the CIA* (New York: Simon and Schuster, 1986), pp. 533–36, 572–77; and Morgan, pp. 66–71. A typical example of the CIA's actions can be found in "International Connections of U.S. Peace Groups," 15 November 1967, National Security file, Intelligence File, box 3, "U.S. Peace Groups—International Connections" folder, Lyndon B. Johnson Library, Austin, Texas. The cover memo from CIA director Richard Helms to President Johnson confirmed that the FBI and the National Security Agency were also deeply involved in such surveillance.
13. Seymour M. Hersh, "Huge CIA Operation Reported in U.S. against Antiwar Forces, Other Dissidents in Nixon Years," *New York Times*, December 22, 1974, p. 1. Despite the title of Hersh's article, the internal spying program had been in effect since the 1950s.
14. Kail, p. 219.
15. Quoted in William M. Hammond, *Public Affairs: The Military and the Media, 1962–1968* (Washington: U.S. Army Center of Military History, 1988), p. 190.
16. Quoted in ibid., p. 191. Emphasis in original.
17. Clarence R. Wyatt, *Paper Soldiers: The American Press and the Vietnam War* (New York: W. W. Norton, 1993), p. 145.
18. Wayne King, "FBI Stand Is Contradicted on Surveillance of Policy Foes," *New York Times*, February 14, 1988, p. A34. For a discussion of the Reagan administration's use of the FBI against foreign policy opponents, see Athan Theoharis, "Conservative

Politics and Surveillance: The Cold War, the Reagan Administration, and the FBI," in *Freedom at Risk: Secrecy, Censorship and Repression in the 1980s*, ed. Richard O. Curry (Philadelphia: Temple University Press, 1988), pp. 259–71.

19. See, for example, the attack on the Center for Defense Information by federal government attorney Michael Fumento, "The Center for Defense Misinformation," *American Spectator*, April 1988, pp. 20–23.

20. U.S. House Committee on the Judiciary, *FBI Investigation of First Amendment Activities: Hearings before the Subcommittee on Civil and Constitutional Rights of the Committee on the Judiciary*, June 21 and 22, 1989, 101st Cong., 1st sess., pp. 1–2.

21. Ibid., p. 5.

22. Ibid., p. 3.

23. Howard Kurtz, "Sen. Simpson Calls Arnett 'Sympathizer,' " *Washington Post*, February 8, 1991, p. B2. Simpson later apologized for using the term "sympathizer," stating that he should have referred to Arnett as a "dupe" or "tool." Alan Simpson, letter to the editor, *New York Times*, March 20, 1991, p. A28. It is interesting that Simpson did not offer even that tepid half-apology until the gulf war was over.

24. Freeland, p. 224.

25. Ibid., pp. 11, 224–25.

26. David Wise, *The Politics of Lying: Government Deception, Secrecy, and Power* (New York: Random House, 1973), p. 30.

27. Janice Castro, "Peace Pact on War Coverage," *Time*, September 3, 1984, p. 73. The attempt to bar foreigners was not merely chauvinism. Military leaders had noted that non-American correspondents had tended to be more critical of U.S. policy in both Korea and Vietnam than their American colleagues. The Sidle panel report stated bluntly that, based on the Pentagon's "public affairs experience in Vietnam," many foreign correspondents "proved entirely reliable; however, some did not." In Pentagonese, "reliable" was essentially a code word for favoring U.S. policy. U.S. Department of Defense, *Report of the Chairman of the Joint Chiefs of Staff, Media-Military Relations Panel* (Sidle panel), August 23, 1984, p. 9.

28. Theodore F. Koop, *Weapon of Silence* (Chicago: University of Chicago Press, 1946), pp. 176–77.

29. Ibid., p. 177.

30. "FCC Refuses CIA Request to Punish ABC," *Dallas Morning News*, January 11, 1985.

31. Bill McAllister, "USIA Labels U.S. Film 'Propaganda,' " *Washington Post*, January 17, 1988, p. A23; and Elizabeth Kastor, "Wick, Heating Up Film Battle," *Washington Post*, July 27, 1988, p. C1.

32. Bob Woodward, "Gadhafi Target of Secret U.S. Deception Plan," *Washington Post*, October 2, 1986; and Jonathan Alter, "A Bodyguard of Lies," *Newsweek*, October 13, 1986, pp. 43–45. For discussions of that episode's larger significance, see Anthony Lewis, "When We Practice to Deceive," *New York Times*, October 6, 1986; and Ted Galen Carpenter, "Secrecy and the Erosion of Democratic Values," *Baltimore Sun*, November 13, 1986.

33. Stansfield Turner, *Secrecy and Democracy: The CIA in Transition* (Boston: Houghton Mifflin, 1985), p. 149.

34. "Framing Leakers as Spies after Morison," *First Principles*, May 1988, p. 3.

35. Gregory F. Treverton, *Covert Action: The Limits of Intervention in the Postwar World* (New York: Basic Books, 1987), p. 186.

36. For example, John Mecklin, the chief information officer at the Saigon mission in the early 1960s, suggested that Washington share classified information only with "responsible journalists." Wyatt, p. 123. At the same time the Kennedy administration was justifying its increasingly restrictive information policy on the Vietnam conflict on the grounds that the national security issues were "a matter of great sensitivity." Wyatt, p. 90.

37. Quoted in Hammond, p. 217.

38. Seymour M. Hersh, *The Price of Power: Kissinger in the Nixon White House* (New York: Summit Books, 1983), pp. 88–92. In a meeting with Nixon and several of his advisers in November 1969, Kissinger reportedly made the bizarre accusation that Kalb was an agent of the Romanian government. Ibid., p. 93. Years later Kalb discussed the issue and suggested why Nixon and his advisers could believe such an improbable charge. Marvin Kalb, "I Was a 'Rumanian Agent,' " *Washington Post*, August 8, 1994, p. A19. On the wiretapping of journalists, dissident government employees, and other foreign policy critics, see David Wise, *The American Police State* (New York: Random House, 1976), pp. 31–106.

39. Heise, p. 134.

40. Mark Hertsgaard, *On Bended Knee: The Press and the Reagan Presidency* (New York: Schocken Books, 1988), p. 234.

41. Quoted in John Lancaster, "Pentagon Drops Security Probe of Professor on Patriot Article," *Washington Post*, March 28, 1992, p. A11.

42. Wise, p. 66.

43. *Gorin v. United States*, 312 U.S. 19 (1941).

44. The *Amerasia* case is discussed in Earl Latham, *The Communist Controversy in Washington* (Cambridge, Mass.: Harvard University Press, 1966), pp. 203–16.

45. A 1984 internal government report asserted that the government already had the legal authority to punish reporters who published classified information, although it would be "politically controversial" to engage in such prosecutions. "U.S. Seeks to Stop Disclosures by Punishing Sources of Leaks," *Dallas Morning News*, December 23, 1984.

46. Weinberger also seemed miffed that the *Post* had not been as "cooperative" as other media outlets. He said it was "the height of journalistic irresponsibility to violate requests that are made." Alex S. Jones, "Pentagon Chief Assails Article on Shuttle Trip," *New York Times*, December 20, 1984. In other words, the press should keep secret whatever the government asks it to and should exercise no independent judgment on the matter.

47. "Weinberger Attacks Post for Story on Spy Satellite," *Dallas Morning News*, December 20, 1984; and Walter Karp, "Liberty under Siege," *Harper's*, November 1985, p. 66. Casey also mentioned the possibility of prosecution to Seymour Hersh because of Hersh's disclosures of U.S. intelligence operations in connection with the Soviets' destruction of Korean Airlines flight 007. "Again, It's Casey at Bat," *U.S. News & World Report*, July 7, 1986.

48. Quoted in Jay Peterzell, "Can the CIA Spook the Press?" *Columbia Journalism Review*, September–October 1986, p. 29. Casey's threats even drew fire from the conservative *Wall Street Journal*, normally a staunchly pro-administration publication. "Traitors and Journalists," editorial, *Wall Street Journal*, May 22, 1986, p. A28.

49. Molly Moore, "Prosecution of Media for Leaks Urged," *Washington Post*, September 3, 1987, p. A4. Odom cited the provision of a 1950 law prohibiting disclosure of "communications intelligence" as his justification.

50. "Do Loose Lips Sink Ships?" *New Republic*, November 18, 1985, p. 7.

51. Quoted in Nat Hentoff, "How We Got an Official Secrets Act," *Progressive*, March 1989, p. 10.

52. Steven Burkholder, "The Morison Case: The Leaker as 'Spy,' " in *Freedom at Risk*, p. 119.

53. Hertsgaard, p. 224. For an indication of how radically the Reagan administration's thesis differed from most previous views of the scope of the Espionage Act and related statutes, see the exhaustive treatment of the subject by Harold Edgar and Benno C. Schmidt Jr., "The Espionage Statutes and Publication of Defense Information," *Columbia Law Review* 73 (May 1973): 930–1087. Edgar and Schmidt emphasized, however, that several provisions of the espionage laws were dangerously vague.

54. Morton H. Halperin and Daniel Hoffman, *Top Secret: National Security and the Right to Know* (Washington: New Republic Books, 1977), p. 116.

55. Both former secretary of state Alexander M. Haig and former secretary of defense James Schlesinger have also endorsed prosecuting reporters who receive classified information to—in Schlesinger's words—"teach other reporters some inhibitions." "The Military and the News Media," Columbia University Graduate School of Journalism Media and Society Seminars, Princeton, N.J., January 1985, edited transcript in "The Pentagon vs. the Press," *Harper's*, November 1985, p. 48.

56. Quoted in Burkholder, pp. 127–28.

Chapter 5

1. "A Basis for Censorship Planning," memorandum from Byron Price to President Truman, August 24, 1945, Presidential Files, box 419, Harry S. Truman Library, Independence, Missouri, p. 6.

2. Letter from Byron Price to Harry S. Truman, August 24, 1945, Presidential Files, box 419, Harry S. Truman Library, Independence, Missouri.

3. "A Basis for Censorship Planning," pp. 1–2.

4. "Censorship Mobilization Planning," National Security Resources Board Document 119, Exhibit D, Harry S. Truman Library, Independence, Missouri, p. 10.

5. Robert Higgs, *Crisis and Leviathan: Critical Episodes in the Growth of American Government* (New York: Oxford University Press, 1987), p. 251.

6. National Security Resources Board, "Mobilization Planning for Censorship," staff study, February 12, 1953, White House Central Files, Confidential File, box 23, Dwight D. Eisenhower Library, Abilene, Kansas.

7. Letter from Lyndon B. Johnson to Theodore F. Koop, February 1, 1967, Confidential File, box 15, Lyndon B. Johnson Library, Austin, Texas; and Minutes of Cabinet Meeting, April 24, 1959, Ann Whitman File, Cabinet Series, box 13, Dwight D. Eisenhower Library, Abilene, Kansas.

8. Department of Defense Directive no. 5230.7 (with changes through 5-21-71), reprinted in U.S. Senate Committee on Governmental Affairs, *Pentagon Rules on Media Access to the Persian Gulf War: Hearing before the Senate Committee on Governmental Affairs*, 102d Cong., 1st sess., February 20, 1991, pp. 833, 835.

9. Department of Defense Directive 5230.7, in ibid., pp. 826–27.

10. David Wise, *The Politics of Lying: Government Deception, Secrecy and Power* (New York: Random House, 1973), pp. 137–38; U.S. House Committee on Government Operations, *U.S. Government Information Policies and Practices—Problems of Congress in Obtaining Information from the Executive Branch (Part 8): Hearings before a Subcommittee*

of the House Committee on Government Operations, 92d Cong. 2d sess., May 12, 1972, p. 2950.

11. Wise, p. 138.

12. Ibid., p. 140.

13. *New York Times Company v. United States,* 91 S. Ct. 2140 (1971), p. 2155. The most thorough discussion of the Pentagon Papers case and its ramifications is Sanford J. Unger, *The Papers and the Papers: An Account of the Legal Battle over the Pentagon Papers* (New York: Columbia University Press, 1989).

14. *Near v. Minnesota ex rel. Olson* 283 U.S. 697 (1931). See also *Bantam Books, Inc. v. Sullivan,* 372 U.S. 58 (1963).

15. *New York Times Company v. United States,* p. 2141.

16. Ibid., p. 2151.

17. Instead, the government unsuccessfully prosecuted Ellsberg and Russo under the Espionage Act. See Peter Schrag, *Test of Loyalty: Daniel Ellsberg and the Rituals of Secret Government* (New York: Simon and Schuster, 1974).

18. *New York Times Company v. United States,* pp. 2165–66.

19. Quoted in A. M. Rosenthal, "The Pentagon Papers," *New York Times,* June 11, 1991, p. A23.

20. Morton H. Halperin and Daniel Hoffman, *Top Secret: National Security and the Right to Know* (Washington: New Republic Books, 1977), p. 9.

21. Ibid., p. 10.

22. For the background of the original Official Secrets Act, see Clive Ponting, *Secrecy in Britain* (Oxford: Basil Blackwell, 1990), pp. 3–5.

23. Ibid., p. 8.

24. For an analysis of the provisions of that act, see David Leigh, *The Frontiers of Secrecy: Closed Government in Britain* (Frederick, Md.: University Publications of America, 1982), pp. 49–52.

25. Harry Howe Ransom, *Can American Democracy Survive the Cold War?* (Garden City, N.Y: Doubleday, 1963), p. 219.

26. Harold Evans, "The Norman Conquest: Freedom of the Press in Britain and America," in *The Media and Foreign Policy,* ed. Simon Serfaty (New York: Free Press, 1991), pp. 193–94.

27. The chilling effect created by that atmosphere of uncertainty is probably more effective in stifling dissent than the relatively infrequent cases of actual prosecution. Leigh, pp. 52, 57–58.

28. Lionel Barber, "U.S. Defense Reporting: A British Perspective," in *Defense Beat: The Dilemmas of Defense Coverage,* ed. Loren B. Thompson (New York: Lexington Books, 1991), p. 138.

29. Ponting, p. 32.

30. Ibid., p. 64.

31. For other highly questionable incidents in which the Official Secrets Act was used against foreign policy critics, see Leigh, pp. 52–55.

32. Ponting, p. 39; and Evans, "The Norman Conquest," pp. 195–97.

33. Peter Wright, *Spycatcher* (New York: Viking, 1987); and "Officially It's Secret," *Economist* January 9, 1988, p. 12. On the *Spycatcher* episode and what it reveals about the repressive British system of information management, see "Not Liberal Yet," *Economist,* December 19, 1987, p. 54; Mel Friedman, "Her Majesty's Censors," *Progressive,* February 1989, pp. 30–33; and James Atlas, "Thatcher Puts a Lid On: Censorship in Britain," *New York Times Magazine,* March 5, 1989, pp. 36–38, 97. Proponents of

press freedoms secured a victory of sorts in November 1991 when the European Court of Human Rights ruled that the British government had violated the rights of three newspapers and ordered the government to pay $180,000 to each of those publications to cover their legal costs. "British Papers Win 'Spycatcher' Case," *Washington Post*, November 27, 1991, p. A14.

34. Ponting, p. 79.

35. Andrew Sullivan, "Big Sister: The 'Authoritarianism' of Mrs. T," *New Republic*, January 2, 1989, p. 8.

36. Dean Acheson, "The Purloined Papers," *New York Times*, July 7, 1971, p. A37.

37. Minutes of the 172d Meeting of the National Security Council, November 23, 1953, p. 10. Ann Whitman File, NSC Series, box 5, Dwight D. Eisenhower Library, Abilene, Kansas. Emphasis added.

38. Ibid., p. 14.

39. Ibid., p. 10.

40. Quoted in Ransom, p. 209.

41. U.S. House Committee on Government Operations, "Availability of Information from Government Departments and Agencies," Report no. 1884, June 16, 1958, pp. 19–20.

42. Quoted in Wise, p. 155.

43. Michael A. Ledeen, "Secrets," in *The Media and Foreign Policy*, p. 129.

44. U.S. Congress, *Report of the Commission on Government Security*, 85th Cong., 1st sess. (1957), pp. 619–20; *Congressional Record*, 85th Cong., 1st sess., vol. 103, pp. 10447–50; and Wise, p. 155.

45. A detailed discussion of that legislation can be found in Jerry J. Berman and Morton H. Halperin, "The Agents Identities Protection Act: A Preliminary Analysis of the Legislative History," in *The First Amendment and National Security* (Charlottesville, Va.: Center for Law and National Security, 1984), pp. 41–55.

46. Ibid., p. 50.

47. *United States v. The Progressive*, 467 F. Supp. 990 (W.D. Wis. 1979).

48. Quoted in Nat Hentoff, "Stifling the Progressive," *Inquiry*, May 14, 1979, p. 7.

49. Quoted in ibid.

50. Nat Hentoff, "How We Got an Official Secrets Act," *Progressive*, March 1989, pp. 10–11.

51. Burkholder, p. 118.

52. Tom Wicker, "Leakers Beware," *New York Times*, December 6, 1985.

53. Quoted in Burkholder, p. 120.

54. Hentoff, "How We Got an Official Secrets Act," p. 10.

55. "Do Loose Lips Sink Ships?" *New Republic*, November 18, 1985, p. 7.

Chapter 6

1. David Halberstam, *The Making of a Quagmire* (New York: Random House, 1964), p. 319.

2. James Aronson, *The Press and the Cold War* (Indianapolis: Bobbs-Merrill, 1970), p. 219.

3. Joseph C. Goulden, *Truth Is the First Casualty: The Gulf of Tonkin Affair—Illusion and Reality* (Chicago: Rand McNally, 1969).

4. William M. Hammond, *Public Affairs: The Military and the Media, 1962–1968* (Washington: U.S. Army Center of Military History, 1988), p. 181.

5. J. Fred MacDonald, *Television and the Red Menace: The Video Road to Vietnam* (New York: Praeger, 1985), p. 175.

6. Aronson, p. 21.

7. Quoted in ibid., p. 226.

8. Most of the print and broadcast media in the United States helped the Kennedy administration perpetuate that myth. One notable exception was NBC correspondent James Robinson. In a "Projection '62" segment televised on January 5, 1962, Robinson bluntly told his colleagues, "American troops in battle uniform, fully armed, are being killed [by] and killing Communist-led rebels in South Vietnam. American officers are in full command authority of important military operations there. And our active military participation in this war is on the increase." Like it not, Robinson concluded, "We are involved in a shooting war in Southeast Asia." Quoted in Mac-Donald, p. 169.

9. Hammond, p. 15.

10. Ibid., p. 13.

11. Clarence R. Wyatt, *Paper Soldiers: The American Press and the Vietnam War* (New York: W. W. Norton, 1993), p. 98.

12. Phillip Knightley, *The First Casualty* (New York: Harcourt Brace Jovanovich, 1975), p. 376.

13. John Mecklin, *Mission in Torment* (New York: Doubleday, 1965), p. xii.

14. Knightley, p. 376.

15. Halberstam, *The Making of a Quagmire*, p. 273.

16. Ibid., p. 269.

17. Quoted in Wyatt, p. 29.

18. Quoted in Morley Safer, "Television Covers the War," in U.S. Senate Committee on Foreign Relations, *News Policies in Vietnam: Hearings before the Senate Committee on Foreign Relations*, August 17 and 31, 1966, 89th Cong., 2d sess., p. 90.

19. Knightley, pp. 379–80; and Halberstam, *The Making of a Quagmire,* pp. 192–93, 266.

20. Joseph Alsop, "The Crusaders," *Washington Post*, September 23, 1963, p. A17.

21. Quoted in Knightley, p. 381.

22. Halberstam, *The Making of a Quagmire*, p. 315. Halberstam left a rather different impression of his views in his later writings. For example, in the early 1970s he stated that "instead of believing that there was a right way of handling our involvement in Vietnam, in the fall of 1963 I came to the conclusion that it was doomed and that we were on the wrong side of history." David Halberstam, *The Best and the Brightest* (Greenwich, Conn.: Fawcett, 1972), p. 814. It is a little difficult to square that recollection with the hostility he expressed about proposals for withdrawal in *The Making of a Quagmire*.

23. Halberstam, *The Making of a Quagmire*, p. 74.

24. Ibid., p. 75.

25. Quoted in Aronson, p. 193. For a discussion of television news coverage of the early stages of the Vietnam War, see MacDonald, pp. 168–77, 205–17.

26. Hammond, p. 73.

27. *Time*, June 10, 1966, quoted in Aronson, p. 232.

28. Quoted in Hammond, p. 160.

29. Quoted in Knightley, p. 382.

30. Hammond, pp. 130–32.

31. David R. Kiernan, "Is the Military Throttling the Media?" *USA Today Magazine*, January 1991, p. 35.

32. Quoted in David Wise, *The Politics of Lying: Government Deception, Secrecy, and Power* (New York: Random House, 1973), p. 311.

33. Quoted in Knightley, p. 353.

34. Hammond, pp. 212–13.

35. Wyatt, p. 154. For a detailed discussion of the Pentagon's reaction to Salisbury's activities, see Phil Goulding, *Confirm or Deny: Informing the People on National Security* (New York: Harper and Row, 1970), pp. 52–92. Salisbury's own account of his reporting from Hanoi and the U.S. government's response is contained in Harrison Salisbury, *Behind the Lines—Hanoi* (New York: New York Times Company, 1967).

36. Loren B. Thompson, "Media versus the Military: A Brief History of War Coverage in the United States," in *Defense Beat: The Dilemmas of Defense Coverage*, ed. Loren B. Thompson (New York: Lexington Books, 1991) p. 44.

37. Knightley, p. 416.

38. Hammond, p. 279.

39. Quoted in Aronson, p. 244. For a detailed account of media coverage of the Tet offensive, see Peter Braestrup, *Big Story: How the American Press and Television Reported and Interpreted the Crisis of Tet in Vietnam and Washington*, abridged (New Haven, Conn.: Yale University Press, 1978).

40. Quoted in Bill Monroe, "Rusk to John Scali: Whose Side Are You On?" *Washington Journalism Review*, January–February 1991, p. 8.

41. Ibid.

42. Clarence Wyatt takes a somewhat different view, contending that Tet was "more climax than cause." He argues that media criticism of the war effort had been growing for months and that public discontent was rising as well. Wyatt, pp. 167–68, 182. Although it is true that criticism had been growing, it became much more pronounced after Tet.

43. Quoted in Ronald H. Spector, *After Tet: The Bloodiest Year in Vietnam* (New York: Free Press, 1993), p. 215. Emphasis in original.

44. Harry Summers, "Turning History Upside Down," *Washington Times*, July 3, 1992, p. F4.

45. Lyndon Johnson, *Vantage Point: Perspectives of the Presidency, 1963–1969* (New York: Holt, Rinehart and Winston, 1971), p. 384.

46. Lyndon Johnson later contended that he and his advisers had actually anticipated a major communist offensive for months. He stated further that the press had been told of that conclusion in a host of "background" briefings. "In those briefings, we had stressed that heavy action could be expected soon." Ibid., p. 380. Given the number of public statements to the contrary throughout late 1967 and early 1968, Johnson's retrospective comments are probably an attempt to whitewash an egregious error in judgment.

47. Message from Wheeler to Westmoreland, March 9, 1967. Quoted in Hammond, p. 281.

48. R. W. Apple, "Vietnam: The Signs of Stalemate," *New York Times*, August 7, 1967, p. A1.

49. Halberstam, *The Best and the Brightest*, p. 785.

50. Hammond, p. 328.

51. Ibid., p. 342.

52. Orr Kelly, "In a Military Sense, The War Is About Won," *Washington Star*, November 7, 1967. Considine is quoted in Hammond, p. 336.

53. It was that growing realization that apparently caused a shift in public opinion toward a more dovish position on the war a few weeks after the Tet offensive. John E. Mueller, *War, Presidents and Public Opinion* (New York: John Wiley & Sons, 1973), pp. 106–7.

54. Quoted in Don Oberdorfer, *Tet!* (New York: Doubleday, 1971), p. 158.

55. "Bloody Path to Peace," editorial, *New York Times*, February 1, 1968.

56. "Misled, in Every Sense," *New Republic*, February 17, 1968, p. 7.

57. Braestrup. p. 511.

58. Henry Kissinger still clung to that argument years later. Henry Kissinger, *White House Years* (Boston: Little, Brown, 1979), p. 252.

59. It has been a long-standing habit of governments to conceal unpalatable information on the bogus grounds that disclosure would aid the enemy. William Howard Russell, generally regarded as the first modern war correspondent, enraged the British military hierarchy by sending the *Times* of London graphic reports of suffering and incompetence during the Crimean War. Lord Ragslan, the commanding general, urged the *Times* to suppress Russell's dispatches on the grounds that they would give aid and comfort to the enemy. As Arthur Lubow points out, however, "The Russians knew how bad conditions were at the front. It was the Britons back home who were in the dark." He notes further that two things happened once they were enlightened: the cabinet fell, "and at the front Britain belatedly introduced military censorship." Arthur Lubow, "Read Some about It," *New Republic*, March 18, 1991, p. 23.

60. Richard Nixon, *No More Vietnams* (New York: Arbor House, 1985), p. 108.

61. Kissinger, pp. 243–44.

62. Wyatt, pp. 201–2.

63. Kiernan, p. 35.

64. Associated Press, "Vietnam Curbs Hit by Newsmen," *Baltimore Sun*, March 18, 1965.

65. Hammond, pp. 144–45.

66. Ibid., pp. 160–61, 193–95.

67. Wyatt, p. 20.

68. Knightley, p. 382.

69. Ibid., p. 403. Actually, that was the system only after December 1965. Beverly Deepe, "Revised Accreditation Plan Outlined for Viet by MACV," *Overseas Press Club Bulletin*, December 18, 1965, p. 3. The previous system, similar to those of earlier wars, was somewhat more rigorous. That the reason for the change was something other than an upsurge of respect for the value of diverse opinions was acknowledged in the Army's official history of media relations. "The old system, with its background checks and sometimes classified files, carried the potential of becoming an embarrassment should a newsman denied access to the war for any reason other than security decide to sue." Hammond, p. 234.

70. Ibid., p. 160.

71. "G.I.'s, in Pincer Move, Kill 128 in Daylong Battle," *New York Times*, March 17, 1968, p. A1.

72. For discussions of the government's disinformation about the original My Lai incident and the subsequent attempts to cover up the atrocity, see Juergen Arthur Heise, *Minimum Disclosure: How the Pentagon Manipulates the News* (New York: W.

W. Norton, 1979), pp. 17–48; and Seymour M. Hersh, *Cover-Up* (New York: Random House, 1972).

73. Hammond, p. 338.

74. Douglas Kinnard, *The War Managers* (Hanover, N.H.: University Press of New England, 1977), p. 175.

75. Hammond, p. 339.

76. Michael Arlen, "The Falklands, Vietnam and Our Collective Memory," *New Yorker*, August 16, 1982, p. 73.

77. Lawrence W. Lichty, "Comments on the Influence of Television on Public Opinion," in *Vietnam as History*, ed. Peter Braestrup (Washington: Woodrow Wilson International Center for Scholars, 1984), p. 158.

78. Hammond, p. 37.

79. Thompson, p. 47.

80. Knightley, pp. 410–11. Similarly, the influence of the anti-war movement on public opinion appears to have been greatly exaggerated; the demonstrations also had virtually no impact on government policy. Melvyn Small, "The Impact of the Antiwar Movement on Lyndon Johnson: A Preliminary Report," *Journal of Peace and Change* 10 (Spring 1984): 1–23.

81. Mueller, *War, Presidents and Public Opinion*, p. 65. See also John E. Mueller, "Trends in Popular Support for the Wars in Korea and Vietnam," *American Political Science Review* 64 (March 1971): 18–34.

82. Quoted in Edward Jay Epstein, *News from Nowhere* (New York: Random House, 1973), p. 9.

83. Quoted in Knightley, p. 411.

84. Ibid.

Chapter 7

1. *Battle Lines: Report of the Twentieth Century Fund Task Force on the Military and the Media* (New York: Priority, 1985), p. 3.

2. Hugh O'Shaughnessy, *Grenada: An Eyewitness Account of the U.S. Invasion and the Caribbean History That Provoked It* (New York: Dodd, Mead, 1984), p. 205. O'Shaughnessy was a British journalist who was in Grenada when the invasion took place.

3. Edward Cody, "U.S. Forces Thwart Journalists' Reports," *Washington Post*, October 28, 1983.

4. Quoted in O'Shaughnessy, pp. 205–6.

5. William E. Farrell, "U.S. Allows 15 Reporters to Go to Grenada for Day," *New York Times*, October 28, 1983; Phil Gailey, "U.S. Bars Coverage of Grenada Action," *New York Times*, October 27, 1983; and "Newsweek Is Dropped from Grenada Visits," *New York Times*, October 30, 1983.

6. Farrell; and Bernard Weintraub, "U.S. Press Curbs: The Unanswered Questions," *New York Times*, October 29, 1983. For a scathing critique of the administration's rationale by a prominent conservative, see William Safire, "Us against Them," *New York Times*, October 30, 1983. Weinberger later claimed that the administration had received "a strong request" from Admiral Metcalf that no press be permitted to land with the military personnel. Believing it "would have been a very bad start" to overrule the mission commander's first recommendation, "I accepted and agreed to [his] request, with the understanding we would make every effort to get the press in at the end of the first day." Weinberger noted, however, that Metcalf did not admit

the press by the end of the first day, "and the Joint Chiefs and I had to direct him to get them in on the second." Although Weinberger's comments seemed designed to put most of the responsibility for the media blackout at Metcalf's door, the secretary betrayed his own anti-media sentiments, stating that the admiral's exclusion request "seemed to me to have considerable justification and reason behind it." Caspar W. Weinberger, *Fighting for Peace: Seven Critical Years at the Pentagon* (New York: Warner Books, 1990), pp. 114–15.

7. Such congressional critics of the administration's exclusion policy as Sens. Nancy Kassebaum (R-Kans.), Edward Kennedy (D-Mass.), and Paul Sarbanes (D-Md.) made similar observations. *Congressional Record* 129 (October 28, 1983): S14877–78; and *Congressional Record* 129 (October 29, 1983): S14961–67.

8. Loren B. Thompson, "The Media versus the Military: A Brief History of War Coverage in the United States," in *Defense Beat: The Dilemmas of Defense Coverage*, ed. Loren B. Thompson (New York: Lexington Books, 1991), p. 49.

9. *Public Papers of the Presidents of the United States: Ronald Reagan, 1983* (Washington: U.S. Government Printing Office, 1985) book 2, p. 1731. Some veteran journalists seemed to have a similar nostalgic view. John Hersey recalled that what impressed him the most when he arrived in the Pacific theater during World War II "was the degree to which I was trusted by the military. The press was far less confrontational back then in its attitude toward government than it has since become, and the assumption on the part of those in command in the Pacific, in its dealings with us was that 'we're all in this together.'" John Hersey, "Print War, Television War," *Wall Street Journal*, December 3, 1991, p. A14.

10. I. F. Stone, "Treating Press Freedom Like Grenada," *Civil Liberties* (Winter 1984): 3.

11. Louis Wolf, "Inaccuracy in Media: Accuracy in Media Rewrites the News and History," in *Freedom at Risk: Secrecy, Censorship, and Repression in the 1980s*, ed. Richard O. Curry (Philadelphia: Temple University Press, 1988), p. 370.

12. H. Norman Schwarzkopf with Peter Petre, *It Doesn't Take a Hero* (New York: Bantam Books, 1992), p. 248.

13. Quoted in Mark Hertsgaard, *On Bended Knee: The Press and the Reagan Presidency* (New York: Schocken Books, 1988), p. 208.

14. Ibid., p. 209.

15. Maxwell D. Taylor, *Swords into Ploughshares* (New York: W. W. Norton, 1972). For examples of Taylor's hostility toward the press, see pp. 411–12.

16. "Q. & A.: Gen. Maxwell D. Taylor," *New York Times*, January 4, 1984.

17. Ibid.

18. Ibid.

19. Stone, p. 3.

20. Nathaniel C. Nash, "Reports of Falklands War Executions Spur Inquiry," *New York Times*, August 23, 1992, p. A13.

21. Quoted in Hertsgaard, p. 211.

22. Arthur A. Humphries, "Two Routes to the Wrong Destination: Public Affairs in the South Atlantic War," *Naval War College Review* 36 (May–June, 1983): 57.

23. Ibid., p. 56.

24. Ibid., p. 57.

25. Ibid.

26. Ibid.

27. Ibid., p. 61.

28. Ibid., pp. 63, 65.

29. Marie Gottschalk, "Operation Desert Cloud: The Media and the Gulf War," *World Policy Journal* 9 (Summer 1992): 451.

30. Quoted in O'Shaughnessy, p. 213.

31. Quoted in Hertsgaard, p. 212.

32. "Times Poll: Bare Majority Backs Grenada News Curbs," *Los Angeles Times*, November 20, 1983, p. A1. Interestingly, a Louis Harris poll taken several weeks later showed that Americans opposed the government's Grenada press ban by 65 percent to 32 percent. Thomas Griffin, "Truce with the Pentagon," *Time*, February 27, 1984, p. 91. However gratifying such sober second thoughts may have been, the damage had already been done.

33. "Censoring the Invasion," editorial, *Washington Post*, October 28, 1983.

34. "Reporting the News in a Communique War," *New York Times*, October 26, 1983, p. A23. Emphasis added.

35. Weinberger, p. 127.

36. Philip Taubman, "Cuban Troops Called Surprise to U.S.," *New York Times*, October 27, 1983; Philip Taubman, "Senators Suggest Administration Exaggerated Its Cuba Assessment, "*New York Times*, October 30, 1983; and Richard Halloran, "U.S. Reduces Force in Grenada by 700; Estimate of Cuban Nationals on the Island Is Also Cut," *New York Times*, October 31, 1983.

37. Quoted in Hertsgaard, p. 233.

38. Loren Jenkins, "Grenada Military Base Found Well Stocked," *Washington Post*, October 29, 1983, p. A1. Jenkins noted that the principal arms shed was barely one-quarter full and that, although some modern, sophisticated arms were stored there, others were antiquated weapons.

39. Remarks during the *Dick Cavett Show*, CNBC, March 4, 1994.

40. "The Battle for Grenada," *Newsweek*, November 7, 1983, p. 75. See also "Bastion Reported to Fall; Battle Goes On," *New York Times*, October 28, 1983.

41. O'Shaughnessy, pp. 214–15.

42. Richard A. Gabriel and Paul L. Savage, "A 'Study in Military Incompetence,' " *Boston Globe*, October 21, 1984, p. A22.

43. O'Shaughnessy, p. 234.

44. Quote in Hertsgaard, p. 233. Emphasis added.

45. U.S. Department of Defense, *Report of the Chairman of the Joint Chiefs of Staff, Media-Military Relations Panel*, August 23, 1984, p. 3. Cited hereafter as the Sidle panel report.

46. Phillip Knightley, *The First Casualty* (New York: Harcourt Brace Jovanovich, 1975), p. 295. The press pool concept appears to have originated with Japan's government during the Russo-Japanese War of 1904–5. Japanese officials used it in much the same way U.S. officials would after Grenada. According to Arthur Lubow, "Promising Western correspondents a trip to the front, the Japanese authorities kept them bottled up in Tokyo for months. When a handful of reporters were at last selected to go to Manchuria, they were detained under tight escort at a risible distance from the fighting." Arthur Lubow, "Read Some about It," *New Republic*, March 18, 1991, p. 24.

47. Sidle panel report, p. 8.

48. Janice Castro, "Peace Pact on War Coverage," *Time*, September 3, 1984, p. 73. The Pentagon embraced a strategy of creative ambiguity on that point. Michael Burch, assistant secretary of defense for public affairs, later stated that the people to serve in the pools would "more or less" be selected by the Pentagon. He added that

although there would be "consultations" with news executives, "the final decisions are ours." Quoted in Charles Mohr, "The Continuing Battle over Covering Wars," *New York Times*, September 14, 1984, p. A24.

49. Sidle panel report, p. 8.

50. Andrew Rosenthal, "News Group Faults Military Delay on Gulf Reports," *New York Times*, July 23, 1987.

51. Quoted in Harry Summers, "Like It or Not, News Media Are Needed," *Air Force Times*, August 19, 1991, p. 63.

52. Sidle panel report, p. 9.

53. Stephen S. Rosenfeld, "In the Gulf: The Wars of the Press," in *The Media and Foreign Policy*, ed. Simon Serfaty (New York: Free Press, 1991), p. 244.

54. Gottschalk, p. 457.

55. Mark Lawrence, "Pentagon Delayed News Reports from Persian Gulf," *Washington Post*, July 23, 1987; and Molly Moore and Eleanor Randolph, "Military and Media: Collision Course in the Gulf?" *Washington Post*, September 1, 1987. Most Pentagon officials, however, believed the pool system worked well in covering the gulf convoying operation. For the view of one such official, see Jeffrey J. Carnes, "The Department of Defense Media Pool: Making the Media-Military Relationship Work," in *Defense Beat*, pp. 156–59.

56. Quoted in "The 'USS Vincennes': Public War, Secret War," ABC News *Nightline*, July 1, 1992, transcript, p. 1.

57. Ibid., p. 2.

58. A typical example was Nancy Cooper et al., "Tragedy in the Gulf," *Newsweek*, July 18, 1988, pp. 19–24.

59. The Navy's case began to leak badly almost immediately. See "A300 Downing Clouds Aegis Capability," *Aviation Week and Space Technology*, July 11, 1988, pp. 17–18; and "Probe Focuses on Iranian F-14 Signal Detected by Cruiser," ibid., p. 21. For the Navy's own investigation of the incident, see Rear Adm. William M. Fogarty, "Formal Investigation into the Circumstances Surrounding the Downing of a Commercial Airliner by the *USS Vincennes*," U.S. Department of Defense, July 28, 1988.

60. John Barry and Roger Charles, "Sea of Lies," *Newsweek*, July 13, 1992, p. 29. Actually, the story that the *Vincennes* was in Iranian waters was first broken by *Chicago Tribune* defense correspondent David Evans, relying primarily on information from British naval sources. Curiously, the story did not receive much play in the United States until the appearance of the much more detailed *Newsweek* account six months later. It did, however, receive some attention in Britain. See Patrick Cockburn, "U.S. Ship 'Was in Iran Waters,' " *Independent*, December 12, 1991, p. 11. A later, more detailed analysis by Evans of the incident and the Navy's concerted effort to neutralize adverse publicity can be found in David Evans, "*Vincennes*: A Case Study," *Proceedings*, August 1993, pp. 49–55.

61. Quoted in John Lancaster, "Adm. Crowe Denies Coverup in 1988 Downing of Iranian Airliner," *Washington Post*, July 7, 1992, p. A12.

62. David C. Martin, "Covering the Pentagon for Television: A Reporter's Perspective," in *Defense Beat*, p. 87.

63. Quoted in John R. MacArthur, *Second Front: Censorship and Propaganda in the Gulf War* (New York: Hill and Wang, 1992), p. 5.

64. Stanley W. Cloud, "How Reporters Missed the War," *Time*, January 8, 1990, p. 61.

65. Ibid.

66. Michael Mossetig, "Panama and the Press," *SAIS Review* (Summer–Fall 1990): 186. See also George Garneau, "Military Press Pool Misses Most of the Action," *Editor and Publisher*, January 6, 1990, pp. 4, 84.

67. Kevin Merida, "The Panama Press-Pool Fiasco," *Washington Post*, January 7, 1990, p. B2.

68. Steven Komarow, "Pooling Around in Panama," *Washington Journalism Review*, March 1990, p. 45.

69. U.S. Department of Defense, "Report on Media Pool Coverage of the Panama Operation," March 20, 1990, p. 2. Emphasis in original.

70. Komarow, p. 52.

71. Quoted in Cloud, p. 61.

72. Quoted in MacArthur, pp. 143–44.

73. Quoted in Cloud, p. 61.

74. Merida, p. B2.

75. Bernard E. Trainor, "The Military's War with the Media: Causes and Consequences," in *Defense Beat*, p. 73.

76. Knightley, p. 323.

77. Ibid., pp. 300–301.

78. Barbara Jamison, "Promises Broken, Illusions Lost," *Nation*, March 15, 1993, p. 337.

79. MacArthur, p. 144.

80. Christina Jacqueline Johns and P. Ward Johnson, *State Crime, the Media, and the Invasion of Panama* (New York; Praeger, 1994), p. 90.

81. Ibid., p. 89.

82. Komarow, p. 52.

83. Quoted in Cloud, p. 61.

84. MacArthur, p. 32.

Chapter 8

1. Pete Williams, "Let's Face It, This Was the Best War Coverage We've Ever Had," *Washington Post*, March 17, 1991.

2. Colman McCarthy, "When the Media Danced to Jingo Bells," *Washington Post*, March 17, 1991.

3. Marie Gottschalk, "Operation Desert Cloud: The Media and the Gulf War," *World Policy Journal* 9 (Summer 1992): 451.

4. Ibid., p. 453.

5. For analyses debunking the "oil domination" thesis, see Doug Bandow, "The Myth of Iraq's Oil Stranglehold," *New York Times*, September 16, 1990; David R. Henderson, "Do We Need to Go to War for Oil?" Cato Institute Foreign Policy Briefing no. 4, October 24, 1990; and David R. Henderson, "The Myth of Saddam's Oil Stranglehold," in *America Entangled: The Persian Gulf Crisis and Its Consequences*, ed. Ted Galen Carpenter (Washington: Cato Institute, 1991), p. 43. Henderson's estimates were confirmed by economists of diverse political persuasions, including Nobel laureates Milton Friedman and James Tobin. Jonathan Marshall, "Economists Say Iraq's Threat to U.S. Oil Supply Is Exaggerated," *San Francisco Chronicle*, October 29, 1990.

6. Tom Marks, "Iraq's Not-So-Tough Army," *Wall Street Journal*, August 21, 1990, p. A14.

7. John J. Mearsheimer, "A War the U.S. Can Win—Decisively," *Chicago Tribune*, January 15, 1991, p. A13.

8. Stephen Budiansky, "A Messy, Dangerous World," *U.S. News & World Report*, August 13, 1990, p. 10.

9. Gottschalk, p. 460.

10. Vincent Carroll, "The Scarcity of Anti-War Editorial Voices," *Washington Journalism Review*, January–February, 1991, p. 14.

11. Gene Ruffini, "Press Fails to Challenge Rush to War," *Washington Journalism Review*, March 1991, p. 21.

12. John R. MacArthur, *Second Front: Censorship and Propaganda in the Gulf War* (New York: Hill and Wang, 1992), p. 43.

13. Indeed, in some journalistic circles the demonizing of Saddam had begun even before the invasion of Kuwait. See, for example, Brian Duffy et al., "The World's Most Dangerous Man," *U.S. News & World Report*, June 4, 1990, pp. 38–51. For a discussion of the effort to demonize Saddam, see Eric Alterman, "Operation Pundit Storm," *World Policy Journal* 9 (Fall–Winter 1992): 605–7.

14. Mark Hertsgaard, "Following Washington's Lead," *Deadline* 6 (January–February 1991): 4.

15. Mark Crispin Miller, " 'Showdown' in Gulf Imagery," *Deadline*, 6 (January–February 1991): 9.

16. A notable exception to the lack of media inquiries into such matters was the article by Glenn Frankel, "Imperialist Legacy: Lines in the Sand," *Washington Post*, August 31, 1990, p. A1.

17. For a good summary of the evidence of Washington's cozy relationship with Saddam, see Stanley Kober, "Appeasement and the Gulf War," Progressive Policy Institute Commentary, July 1992.

18. William A. Dorman, "The Forgotten War," *Deadline* 6 (January–February 1991): 13.

19. MacArthur, *Second Front*, p. 68.

20. John R. MacArthur, "Remember Nayirah, Witness for Kuwait?" *New York Times*, January 6, 1992, p. A17.

21. Clifford Krauss, "Congressman Says Girl Was Credible," *New York Times*, January 12, 1992, p. A11.

22. MacArthur, *Second Front*, pp. 59–61, 63–64.

23. Ibid., p. 67. The interview with the Palestinian doctor ran on page 13 of the *Seattle Times* on September 30 but was not picked up by other papers. A brief story including comments by Icelandic physician Dr. Gisli Sigurdsson ran on page 7 of the December 10 edition of *USA Today*. Again, the other major metropolitan dailies, the principal news magazines, and the television networks failed to mention such rebuttals.

24. The government continued to circulate the baby incubator charges, however. A report prepared in early 1992 by Army investigators at the behest of the State Department concluded that 120 babies were left to die after being removed from incubators that were then taken to Iraq. U.S. Department of the Army, "Report on Iraqi War Crimes (Operation Desert Shield/Desert Storm) [Unclassified Version]," January 8, 1992, pp. 9, 36. Again, the "evidence" consisted of statements from alleged eyewitnesses obligingly provided by the Kuwaiti government plus post facto records supplied by the government-operated hospital in Kuwait City.

Interestingly, the Army report was not made public until March 1993. According to a "senior official" who was privy to the original decision to withhold the report, the Bush administration had refused to declassify the document out of concern that the information would damage Bush's reelection bid by underscoring his failure to drive Saddam from power. John Lancaster, "Administration Releases Report on Iraqi War Crimes in Kuwait," *Washington Post*, March 20, 1993, p. A18. The incident provides yet another example of how the veil of "national security" is used to protect personal or political reputations.

25. Knightley, p. 217.

26. Even though the administration considered press and congressional support for its policies desirable, it did not view either one as indispensable. Indeed, President Bush made it clear on several occasions that he was prepared to act against Iraq even without congressional authorization—and quite likely to do so even in defiance of an explicit congressional prohibition. See Doug Bandow, "The Persian Gulf: Restoring the Congressional War Power," in *America Entangled*, pp. 97–104. See also Fred Barnes, "The President's Men," *New Republic*, February 4, 1991, pp. 15–16. Supporters of the war boasted of how Bush maneuvered the nation toward war through a series of unilateral steps, while anti-war spokesmen decried yet another precedent of unbridled and unconstitutional presidential warmaking. Both sides agreed, however, that the president had never been willing to brook opposition to his course. See Charles Krauthammer, "Bush's March through Washington," *Washington Post*, March 1, 1991, p. A15; and Anthony Lewis, "On His Word Alone," *New York Times*, January 12, 1993, p. E19.

27. MacArthur, *Second Front*, pp. 6–7.

28. Gen. H. Norman Schwarzkopf later contended that U.S. reporters had "had unprecedented access to Saudi Arabia." H. Norman Schwarzkopf with Peter Petre, *It Doesn't Take a Hero* (New York: Bantam Books, 1992), pp. 343–44. Given the history of the Riyadh government, that was not saying very much. Schwarzkopf also stated that on one occasion in August the Saudi regime had decided to ask all reporters to leave, but the U.S. Central Command had "interceded successfully on their behalf" (p. 344). The U.S. action was less altruistic than it might have seemed, however. In marked contrast to the Grenada and Panama operations—quick, decisive interventions that did not require sustained public support to be successful—the Persian Gulf military enterprise was certain to be a much larger and more time-consuming affair. Public support (or at least acceptance) was, therefore, essential, and that was not likely to be forthcoming if there was a complete news blackout. Schwarzkopf and his friends needed the media—as long as they continued to provide the right kinds of stories.

29. For a discussion of "Annex Foxtrot" and its significance, see Jason De Parle, "Military Decisions Leading to Gulf War Censorship," in *The Media and the Gulf War: The Press and Democracy in Wartime*, ed. Hedrick Smith (Washington: Seven Locks, 1992), pp. 18–26.

30. Quoted in Michael Hill, "Re-Examining Reporting of the Gulf War," *Baltimore Sun*, August 2, 1992, p. M-1.

31. Malcolm W. Browne, "The Military vs. the Press," *New York Times Magazine*, March 3, 1991, p. 28.

32. Jason De Parle, "Long Series of Military Decisions Led to Gulf War News Censorship," *New York Times*, May 5, 1991, p. A1.

33. Sydney H. Schanberg, "Censoring for Political Security," *Washington Journalism Review*, March 1991, p. 24.

34. Quoted in MacArthur, *Second Front*, p. 9.

35. Ibid., p. 8.

36. William M. Hammond, *Public Affairs: The Military and the Media, 1962–1968* (Washington: U.S. Army Center of Military History, 1988), p. 322.

37. Quoted in MacArthur, *Second Front*, p. 171. *Newsweek*'s David Hackworth aptly described the escort system as having "a thought control policeman guiding [report ers'] every moment." *America's Defense Monitor*, PBS, August 11, 1991, transcript, p. 9.

38. Quoted in "Military Obstacles Detailed," *Editor and Publisher*, July 13, 1991, p. 9.

39. Howard Kurtz, "News Media Ask Freer Hand in Future Conflicts," *Washington Post*, July 1, 1991, p. A4. For General Schwarzkopf's defense of the military command's cooperation with Saudi efforts to ban any press coverage of religious celebrations, see Schwarzkopf and Petre, pp. 396–97.

40. PBS president Larry Grossman later stated that "to me the most interesting aspect of this war was the fact that the screen was filled up by material—briefings, press conferences, videotapes—that were supplied by the government." "The Media at War: The Press and the Persian Gulf Conflict," Gannett Foundation Report, June 1991, p. 65.

41. MacArthur, *Second Front*, p. 146, 196.

42. Stanley W. Cloud, "Covering the Next War," *New York Times*, August 4, 1992, p. A19.

43. Browne, p. 45.

44. Kurtz, "News Media Ask Freer Hand in Future Conflicts," p. A4.

45. Christopher Hedges, "The Unilaterals," in *The Media and the Gulf War*, pp. 151–52. In another revealing example of the quisling status accepted by some press pool members, Hedges reported that when he protested his treatment to the military officer in charge, "one of the pool reporters told me to be quiet. 'You can't talk to him like that,' he said. 'They'll take away your credentials for good'" (p. 152).

46. MacArthur, *Second Front*, pp. 183, 202; Yant, pp. 30–31; and Edith Lederer, "Press Pool Hassles," *Editor and Publisher*, February 16, 1991, p. 10.

47. David H. Hackworth, "Learning How to Cover a War," *Newsweek*, December 21, 1992, p. 32.

48. Schanberg, p. 25. For Fisk's account of the incident, see Robert Fisk, "Out of the Pool," *Mother Jones*, May–June 1991, p. 57.

49. MacArthur, *Second Front*, p. 182.

50. Quoted in ibid., pp. 182–83.

51. Browne, p. 29.

52. Gottschalk, p. 459.

53. Frank A. Aukofer, testimony, in U.S. Senate Committee on Governmental Affairs, *Pentagon Rules on Media Access to the Persian Gulf War: Hearing before the Senate Committee on Governmental Affairs*, 102d Cong., 1st sess., February 20, 1991, p. 2.

54. Quoted in MacArthur, *Second Front*, p. 197.

55. Browne, p. 44.

56. Quoted in MacArthur, *Second Front*, p. 28.

57. Quoted in Howard Kurtz, "U.S. Lets Some News Filter through the 'Blackout,' " *Washington Post*, February 25, 1991, p. A18.

58. Michael Getler, "Do Americans Really Want to Censor War Coverage This Way?" *Washington Post*, March 17, 1991, p. D1.

59. Jonathan Alter, "Clippings from the Media War," *Newsweek*, March 11, 1991, p. 52.

60. Gottschalk, p. 455.

61. Quoted in MacArthur, *Second Front*, pp. 155–56.

62. A congressional report released in April 1992 concluded that there were only 183,000 Iraqi troops in place in the Kuwait theater of operations when the "coalition" ground offensive began. Gottschalk, p. 452. John Heidenrich, a former military analyst with the Defense Intelligence Agency, concedes, "Because of massive desertion, the total Iraqi force probably fell below 300,000 troops—perhaps even below 200,000 troops." John G. Heidenrich, "The Gulf War: How Many Iraqis Died?" *Foreign Policy* 90 (Spring 1993): 115.

63. Quoted in Yant, p. 143.

64. Susan Sachs, "Allies Faced Ghost Army," *Newsday*, March 1, 1991, p. 17. Another official conceded that the Pentagon continued to feed stories that hyped the military capabilities of the Iraqi army—even after the air war had pulverized it—specifically to keep public support for Operation Desert Storm at a fever pitch. Paul Bedard, "Iraqi Build-Up Partially Fictional," *Washington Times*, March 5, 1991, p. A10. A study commissioned by the Gannett Foundation also found that "the military used the news media effectively during the period immediately before the ground offensive to spread disinformation to the Iraqis. During that time, military officials fed news-hungry journalists false information about how it would be carried out. Endless reports based on those briefings soon appeared in the press. . . . Thus, in the end, Pentagon officials succeeded not only in censoring media coverage of the gulf war but also in making what coverage there was inaccurate in ways that suited the military's purposes." "Media at War," p. 20.

65. Yant, pp. 91–92.

66. Ibid., p. 21.

67. John Heidenrich, however, argues that civilian deaths directly attributable to the bombing campaign were probably fewer than 1,000. He also contends that the number of Iraqi soldiers killed may have been as low as 1,500—although he concedes that a "maximum" figure of 9,500 is also possible. Heidenrich, pp. 117–19, 123. Since Heidenrich's policy agenda centers around the notions that it is possible to wage modern war "without excessive brutality" and that the gulf war proves that proposition, his sanguine estimates of Iraqi casualties should be viewed with some caution. For other accounts and estimates of civilian deaths from the air war, see Middle East Watch, *Needless Deaths in the Gulf War: Civilian Casualties during the Air Campaign and Violations of the Laws of War* (New York: Human Rights Watch, November 1991); and Greenpeace, *The Body Count* (Washington: Greenpeace, 1992).

68. Barton Gellman, "U.S. Bombs Missed 70% of Time," *Washington Post*, March 16, 1991, p. A1. Even the much-touted accuracy of the Tomahawk cruise missiles proved to be overrated. As the war progressed, they began hitting an increasing number of incorrect targets because their preprogrammed digital maps became outdated once key landmark buildings had been destroyed. Yant, p. 117.

69. Alberto Ascherio et al., "Effect of the Gulf War on Infant and Child Mortality in Iraq," *New England Journal of Medicine*, September 24, 1992, pp. 933–34. The Greenpeace study estimated that at least 70,000 Iraqi civilians had perished as a result of inadequate medical care, poor food distribution, and other conditions resulting from the bombing campaign's devastation. Greenpeace, pp. 1–2.

70. Yant, p. 28.

71. Gregg Easterbrook, "Operation Desert Shill," *New Republic*, September 30, 1991, p. 42. Some graphic scenes of Iraqi casualties were shown on a PBS special, "After the War," hosted by Bill Moyers. The audience for that program, however, was a tiny fraction of those who watched sanitized war footage on the "big three" networks and CNN. Moreover, the special aired weeks after the end of the war, when most Americans' interest in the conflict had waned considerably.

72. Howard Kurtz, "Sen. Simpson Calls Arnett 'Sympathizer,' " *Washington Post*, February 8, 1991, p. B1.

73. Richard Zoglin, "It Was a Public Relations Rout, Too," *Time*, March 11, 1991, p. 56.

74. Quoted in Gottschalk, pp. 429–30. CBS News anchor Dan Rather was more critical of both the government's restrictions and the media's performance, but his assessment of the nature of the principal "damage" was peculiar. In his view, "too much censorship, too many unnecessary controls and ill-conceived policies concerning the flow of information, fogged up a story of great courage, great strategy that worked, and a mighty triumph." Dan Rather with Mickey Herskowitz, *The Camera Never Blinks Twice* (New York: William Morrow, 1994), p. 224. The notion that the main problem with the media's coverage of the gulf war was that the American people did not get an adequate picture of the extent of the U.S. military victory suggests that Rather, like many other journalists, still does not understand the problem.

75. David S. Broder, "The War Story," *Washington Post*, March 20, 1991.

76. Gottschalk, p. 454.

77. "The Media at War," p. 91. The poll was conducted by Times-Mirror on January 25–27, 1991.

78. Yant, p. 17.

Chapter 9

1. Quoted in Howard Kurtz, "News Chiefs Vow to Resist Pentagon War Coverage Rules in the Future," *Washington Post*, May 14, 1991, p. A4.

2. Text in Howard Kurtz and Barton Gellman, "Guidelines Set for News Coverage of Wars," *Washington Post*, May 22, 1992, p. A23.

3. Quoted in ibid.

4. Marie Gottschalk, "Operation Desert Cloud: The Media and the Gulf War," *World Policy Journal* 9 (Summer 1992): 478.

5. "Defense Department Proposes Rules on Covering War," *Washington Post*, September 25, 1992, p. A23.

6. "Are Pools Necessary?" editorial, *Editor and Publisher*, December 12, 1992, p. 8.

7. Quoted in Janice Castro, "Peace Pact on War Coverage," *Time*, September 3, 1984, p. 73.

8. U.S. Department of Defense, "Report on Media Pool Coverage of the Panama Operation," March 20, 1990, p. 3.

9. Quoted in George Garneau, "Panning the Pentagon," *Editor and Publisher*, March 31, 1990, pp. 11–12.

10. Sydney Schanberg, "Media Hold Power to Shed War Blinders," *Newark Star-Ledger*, September 5, 1991, p. 21.

11. Howard Kurtz, "TV Viewers Join Military Critics of Media Spectacle on the Beach," *Washington Post*, December 10, 1992, p. A33. Cynics in the media "suggested

the Pentagon had planned its press policy to show the chaos of unrestricted coverage," ABC News correspondent Jeff Greenfield observed. "If there had been such a plot, the press' behavior made it work to perfection." Ibid.

12. Debra Gersh, "It's Hollywood! No, It's Somalia!" *Editor and Publisher*, December 19, 1992, p. 9. Georgiana Vines, president of the Society of Professional Journalists, even charged that the Pentagon knew at least two days in advance that there would be reporters on the beach, yet failed to voice any objections. Similarly, CNN vice president for news Ed Turner observed, "No one should have been surprised that there was a crowd of journalists on the beach, because they were told what time and where, and encouraged to be there in briefings by the Pentagon and State Department." Ibid. See also "Too Many Lights? It Was a Pentagon 'Photo Op'!" editorial, *Long Island Newsday*, December 10, 1992, p. 64.

13. John Lancaster, "Hitting the Beach in the Glare of the Night," *Washington Post*, December 9, 1992, p. A1. Emphasis added.

14. David H. Hackworth, "Learning How to Cover a War," *Newsweek*, December 21, 1992, p. 32.

15. Howard Kurtz, "No American Journalists Reporting from the Scene," *Washington Post*, October 6, 1993, p. A13.

16. Ibid.

17. Howard Kurtz, "White House Aide Sent to Somalia to Deal with Press," *Washington Post*, October 14, 1993, p. A22.

18. Kurtz, "No American Journalists."

19. See, for example, Rakiya Omaar and Alex de Waal, "Somalia's Uninvited Saviors," *Washington Post*, December 13, 1992, p C1.

20. See, for example, Anna Husarska, "The Bodyguards," *New Republic*, February 15, 1993, p. 20.

21. Douglas Waller, "Everyone Is Sniping at the Marines," *Newsweek*, December 28, 1993.

22. For a discussion of the various *mujahadeen* factions and their rather unsavory political agendas, see Ted Galen Carpenter, "The Unintended Consequences of Afghanistan," *World Policy Journal* 11 (Spring 1994): 76–87.

23. Richard Falk, "Hard Choices and Tragic Dilemmas," *Nation*, December 20, 1993, p. 761.

24. A rare exception was Alexander Cockburn, "Beat the Devil," *Nation*, December 21, 1992, pp. 762–63.

25. One of the few media accounts to pay attention to the growing friction between the inhabitants of Somaliland and UN officialdom was Donatella Lorch, "In Another Part of Somalia, Resentment of the UN," *New York Times*, September 30, 1993, p. A3. Lorch's account was detailed and insightful, but it did not appear until long after the U.S.-UN mission in Somalia had turned into a debacle. Such belated coverage was symptomatic of the press's larger failure to help the American public to understand Somalia's complex society and politics.

26. For a discussion of the Clinton administration's decision to place U.S. troops under UN command in the Somalia peacekeeping mission, which put those troops in grave peril, see Kent DeLong and Steven Tuckey, *Mogadishu: Heroism and Tragedy* (Westport, Conn.: Praeger, 1994).

27. For an impressive exception, see the various articles by Michael Maren in the *Village Voice*, especially "The Somalia Experiment," *Village Voice*, September 28, 1993, pp. 33–39. Some of the later articles by *Washington Post* correspondent Keith Richburg

also significantly advanced readers' understanding of Somalia's diverse political landscape.

28. Quoted in Keith B. Richburg, "Stuck in Somalia?" *Washington Post,* September 21, 1993, p. A1.

29. Sylvia Poggioli, "Scouts without Compasses," *Nieman Reports* 47 (Fall 1993): 17.

30. For a discussion of Tito's policies and their consequences, see Dusko Doder, "Yugoslavia: New War, Old Hatreds," *Foreign Policy* 91 (Summer 1993): 10–19.

31. International Institute for Strategic Studies, *The Military Balance, 1992–1993* (London: Brassey's, 1992), pp. 51, 87.

32. Daryl G. Press, "What's Happening in Bosnia Is Terrible, But It's Not Genocide," *Christian Science Monitor,* September 26, 1993, p. E4. Furthermore, ethnically motivated killing is not confined to Serb forces. Croat and Bosnian Muslims also commit such atrocities, although that fact is generally lost in the barrage of stories about Serbian crimes. For a rare example of a story focusing on Serbs as victims, see John F. Burns, "In Muslim Town, Serbs Pay the Price," *New York Times,* March 9, 1993, p. A6. Even in that case, however, the implied message was that if Serb forces had not engaged in "ethnic cleansing," the Muslims would not have "retaliated" by killing innocent Serb civilians. Anyone familiar with the long history of violence in the Balkans will be at least skeptical of that thesis. For a more detailed discussion of Croat and Muslim atrocities, see "Bosnia-Hercegovina: Abuses by Bosnian Croat and Muslim Forces in Central and Southwestern Bosnia-Hercegovina," *Helsinki Watch Report* 5, issue 18, (September 1993).

33. Andrew Bell-Fialkoff, "A Brief History of Ethnic Cleansing," *Foreign Affairs* 72 (Summer 1993): 110–21.

34. Larry Collins and Dominique Lapierre, *Freedom at Midnight* (New York: Simon and Schuster, 1975), pp. 329–98. A similar although less bloody expulsion of populations occurred after the UN-mandated partition of Palestine into Arab and Jewish states. Some 700,000 Palestinians ultimately fled their homes—many in response to terrorist campaigns conducted by Israeli paramilitary organizations.

35. Alfred M. de Zayas, *Nemesis at Potsdam: The Anglo-Americans and the Expulsion of the Germans* (London: Routledge & Kegan Paul, 1977).

36. Poggioli, p. 19.

37. United Nations High Commissioner for Refugees, Office of the Special Envoy for Former Yugoslavia, "Information Notes on Former Yugoslavia," January 22, 1993, pp. 6–7.

38. "U.N. Accuses All Sides of Rape," *Washington Post,* January 30, 1993, p. A16.

39. Quoted in "For the Record," *Washington Post,* February 24, 1993, p. A16.

40. Quoted in Manuela Dobos, "The War in Bosnia," *Peace and Democracy News* 7 (Summer 1993): 17.

41. For examples of accounts that explicitly compare the events in the former Yugoslavia with the Holocaust, see Anthony Lewis, "Waiting for Clinton," *New York Times,* April 19, 1993, p. A19; Zbigniew Brzezinski, "Never Again—Except for Bosnia," *New York Times,* April 22, 1993, p. A25; Patrick Glynn, "See No Evil," *New Republic,* October 25, 1993, p. 23; and Roy Gutman, *Witness to Genocide: The 1993 Pulitzer Prize-Winning Dispatches on the "Ethnic Cleansing" of Bosnia* (New York: Macmillan, 1993), passim. For criticisms of such comparisons, see Richard Cohen, "It's Not a Holocaust: Rhetoric and Reality in Bosnia," *Washington Post,* February 28, 1993, p. C1; and Erwin Knoll, "The Uses of the Holocaust," *Progressive,* July 1993, pp. 15–16.

42. Lewis MacKenzie, testimony, in U.S. Senate Committee on Armed Services, *Situation in Bosnia and Appropriate U.S. and Western Responses: Hearing before the Senate Committee on Armed Services*, 102d Cong., 2d sess. August 11, 1992, pp. 50–61.

43. "Bosnia's Brutal Camps," *New York Times*, editorial, January 26, 1993, p. A22.

44. The *Times* news stories on the other hand were a mixed lot. Some of those accounts reflected a clear anti-Serb bias while others—especially those by David Binder—were fairly balanced.

45. Peter Brock, "Dateline Yugoslavia: The Partisan Press," *Foreign Policy* 93 (Winter 1993–94): 153–54. Brock made a factual error concerning his assertion about the first photo and caption. They appeared in *Newsweek*, not *Time*.

46. Roy Gutman, letter to the editor, *Foreign Policy* 94 (Spring 1994): 160–61.

47. Charles Lane, "Washington Diarist: War Stories," *New Republic*, January 3, 1994, p. 43; and Charles Lane, "Brock Crock," *New Republic*, September 5, 1994, pp. 18–21.

48. Editor's Note, *Foreign Policy* 97 (Winter 1994–95): 185.

49. Ibid.

50. Lane, "Brock Crock," p. 20. In his earlier analysis, Lane also conceded that many reporters had become "emotionally involved" in the story and that the preponderance of Serb abuses "led some of us to hope that the West would ride to the rescue." That comment suggested a policy agenda that was likely to color his analysis of the conflict. Lane, "Washington Diarist," p. 43.

51. Brock, p. 164.

52. "Reaction to the Sarajevo Marketplace Shelling," February 7, 1994, U.S. Department of State *Dispatch*, February 14, 1994, p. 82.

53. For a concise and balanced discussion of the uncertainties that still surround the marketplace incident, see David Binder, "Anatomy of a Massacre," *Foreign Policy* 97 (Winter 1994–95): 70–78.

54. Nikolaos A. Stavrou, "The Balkan Quagmire and the West's Response," *Mediterranean Quarterly* 4 (Winter 1993): 35.

55. Even the U.S. State Department, in a rare movement of balance and candor, conceded that point. Ralph Johnson, principal deputy assistant secretary of state for European and Canadian affairs, told the Senate Foreign Relations Committee in October 1991, "The policies of the Croatian government toward the Serbian minority do not justify Serbia's actions, but they have contributed to the atmosphere of tension and recrimination that led to violence." Ralph Johnson, "U.S. Efforts to Promote a Peaceful Settlement in Yugoslavia," U.S. Department of State *Dispatch*, October 21, 1991, p. 784. Of course, at the time Johnson made that admission, Washington was still clinging to the policy of maintaining a united Yugoslavia and thus wished to placate Belgrade. Once the United States concluded that the Yugoslav federation was doomed, such reasonably fair assessments virtually disappeared.

56. The Croatian government's penchant for resurrecting the symbols of the fascist era has not decreased. In May 1994 Zagreb replaced its currency, the dinar, with the kuna—the same name the Ustasha republic used for its currency in World War II. John Pomfret, "New Croatian Money Anathema to Serbs," *Washington Post*, May 31, 1994, p. A12; and Roger Cohen, "Croatia's Currency's Name Protested," *New York Times*, May 28, 1994, p. A3.

57. Jonathan C. Randal, "Croat, Muslim Forces Turn Guns on Each Other in Central Bosnia," *Washington Post*, April 20, 1993, p. A16; John F. Burns, "Beleaguered Bosnia Faces New Battle against Croats," *New York Times*, April 20, 1993, p. A10; and Jonathan C. Randal, "Croat-Muslim Combat in Bosnia Reaches New Ferocity," *Washington Post*,

April 21, 1993, p. A21. For an example of the new, disillusioned media interpretation of Croatian conduct and motives in Bosnia, see Rod Norland and Charles Lane, " 'Kill All the Muslims': While the World Focuses on Serb Atrocities, the Croats Get Away with Murder," *Newsweek*, June 7, 1993, p. 28.

58. Steve Coll, "Franjo Tudjman, at War with History," *Washington Post*, March 1, 1993, p. B1.

59. John Pomfret, "Bosnian Mourns 'Tragic Reality' of Partition," *Washington Post*, July 6, 1993, p. A1. Pomfret also mentioned that Izetbegovic was "a careworn, rumpled man with sad, kindly eyes." For a more realistic assessment of Izetbegovic, including the highly authoritarian comments and religiously intolerant comments made in his 1970 book, *The Islamic Declaration: A Programme for the Islamization of Muslims and the Muslim People*, see Michael Mennard, letter to the editor, *Foreign Policy* 93 (Winter 1993–94): 183–84. Mennard is a former U.S. Foreign Service officer with extensive experience in the Balkans.

60. For examples of the U.S. government's interpretation, see Edward J. Perkins, "Aggression by the Serbian Regime" (statement by the U.S. Permanent Representative to the United Nations before the UN Security Council, May 30, 1992), U.S. Department of State *Dispatch*, June 8, 1992, p. 448; George Bush, "Containing the Crisis in Bosnia and the Former Yugoslavia," U.S. Department of State *Dispatch*, August 6, 1992, p. 617; and Lawrence Eagleburger, "Intervention at the London Conference on the Former Yugoslavia," U.S. Department of State *Dispatch*, August 31, 1992, p. 673.

61. For a concise discussion of the Muslim-Croat power play and the inherent political fragility of Bosnia, see Aleksa Djilas, "The Nation That Wasn't," *New Republic*, September 21, 1992, pp. 25–31.

62. Paul Lewis, "2 Leaders Propose Dividing Bosnia into Three Areas," *New York Times*, June 17, 1993, p. A3.

63. Poggioli, p. 19.

64. Paul T. Lewis, "Bosnian Leader Goes to Geneva for Start of Talks," *New York Times*, July 27, 1993, p. A3. Interestingly, only the map of the two partition plans accompanying Lewis's article conveyed the more hard-line position adopted by the Croats. The text of the article did not mention that detail.

65. Examples of the continuing double standard in evaluating Serb and Croat actions included "Is Croatia Going the Way of Serbia?" editorial, *Washington Times*, July 14, 1993, p. G2; and Anna Husarska, "Why Help Somalia but Not Bosnia?" *Washington Post*, July 23, 1993, p. A23. The interventionist media's favorite Balkan policy expert, George Kenney, took the double standard to new heights when he advocated sending in an additional 10,000 UN peacekeepers. "If Croatia balks, threaten sanctions. If the Serbians balk, threaten war." George Kenney, "From Bosnian Crisis to All-Out War," *New York Times*, June 20, 1993, p. E17.

66. "Relief for Bosnia," editorial, *Washington Post*, November 21, 1993, p. C6.

67. Richard Cohen, "Considering an Air Strike," *Washington Post*, April 7, 1993, p. A27.

68. A typical example of the *Times*'s "balance" on the Yugoslavian crisis was the op-ed page of April 22, 1993, which featured an article by former national security adviser Zbigniew Brzezinski advocating bombing Serbian targets and arming Bosnian government forces and another article by British M.P. Winston S. Churchill advocating arming Bosnian government forces and bombing Serbian targets.

69. The first NBC/*Wall Street Journal* poll, taken in December 1992, asked, "Do you favor or oppose the United States sending troops to Yugoslavia to help stop the

civil war there?" Sixty-two percent of respondents opposed sending troops, only 26 percent endorsed the step. A Harris poll conducted at the same time asked, "Do you favor or oppose sending U.S. forces to restore peace and assure humanitarian aid in Bosnia?" Although that wording (by invoking the goal of humanitarian aid) was more likely to elicit a positive response, the survey still found just 42 percent in favor, while 45 percent were opposed. "Opinion Outlook," *National Journal*, January 16, 1993, p. 157. An NBC/*Wall Street Journal* poll conducted in March 1993 asked, "President Clinton has said the U.S. would be willing to send some ground troops to Bosnia as part of a peacekeeping force. Do you favor or oppose using American ground troops in such an operation?" Despite invoking the president's prestige and stressing that U.S. intervention would be part of a "peacekeeping" mission—implying that fighting would have already ceased—the poll still found 51 percent opposed and only 41 percent in favor. *Wall Street Journal*, March 19, 1993, p. A12.

70. George D. Kenney, "Bosnia: Appeasement in Our Time," *New York Times*, August 30, 1992, p. C7.

71. Letter to the editor, *Foreign Policy* 94 (Spring 1994): 162. An exhaustive study by British journalist Nick Gowing reached essentially the same conclusion. Nick Gowing, "Instant Pictures, Instant Policies?" *Independent* (London), July 3, 1994, p. 14. For a further analysis of the pervasive media bias, see Stavrou, pp. 28–29.

72. Letter to the editor, *Foreign Policy*.

Chapter 10

1. Robert C. Hilderbrand, *Power and the People: Executive Management of Public Opinion in Foreign Affairs, 1897–1921* (Chapel Hill: University of North Carolina Press, 1981), p. 204.

2. Floyd Abrams, "Will the First Amendment Survive the 1980's?" *Vital Speeches of the Day*, April 15, 1985, pp. 410–13.

3. Thomas I. Emerson, "National Security and Civil Liberties," in *The First Amendment and National Security* (Charlottesville, Va.: Center for Law and National Security, 1984), p. 84.

4. Sydney Schanberg, "Censoring for Political Security," *Washington Journalism Review*, March 1991, p. 24.

5. Ibid.

6. Barry Zorthian, "Now, How Will Unfettered Media Cover Combat?" *New York Times*, September 12, 1984, p. A31.

7. Bernard E. Trainor, "The Military's War with the Media: Causes and Consequences," in *Defense Beat: The Dilemmas of Defense Coverage*, ed. Loren B. Thompson (New York: Lexington Books, 1991), p. 78.

8. William E. Odom, "U.S. Intelligence: Current Problems in Historical Perspective," in *The Media and Foreign Policy*, ed. Simon Serfaty (New York: St. Martin's, 1991), p. 162.

9. Jonathan Alter, "Clippings from the Media War," *Newsweek*, March 11, 1991, p. 52.

10. Ibid.

11. James T. Bennett and Thomas J. DiLorenzo, *Official Lies: How Washington Misleads Us* (Alexandria, Va.: Groom Books, 1992).

12. *Bartlett's Familiar Quotations*, 16th ed., ed. Justin Kaplan (Boston: Little, Brown, 1982), p. 687.

13. Senate Standing Committee on Constitution and Legal Affairs, *Freedom of Information* (Canberra: Australian Government Publishing Service, 1979), p. 2.

14. Letter from Madison to W. T. Barry, August 4, 1822, in *The Complete Madison*, ed. Saul K. Padover (New York: Harper, 1953), p. 337.

15. Caspar W. Weinberger, "A Free Press and National Security," *Defense*, October 1985, pp. 2–3.

16. David R. Kiernan, "Is the Military Throttling the Media?" *USA Today Magazine*, January 1991, p. 35.

17. James Russell Wiggins, *Freedom or Secrecy*, rev. ed. (New York: Oxford University Press, 1964), p. 232.

18. An excellent discussion of that phenomenon can be found in Robert Higgs, *Crisis and Leviathan: Critical Episodes in the Growth of American Government* (New York: Oxford University Press, 1987).

Epilogue

1. Rowan Scarborough, "Media Blamed for Confusion about U.S. Mission in Haiti," *Washington Times*, October 3, 1994, p. A20; and Art Pine, "U.S. Military Leaders Face Familiar and Formidable Foe—the Free Press," *Los Angeles Times*, October 6, 1994, p. A6.

2. "Military Censorship Lives," editorial, *Washington Post*, September 21, 1994, p. A22.

Index

About the Author

Ted Galen Carpenter is director of foreign policy studies at the Cato Institute. He is the author of *Beyond NATO: Staying Out of Europe's Wars* and *A Search for Enemies: America's Alliances after the Cold War* and the editor of five books on defense and foreign policy issues.

He has contributed chapters to 15 books on international relations, and his articles have appeared in numerous policy journals including *Foreign Affairs, Foreign Policy, World Policy Journal, International History Review, National Interest,* and *Journal of Strategic Studies.*

Carpenter received his B.A. and M.A. in U.S. history from the University of Wisconsin at Milwaukee and his Ph.D. in U.S. diplomatic history from the University of Texas.

Cato Institute

Founded in 1977, the Cato Institute is a public policy research foundation dedicated to broadening the parameters of policy debate to allow consideration of more options that are consistent with the traditional American principles of limited government, individual liberty, and peace. To that end, the Institute strives to achieve greater involvement of the intelligent, concerned lay public in questions of policy and the proper role of government.

The Institute is named for *Cato's Letters*, libertarian pamphlets that were widely read in the American Colonies in the early 18th century and played a major role in laying the philosophical foundation for the American Revolution.

Despite the achievement of the nation's Founders, today virtually no aspect of life is free from government encroachment. A pervasive intolerance for individual rights is shown by government's arbitrary intrusions into private economic transactions and its disregard for civil liberties.

To counter that trend, the Cato Institute undertakes an extensive publications program that addresses the complete spectrum of policy issues. Books, monographs, and shorter studies are commissioned to examine the federal budget, Social Security, regulation, military spending, international trade, and myriad other issues. Major policy conferences are held throughout the year, from which papers are published thrice yearly in the *Cato Journal*. The Institute also publishes the quarterly magazine *Regulation*.

In order to maintain its independence, the Cato Institute accepts no government funding. Contributions are received from foundations, corporations, and individuals, and other revenue is generated from the sale of publications. The Institute is a nonprofit, tax-exempt, educational foundation under Section 501(c)3 of the Internal Revenue Code.

CATO INSTITUTE
1000 Massachusetts Ave., N.W.
Washington, D.C. 20001